M000316837

To Live in the Center of the Moment

AGE STUDIES
Anne M. Wyatt-Brown, Editor

To Live in the Center of the Moment

Literary Autobiographies of Aging

Barbara Frey Waxman

UNIVERSITY PRESS OF VIRGINIA

Charlottesville and London

Acknowledgments for previously published material appear on page x, which constitutes an extension of the copyright page.

THE UNIVERSITY PRESS OF VIRGINIA
© 1997 by the Rector and Visitors of the University of Virginia
All rights reserved
Printed in the United States of America
First published 1997

⊗ The paper used in this publication meets the minimum requirements of the American National Standard for Information Sciences— Permanence of Paper for Printed Library Materials, ANSI Z39.48-1984.

Library of Congress Cataloging-in-Publication Data
Waxman, Barbara Frey.
   To live in the center of the moment : literary autobiographies of aging / Barbara Frey Waxman.
      p.   cm. — (Age studies)
   Includes bibliographical references (p.) and index.
   ISBN 0-8139-1757-3 (cloth : alk. paper)
   1. American prose literature—20th century—History and criticism.
2. Authors, American—20th century—Biography—History and criticism.   3. Old age in literature.   4. Aging in literature.
5. Autobiography. I. Title. II. Series.
PS366.A88W38   1997
818'.540809354—DC21   97-25380
                                               CIP

For Linda and Allen, Alan and Flo,
Sandy and Sanford, and Ellen

and in memory of
Harvey Braaf

Contents

Acknowledgments

I began work on this book in the fall of 1992, with the help of my department chair at the time, Dr. Jo Ann Seiple (now Dean of the College of Arts and Sciences at University of North Carolina-Wilmington). She gave me time for reading and reflection that semester, time to search for autobiographies that grappled with important issues of aging and mortality, autobiographies that envisioned new meanings of old age, autobiographies that described how to intensify time and spiritualize life. For this intensive time of reading and reflection I am grateful. Thanks also to my friend Renée Hartman, who is very good at helping me to search for the books I need.

This book comes out of my work on novels of aging and out of my own aging, but also out of working with students at my university. Students in my seminars on autobiography and on the literature of aging (especially my students in Eng. 390, The Older Generation in Literature, in the fall of 1996) inspired me to delve into these autobiographies of aging after we had discussed the books in class to introduce them to the "foreign country" of old age. Thanks go to Mary Ann Burrell, Steve Dugan, Holly Henderson, Rhonda Limoges, Joey Szalkiewicz, and Barry Wood for their responses to the chapter on May Sarton's *At Seventy*.

Thanks go also to Anne Wyatt-Brown for her encouragement of my project, for her suggestions to improve it, and for her own inspiring work in literary gerontology. I am grateful for her support and for the support of Nancy Essig, director of the University Press of Virginia.

To my colleagues in the English department's Works in Progress Association goes my appreciation for their comments on my manuscript's introduction. Thanks to Lindsay Aegerter, Bill Atwill, Todd Berliner, Ele Byington, Janet Ellerby, Carol Ellis, Keith Newlin, Dan Noland, Kathy Rugoff, and Sally Sullivan. Thanks to my chair, Phil Furia, for departmental budget support for printing and reproduction costs. A special thank-you to Paul Wilkes for offering very instructive suggestions for revision of my introduction.

Last but certainly not least, my appreciation to Robert Waxman, my husband, for his continuing encouragement of my work and to Dina and Daniel for their patience in waiting for Mom when she was (perennially) late in picking them up.

Quotations are printed by permission.

Excerpts from *The Summer of the Great-Grandmother* by Madeleine L'Engle. Copyright © 1974 by Crosswicks, Ltd. Reprinted by permission of Farrar, Straus & Giroux, Inc. British Commonwealth rights granted by permission of Lescher & Lescher, Ltd.

Excerpts from *The Measure of My Days* by Florida Scott-Maxwell. Copyright © 1968 by Florida Scott-Maxwell. Reprinted by permission of Alfred A. Knopf, Inc. British Commonwealth rights granted by permission of Hilary Henderson.

Excerpts from *Coming into the End Zone: A Memoir* by Doris Grumbach. Copyright © 1991 by Doris Grumbach. Reprinted by permission of W. W. Norton & Company, Inc.

Excerpts from *At Seventy* by May Sarton. Copyright © 1984 by May Sarton. Reprinted by permission of W. W. Norton & Company, Inc.

Excerpts from *The Cancer Journals* by Audre Lorde. Copyright © 1980 by Audre Lorde. Reprinted by permission of Aunt Lute Books and the Charlotte Sheedy Literary Agency, Inc.

Excerpts from "Generations: A Memoir" copyright © 1987 by Lucille Clifton. Reprinted from *Good Woman: Poems and a Memoir 1969–1980,* by Lucille Clifton, with permission of BOA Editions, Ltd., 260 East Ave., Rochester NY 14604.

To Live in the Center of the Moment

Introduction: Reading Literary
Autobiographies of Aging

Myself as Middle-Aged Reader and Reader-Response Theory

I COME TO THE TOPIC of this book from an entirely interested perspective: I am middle-aged, forty-nine at this writing. Middle age is that time when people are about to enter "the portals of elderhood" (Schachter-Shalomi and Miller, 248), a time when many become anxious about their own impending old age as they increasingly involve themselves with aging parents and other elderly relatives and friends. These anxieties are fed by America's youth-worshipping tendencies. I confess to having entertained fearful associations of old age with deterioration, infirmity, dependency, and fixations on the past that deny the possibilities of a future. This book is in part an attempt to interrogate such associations. I do so by reading and writing about a literature that closely examines aging.

As an English professor and inveterate reader of the Sunday *New York Times Book Review* and of countless publishers' catalogs, I am witnessing a new wave of American literary history, the emergence of this evocative literature of aging. Especially of interest to me is the autobiography of aging,

I

Discuss: Women's power resides in their youthful appearance. Where else might power reside, and how might the lives of older women teach us to use it?

which reflects another current literary trend, the ascension of the memoir and other forms of autobiography into the literary canon and onto the public's bookshelves. Contemporary American autobiographers of aging make elders strong protagonists instead of relegating them to roles as antagonists, sidekicks, or invisible demons. They depict elders' lives, their own lives and those of their age cohort, in innovative ways, challenging the mainstream cultural assumption that entry into old age means the end of vital engagement with life. Since I have written elsewhere (1990) about the novel of aging as ripening, exploring the *Reifungsroman* as an extension of the *Bildungsroman*, and since I have more recently delved into autobiography in the classroom and in my scholarly work, I turn here from novels of aging to autobiographies of aging.

I read and respond to *literary* autobiographies here, those on and by professional authors who inhabit the "foreign country of old age" (May Sarton's phrase). These literary autobiographies of aging challenge negative cultural associations about elders and old age. I have found that they provide a dialectic with my personal stereotypes of elders and my culture's paradigms of senescence as Golden Pond passivity or nursing-home helplessness. Freud's theories of human development, including his view that old age means the tragic loss of productivity, have compounded the negative views of aging that operate in our thinking (Woodward, 37). Capitalism has also contributed to American culture's ageism by valuing only people who are productive in the narrow senses of earning power, profit gains, and achievement of financial success. I grapple with these messages that old age means the end of productivity and the weakening of physical, intellectual, and political powers—especially for women whose power often resides in (youthful) appearance. I want to challenge these messages by responding to literary autobiographies of aging.

It is my contention that autobiographies of aging and literary criticism's readings of these autobiographies can transform our fear of aging and our wariness of elders. As I seek changes in attitudes, I take as my premise critic Louise Rosenblatt's assertion that "literature contributes to the enlargement of experience. We participate in imaginary situations, we look on at characters living through crises" (37). Rosenblatt identifies as "the literary experience" a potentially transformative aesthetic transaction between reader and text. I consider in this book how, given certain nameable tendencies and as-sumptions in our culture and within an individual reader (in particular, my-self), one might respond to a literary experience with, for example, an eccentric elderly character, a plot event such as the incapacitating illness of an elderly parent, or the processes of deciding about caregiving and living wills. If I can demonstrate how or why I respond to these texts as I do and how they have changed some of my accustomed thinking about old age, then I will be able to ascribe to these texts the potential to change other minds about elders, to revalue old age as a rich time to be alive.

My purposes in this book, thus, are to understand the complex trans-actions between myself-as-reader and these provocative texts; to construct readings of the texts that appreciate their literary, psychological, and philo-sophical powers, their potential to foster change; to present a cultural critique of society's ageism; and to contribute to the transformation of negative atti-tudes about old age and the elderly. *Ageism*, a term coined by psychiatrist and gerontologist Robert N. Butler, means prejudice against the aged and marginalization of the old in society. Ageism seems endemic to American society, especially if we contrast our attitudes toward the old to the ways in which many African cultures as well as China and Japan revere their elderly. Ageism is an oppressive disposition that not only mars the contentment of the elderly, but that also willfully rejects the intellectual and spiritual contri-butions elders can make to society. It deserves to be interrogated.

In confronting our culture's ageism, however, I am aware of the timely warning of gerontologist Thomas R. Cole. In his 1992 book, *The Journey of Life*, which examines the historical meanings of middle and old age, Cole argues that substituting for ageism the coercive and false expectation of a perfectly healthy and prosperous old age earned through work and self-discipline perpetuates a dualistic construction of a "good" versus a "bad" old age, one that avoids confrontation with the existential issues of aging and helps to create spiritual vacancy in old age (91, 229, 233). In the discussions of autobiographies of aging that follow, I interrogate ageism by celebrating the writers' portrayals of old age's opportunities to fashion a new self and to contribute to society (Cole, 220). But I temper this celebration with an exami-nation of the works' realistic depictions of old age's limitations and losses and of the conflicts between the generations. I also discuss the works' angst-filled grappling with existential issues of aging. In other words, I examine works whose perspectives on aging include its horrors, its pleasures, and its opportunities.

I would like to speculate on how readers of different ages and experiential backgrounds might respond to these texts in order to test the autobiographies' power to reach diverse audiences and change them. However, I cannot know the exact situatedness of any one reader, nor can I determine who is each author's "immanent reader" (Bakhtin's term), "the imaginary auditor in relation to whom the author positions herself and orients her discourse" (Kaminsky, 85). So, I rely on myself as reader in this study, cognizant of some, not all, of the cluster of factors that determine my ways of reading and my range of responses to texts.

It is an axiom among literary critics and theorists that a reader's response to a text reveals as much about that reader—family background, education, values, life experiences, membership in various communities, personal needs, and the times in which she or he is living—as it does about the text. David Bleich has said, "Every linguistic act has cognitive, expressive, interpersonal, and ethical dimensions that render such acts subjective" (1978, 28). The act of responding to literature is subjective in that it gives us a unique means of seeing our cultural and political situatedness (Bleich 1988, xiii). In addition to the cultural and political contexts of a reader's response to texts, Rosenblatt names some internal factors: "The reader brings to the work personality traits, memories of past events, present needs and preoccupations, a particular mood of the moment, and a particular physical condition. These and many other elements in a never-to-be-duplicated combination determine his response to the peculiar contribution of the text" (30–31).

These ideas of Bleich and Rosenblatt articulate reader-response theory, which emphasizes the reader's role in formulating meanings of texts. Because I use reader-response theory as one of two lenses through which to examine autobiographies of aging (the other is the feminist lens, more of which later), let me situate myself as reader in more detail than I have already done, shaped not only by my age, gender, and profession, but also by my membership in particular subcultures or interpretive communities. The latter term was coined by critic Stanley Fish to signify "a community of readers sharing a set of interpretive strategies in common" (Dasenbrock, 274). Unlike the

How have the interp. Comm. you have been exposed to
taught you to "read" aging & old people?

5

INTRODUCTION

hegemonic American culture, these groups have taught me some positive ways to "read" aging and old folks, in literary texts and in life texts.

Aging as Positive, Elders as Wise

I developed generally positive associations with old age from the subculture of my religious tradition, Judaism. The Jewish tradition in which I was raised connects long life with the potential for attaining wisdom (Isenberg, 153) and honors its elders for their wisdom and virtue. Judaism is certainly not alone in saying that the elders of the community should be respected; many traditional immigrant communities in America as well as African-American and Native American groups also teach respect for elders and have specific ways of implementing this teaching. My own Jewish community puts this teaching into practice by encouraging its members to remember our elders' good deeds and wise teachings at *Yizkor*, the memorial segment of the worship service held on four major holidays in the Jewish calendar (Yom Kippur, Shemini Atzeret, Passover, Shavuot). Many Jews, even those (like my own father) who do not celebrate Jewish holidays or perform other Jewish rituals, *do* remember loved ones' exemplary deeds on the anniversary of their deaths and light a memorial candle (*Yahrzeit*) for the deceased. Through these acts, we hope to let the example of their lives be a blessing in our own lives, to have them serve as an inspiration to our learning and good deeds.

Additionally, as Sheldon Isenberg notes, the prophetic tradition (the teachings of Isaiah, Ezekiel, Jeremiah, etc.) enjoins us to treat our elderly with respect while they are still alive: "The prophetic tradition teaches that mistreatment of the elderly by any human community is a sign of being outside God's will, devoid of any morality" (154). Yes, there may be a few crotchety elders like Job in the Hebrew Scriptures and a few passages, such as in Ecclesiastes, where aging is not associated with anything but death (Isenberg, 155). Yet the prevailing outlook of this interpretive community toward aging and the old is, for me, quite positive, creating good images of elders for me to work with as I read autobiographies of aging.

Jewish tradition provides the backdrop for the positive associations with old age that I derive from another interpretive community: that of my extended family and kinlike friends. This support network is the source of affectionate relationships I have had with actively engaged, life-affirming elders. I greatly admire these elders; they inhabit my past and dwell in my present. They include some elders no longer living but much in my memory: my maternal grandmother, Eva Levine; my father, Ozzie Frey; my father-in-law, Louis Waxman; and Shirley Levins, the mother of my sister-in-law, Flo Frey. They also include the living, such as Elsie Hartman, the ninety-one-year-old mother of my friend Renée Hartman. I think also of other relatives and friends, active people in their sixties and seventies, business people and writers, voracious readers and gourmet cooks, hikers and tennis players, swimmers and docents at museums, art aficionados and world travelers, community volunteers and clay potters. These are some of the activities of my aunts and uncles Rita and Larry Mankoff and Jack and Lillian Levine, my stepmother, Ina Frey, as well as colleagues retired from the university, Sylvia Polgar and Bob Byington. And the list goes on.

All these people are, or were until their death, energetic, productive, and committed to making the most of their time on earth; they affirm the sentiments of May Sarton, who writes in her journal, *After the Stroke,* "I do not *want* to relive the past. . . . I want to live in the instant, the very center of the moment" (48). To live in the center of the moment is to reject our culture's view of time as a linear regression into old age and death. Instead, it is to intensify and spiritualize time in later life. The elders I mention here have done just that. Relationships with these elders lessen my fears of aging, increase my receptivity to autobiographies of aging, and influence my interactions with textual elders in this book. Their lives have made me wonder: How does one get to be like these elders? How does one develop the courage to face the specters of old age and stare them down? How does one reject the association of old age with deterioration and connect aging with productivity and philosophical ripening? How does old age become what Marc Kaminsky has described as a "'career'—one in which the fortunate few attain great wisdom and prestige" (41)?

In part, this book is a search for answers to these and other questions about how to age "successfully." On the other hand, this book scrutinizes sociology's normative paradigm of successful aging, questioning what constitutes success in old age and whether there is—or should be—*one* way to age successfully. Cole has eloquently argued for a *diversity* of views on successful aging, "morally compelling social practices" and "existentially nourishing views of aging" that encourage individual growth while acknowledging the natural limits of one's life course (230, 239, 251). The literary autobiographies I examine here offer diverse views of successful aging and also diverse ways to transform ageist attitudes.

Feminist Lenses to View Autobiographies of Aging

I have been considering the personal influences on my perspective as a reader. However, my scholarly training and reading also exert an influence. I read these texts of aging as a feminist literary critic. The "academy" of feminist scholars is an interpretive community to which I have belonged for twenty-five years, and this community's belief in empowerment for oppressed groups guides my reading of texts about oppressed elders. I have been interested throughout my career in the interlocking oppressions of gender and age as well as of gender and race or ethnicity. I am concerned with the damaging impact of these oppressions on our society. I want to call people's attention to sexism, racism, and ageism through literary analysis, which can uncover and challenge our culture's biases. Most feminist critics focus on gender issues as they intersect with race and class issues. I give priority to age in this study to compensate for other literary critics' and theorists' neglect of it; we critics need to raise readers' awareness of ageism and the harm it does before we can enlist their aid in diminishing its strength.

This book, then, clearly has a social aim. Frank Lentricchia in *Criticism and Social Change* has linked literary criticism with social criticism and has proclaimed social change the preeminent mission of literary criticism. Elizabeth A. Meese has described feminist theorists' special potential for subversion of oppressive social institutions and prevailing attitudes: "Because we have been culturally constituted as the 'Other,' we have the potential as a group . . . for disloyalty" (147). With Meese, I believe that feminists as a group are "disloyal" to all forms of oppression in our culture. And like Lentricchia, I link literary criticism with social criticism as my professional responsibility. Thus, I question our culture's traditional negative notions about aging as dependency and decline, especially the ideas of our Anglo-American Victorian forefathers (Cole, 136, 140), for whom old age was a chronic illness that was

Discuss: How is gender a cultural construct? how is age?

"an embarrassment to the new morality of self-control" (91). I take the confrontation with these ageist notions as an important feminist mission of this study. Together with the autobiographers who chronicle aging, I want to create "a collective will for change" (Lentricchia and McLaughlin, 37) by challenging hostile or fearful attitudes toward elders and aging.

Examining gender issues in aging reveals how women and men age differently in the texts and how ageism and sexism work together to oppress elders, damaging identities already made fragile by illness and age's debilitating changes. Kaminsky, in his study of anthropologist Barbara Myerhoff, notes that Myerhoff argued thirty years ago for gender as an important factor in understanding aging; Myerhoff recognized that "aging, if it is to be adequately studied, must be understood as a gendered process" (Kaminsky, 76). Susan Groag Bell and Marilyn Yalom, literary critics who offer feminist readings of autobiography, similarly note that gender is a cultural construct that shapes one's identity *across the life span;* human beings who endure "the vicissitudes of puberty, adolescence, young adulthood, work, family, mid-life and aging . . . are constantly negotiating gender issues" (6). Like gender, age is a cultural construct. Autobiographies of aging focus on how elders recast the gender roles enacted by more youthful members of society, particularly those within the family. They also explore how relations between older men and women are renegotiated in nonfamily contexts. My approach to these texts is to investigate the oppressive aspects of these renegotiated gender roles/ rules and also to celebrate their liberating aspects. In some ways old women endure fewer gender constraints than young women.

One gender issue often emphasized in autobiographies of aging involves the aging body, especially as perceived by our culture. Literary autobiographies of aging attend carefully to the body: the limits age imposes on mobility, the lessening of strength and endurance, the vulnerability to illness, the increasing unreliability of the senses and the memory. As French feminist critics might say, these autobiographers "write the body" of aging women— and men. Sometimes they invoke the body as the prime determinant of elders' destinies. Kathleen Woodward objects to such a depiction of aging in these texts: "the problem here is in part precisely that of *representing aging primarily in terms of the body.* What of the psyche?" (18–20). Emphasizing the psyche, Woodward gives a psychoanalytic reading of aging in several fictional texts.

Autobiographers like Doris Grumbach refuse to let me forget the physical aspects of aging—for example, that one cannot move with as much energy, grace, and independence at seventy as one could at fifty (except perhaps in the water). But like Woodward, I want to "read" beyond the body to the aged male and female psyches created in the autobiographical texts I also want to learn about the spiritual dimension of these elders, about common yearnings of aged souls, the desire "to move *toward* something as one grows older—a unit of understanding, God, expiation of guilt, renewal of innocence, or restoration of self" (Cole, 242).

As this quotation suggests, spiritual thinking and experiences may be more prevalent as people age, and many literary autobiographers reflect this prevalence. I explore the spiritual components of elders' lives in these texts, their religious and secularized spiritual hungers and quests. I want to show how these questers resist the biological essentialism to which the old are subject. G. Stanley Hall, in his book *Senescence: The Last Half of Life,* wrote in 1922 that the tendency of old age was "not letting go but taking hold of life—synthesizing experience, drawing the 'moral of life,' giving 'integrity to the soul'" (quoted in Cole, 220). This tendency is apparent in contemporary literary autobiographies. Readers' exposure to literary elders' spiritual blooming might revise their stereotyped conceptualization of old age as sterile desert.

Autobiography, Biography, and Dialogic Voices

Besides exploring these themes and characterizations of aging and their impact on readers, with the aid of feminist and reader-response theory, I address two other esthetic issues. The first issue or complex of issues involves autobiography and biography as genres. Although in the past historians, social scientists, and literary critics have separated these two genres as differently motivated and differently constituted, more recently literary theorists conflate the two as varieties of self-reflexive life writing. I agree with them. These critics note that biographers narrating others' lives subjectively choose their subjects, attracted to them out of their own needs, identifying with them as they construct their subjects' lives, and revealing their own personalities in what they construct. Bell and Yalom describe the reciprocity of this textual relationship between biographer and subject: "Biographers often have spe-

Auto/biog. as genre.

cial affinities with their subjects . . . , and they sometimes discover further confirmation of what attracted their interest in the first place—i.e., the distinctive characteristics of appropriate role models, alter egos, foremothers, forefathers, or even explanations for their own personal problems" (3). Hence, autobiography often "masquerades" as biography (4).

Autobiography by elders also partakes of biography's attributes as older autobiographers often portray and pay tribute to those people who have shaped their lives, values, and beliefs. Middle-aged autobiographers, for example, often depict their parents as role models of aging. Many autobiographies of aging also contain biographical portraits of "the 'professional elder,' who exemplifies the range of practices that can teach us how to age well . . . the spiritual mentor, the wise old man [or woman]" (Kaminsky, 35–36). When I use the term *autobiography*, then, I assume that it also includes biographical concerns and that *biography* similarly reflects autobiographical impulses.

For the term *autobiography*, furthermore, I prefer an inclusive understanding of a wide range of forms, such as the diary, the journal, the memoir, and the more conventional chronological narrative of the life history. I examine all these kinds of autobiography in this book, except for the chronological narrative that spans an entire life history because it tends to de-emphasize the last stage of life. For this book, I have selected autobiographical narratives that focus not on the broad sweep of a person's life but on the period in which aging or senescence becomes central to the subject's definition of self.

Because autobiographical subjects live within cultures, autobiographies are never written in a cultural vacuum. What are the cultural implications of the recent proliferation of autobiographies of aging? Literary critic Ralph Cohen has noted that there are different social and historical purposes for different genres, that genres are "bound up in historical and social processes" (quoted in Bleich 1988, 115–16). We are witnessing the aging of our culture's adult population and readers' increasing need to educate themselves about old age. They seek others' expertise and "firsthand" experiences, purchasing self-help books in which they may read different interpretations of aging, watching television programs about "golden girls" or attending movies about "grumpy old men" who find late-life love. Readers create the demand for the autobiography of aging, and the media reinforce the demand. Whereas fifty or even twenty years ago popular autobiographies often portrayed the youthful protagonist's coming of age, entry into vigorous maturity, and assumption of his or her active place in society—such as Richard

Wright's *Black Boy,* Maxine Hong Kingston's *The Woman Warrior,* and Richard Rodriguez's *The Hunger of Memory*—now writers and publishers turn out autobiographies emphasizing the later liminal phase: ripening into senescence.

Connected to these historical and cultural points about literary genres is Bleich's observation that critics identifying literary genres are naming the various sorts of writing used in their society in order "to identify its actions and to regulate its social developments" (1988, 119). This book examines autobiographical "names" that American society uses to label its social trends concerning elders, its actions and attitudes about such things as caregiving to the elderly by families, the medical establishment, religious institutions, and social agencies; ethical and psychological issues of this caregiving role; definitions of work as age related and the issue of mandatory retirement; and conceptualizations of emotional and spiritual growth in old age. In this book, I explore how the autobiographies name aging processes and depict older people, and how they represent the controllers of social developments concerning "successful" aging.

I do not always assume, however, that these autobiographies' depictions of old people and aging are completely accurate or true to a referential reality. This is an important issue associated with autobiography as genre. Despite an author's intention of factual accuracy, the very nature of autobiography is "in its deepest sense a special kind of fiction, its self and its truth as much created as (re)discovered realities" (Eakin, ix). In each chapter, I explore questions about autobiography's construction of reality and truthfulness. In a self-portrait of an elder, for example, which self is represented? How many other selves are repressed? Assuming that multiple selves make for competing truths, who, for instance, is the seventy-year-old May Sarton in her private life and in her published journal, *At Seventy*? How does she at seventy differ from Sarton in her middle years and incorporate aspects of her earlier self? Can readers trust the insights offered by Sarton and other authors about old age's opportunities and challenges? Can the elders portrayed serve as guides to readers navigating through middle and old age?

If these autobiographical portrayals of elders and aging can offer no "guarantee of [their] ethnographic value" (Eakin, xix), are the texts still capable of changing readers' attitudes about old age? Paul John Eakins's reader-based poetics of autobiography can help us answer this question in the affirmative. Influenced by reader-response theory, such a poetics suggests that authors,

Per ques. for anal.

define: "Senescence"

Discuss: Referentiality of autobiog. texts. How important + why?

12

INTRODUCTION

themselves readers who want to believe in the referentiality of the autobiographical text, capitalize on readers' desire to believe by carefully constructing a fictive, but believable, textual self (xxiii). Since autobiographers
are motivated by their own desire to believe in the referentiality of autobiographical texts, they strive in their writing for realistic correlations between
text and life.

This reader-based poetics of autobiography also argues that readers of
autobiography identify with the autobiographer: "the reader, perhaps especially the critic, is potentially an autobiographer himself or herself" (Eakin,
xxiii). This identification between autobiographer and reader or critic aug-
ments the transformative effect of the literary experience. Such identification
between readers of diverse ages and older autobiographers may lead to
broader understanding of elders' humanity and to greater appreciation of the
spiritual intensity of many individuals in later life.

As a critic of autobiographical texts, I confess to identifying actively with
the elderly autobiographical narrators and the middle-aged biographical narrators who write of their elderly parents. It is one of the key reasons I wrote
this book. I also share the desire to write parts of my life as I respond to these
emotionally resonant autobiographies. I cannot, for example, react to Philip
Roth's narrative of his father Herman's final illness without juxtaposing it to
my experiences of my father's last months. Like Philippe Lejeune, I affirm
the critic's impulse to self-disclosure: "at the very heart of the desire to read
[is] a desire to speak [one]self"; this self-reflexive criticism is labeled by
French critic Jean-Michel Olivier as *l'autobiocritique* (Eakin, xxiv). Self-
reflexive disclosures season my responses to all the forms of autobiography
that I discuss in this book. This reader-based poetics of autobiography enables me to examine the effects of these texts on my attitudes toward aging.

Besides genre, there is a second esthetic issue to consider in examining
these texts: the dialogic element of their discourse. Bakhtin's notion of *heteroglossia* is useful here. *Heteroglossia* is linguistically exhibited as "a diversity
of social speech types . . . and a diversity of individual voices. . . . [creating]
stratification of any single national language into social dialects, characteristic group behavior, professional jargons, generic languages, languages of generations and age groups . . . languages that serve the specific sociopolitical
purposes of the day" (262–63). It is pertinent that among the diverse voices
and jargons Bakhtin lists are those of different generations or age cohorts;

Heteroglossia in autobiography

these are among the diverse dialogic voices of the autobiography of aging, and they do serve particular "sociopolitical purposes of the day," revealing areas of tension in the voices of different generations, uncovering elders' own ideological values and goals in contestation with those of youth and middle age (271–72). Bakhtin seems to imply that the tension of these contesting voices is not only between the generations but also within each generation (and, I would add, within many an individual, too). These endlessly multiple dissonances are worth investigating in order to appreciate just how complex autobiographies of aging are and how skilled they are in presenting the complexities of aging.

I try to note the dialogic qualities of these autobiographies of aging, the contesting voices of youth, middle age, and old age, the jostling of male and female elders, the ill and the healthy, the marginalized and the accepted, and the warring interior voices of elders. I explore the contradiction-ridden, tension-filled voices of autobiographical texts on aging to help readers see the problematic nature of aging in our culture, the inconsistent and contending attitudes about old age. Some voices offer grim perspectives, outmoded but still influential, while other voices are more positive and in early stages of formation.

That our attitudes are neither monolithic nor stable is actually encouraging for critics who would transform harmful and oppressive hegemonic attitudes. True, the *heteroglossia* cannot be converted into a harmonious choir because we are forever dealing with distinctions of age, gender, race, and class. It is unlikely that we will ever achieve the society envisioned by Simone de Beauvoir in *The Coming of Age,* where each individual would "be an active, useful citizen at every age" (806). What we must not countenance, however, is the silencing of any generational voices. This book and the texts it examines vigorously give utterance to concerns, values, and feelings that are of importance to all the generations.

A Thematic Approach to Autobiographies of Aging

A word about this book's organization. Each chapter focuses on two or more autobiographies of aging that I compare thematically. Different organizational schemes would, of course, be possible, such as the kind that categorizes the works according to the chronological age group or groups depicted by the autobiographer. Such a scheme might have been useful in helping to define what aging is and how meanings of aging change at different crossroads of old age. However, that is not my main goal in this book. Instead, I want to emphasize the literariness of the books selected for examination, to address literary themes and other uses of language, and to explore the influences of race, class, and gender on the literary language of aging. I want to show how these autobiographies' *literariness* has changed some of my negative thinking about old age. I believe that language can reshape aging readers' identities and recast the ways in which we experience aging. A thematic arrangement of the texts, in my view, emphasizes these transformative literary qualities more than a chronological arrangement, while still allowing room for study of the works' definitions of aging.

A thematic arrangement allows me to compare how the autobiographers convey a "message" about aging, and how a reader might react to the message as well as to the medium in which it is conveyed. With works arranged together that share a theme, for example, I can readily observe and compare in the texts diverse descriptions of characters across the generations and of events marking the passage into old age; personalized uses of flashbacks, flashforwards, and the interweaving of dialogic voices; and unique imbrications of imagery about the aging body, mind, and soul that reinvent our ways of perceiving elders. This thematic arrangement may also highlight the fact that the "factual" age of an older protagonist or autobiographer is less of a determining factor in how that person lives or writes about aging than is that person's values, self-image, and outlook toward old age.

This thematic arrangement does lead to some overlapping of materials in the chapters. Because several of the works explore more than one major theme, those works could have been assigned to more than one chapter. Sometimes I call further attention to the overlapping, ignoring the chapter divisions and seeking new constellations of knowledge by comparing the autobiographies across chapters. The overlapping encourages me to note the autobiographers' shared quests for the meanings of a good old age and similar identification of aging's characteristics, even though their cultural contexts and biological ages may differ.

These are the main themes structuring the book. Relationships between increasingly frail elderly parents and their middle-aged children are the sub-

ject of the first chapter. I explore two biographies that are also overtly autobiographical, Philip Roth's *Patrimony* and Madeleine L'Engle's *The Summer of
the Great-Grandmother.* Both works focus on one elderly parent as biographical subject, from the narrative perspective of the middle-aged child. How
family traditions and history are cherished, the exchange of subject-positions
between parents and their adult children, the concept of a good death, and
the struggles of an orphaned adult are some of the topics I consider in this
chapter. I could have placed Lucille Clifton's *Generations* in this chapter because it also traces family history and reflects upon the deaths of her parents.
However, I assigned it to another chapter (chapter 3) because Clifton did not
focus on just one family member, as L'Engle and Roth did, and also because,
unlike L'Engle's and Roth's works, her narrative features race in relation to
age (more on this issue shortly).

Turning seventy, a major liminal experience, is the subject of the works I
discuss in the second chapter. I first consider why turning seventy has significance in our culture and in literary autobiographies of aging. Then I compare
Doris Grumbach's memoir, *Coming into the End Zone,* with May Sarton's journal, *At Seventy.* I note that themes of work and love are prominent in both
works' characterizations of the "state of being seventy," and I speculate on
why being seventy reemphasizes the importance of both elements in a person's life. I also attempt to characterize the unique wisdom of the seventy-
year-old. This chapter, in addition, examines differences between the journal
and the memoir and the varied reactions readers might have to the two
forms.

Chapter 3 shifts the focus to race as a factor in aging. After a brief discussion of two autobiographical texts written by W. E. B. Du Bois when he was
an old man, I focus on discussions of autobiographical prose by two African-
American poets: Audre Lorde's *Cancer Journals* and Lucille Clifton's *Generations.* Race and gender in combination with middle age are the lenses through
which I view both Lorde and Clifton. Maya Angelou's collection of autobiographical essays, *Wouldn't Take Nothing for My Journey Now,* another variation
on the forms of autobiography selected for this book, allows me to reflect
further upon how African-American race, gender, and age dialogue with one
another. I also examine a traditional American Indian (Alaskan Athabascan)
legend, *Two Old Women,* which has been recast by a contemporary Athabascan writer, Velma Wallis. Wallis frames the tale with some autobiographical

materials, mainly about herself in relation to her mother, and this interesting blend of folk fiction with autobiography tests some autobiographical theories, as well as giving us another view of the intersections between race and age.

I decided to juxtapose these texts to each other, although I knew I ran the risk of being criticized for "ghettoization," because I had discovered significant differences in the ways these writers of color respond to aging, and I wanted to emphasize their contrasts to the white American writers under discussion. In general, Lorde, Clifton, Angelou, and Wallis, especially the three African Americans, are much more optimistic about aging than are the mainstream American writers and do not view it as a form of oppression. For these writers, race is a more compelling source of oppression and often eclipses discussions of age. Readers can better appreciate these different approaches to aging by following discussions of the works within the same chapter. Occasionally, I compare Clifton to autobiographers in other chapters who write about their aged parents, such as L'Engle, Roth, and Donald Hall, using the overlapping feature of the book's organizational scheme to counter the effects of "ghettoization."

In the final chapter I examine in more depth what is hinted at in the earlier chapters: the philosophical and quasi-mystical element of the autobiography of aging and the representation of elders as sages and sibyls. The authors I discuss in this chapter represent old age as offering "new opportunities for healing our culture's split between mastery and mystery"; for them, old age is both a puzzle to be solved and a mystery that should remain ambiguous (Cole, xx–xxi). Reflections upon time, meaningful work and leisure activities, mortality, transcendence, intensity of being, and clarity of vision preoccupy fifty-year-old Howell Raines in *Fly Fishing through the Midlife Crisis,* sixty-three-year-old Donald Hall in *Life Work,* and octogenarian Florida Scott-Maxwell in *The Measure of My Days.* I consider their insights, how they portray aging, and how they create new meanings in their own lives. I also examine how their literary methods affect me, a reader in search of spiritual guidance and reassurance as I age.

A brief afterword extends chapter 4's discussion of the philosophical musings of aging autobiographers by concentrating more on gender considerations in these texts. Furthermore, I return to *l'autobiocritique* to gauge my own receptivity to the texts' treatment of time and mortality, given my age, my "orphaned adult" status (Marc D. Angel's term), and my reflections upon the recent death of a middle-aged member of my family.

Why Literary *Autobiographies of Aging?*

The autobiographies of aging I selected for this book have one important element in common: they are powerfully conceived works written by professional, imaginative writers who have had extensive writing careers. I could have chosen autobiographies from an increasing number being written by elders who have not had serious careers as authors. However, I wanted to study self-consciously literary autobiographies because I think such works are received differently by readers. Admitting my bias as a literary critic in favor of *literary* nonfiction, I think that autobiographies by poets, dramatists, and fiction writers are usually more pleasurable to read, more articulate, more imaginative, and more scrupulously analytical about the experience of aging after a lifetime of self-analysis and linguistic analysis of other people. They are also potentially more transformative of sociopolitical attitudes about aging because of their sophisticated narrative methods, depth of characterizations, and rich descriptive powers. In other words, they are more capable of creating "literary experiences" for readers, more skilled at transporting readers into the foreign country of old age.

These literary autobiographies also represent imaginative and diverse approaches to successful aging, as Cole calls for; I agree with Cole that we readers, also a diverse group, do not want to accept just one paradigm of successful aging. I selected these particular works, finally, because they depict a variety of elders: male and female; middle-aged, young-old and frail old; gay and straight; African-American, American Indian, Jewish American, and Anglo-American. They therefore present a range of reflections upon the negative and positive aspects of late life.

So I offer this study of literary autobiographies of aging by writers of professional repute, writers whose diverse backgrounds and imaginative, active careers have enabled them to create fresh, even visionary, portraits of aging for the twenty-first century.

1

Elderly Parents Seen through Middle-Aged Children's Eyes

WITH THE INCREASED medical technology that keeps many Americans alive well into their eighties comes the problem that often people in their eighties are ill or frail and must depend on others for their daily care. Contrary to what the media would have us believe about nursing homes as major caregivers for elders, most elders (about 90 percent) are cared for in their homes by family members, at times with some paid professional assistance. Nursing homes are used only briefly or intermittently for acute care and convalescence. Autobiography has begun to explore some of the important ramifications of parents' increasing longevity: the changing roles of aging parents and their adult children (themselves normally middle-aged or young-old); moral, psychological, and economic issues of eldercare; children's conflicted, often negative, attitudes toward the aging of parents; and, on the positive side, increased opportunities for elders to pass down their philosophical wisdom and spiritual advice to the younger generations, so that both groups may reconceptualize old age. These issues, and more, are aired in intimate, sometimes anguished, self-reflexive, and meditative narratives offered by adult children of dependent parents.

Besides taking up the pen to ventilate the complex feelings and ethical issues elicited by becoming parent to one's parent and of having to witness the deterioration of a loved one, the authors of these autobiographies of aging often have the traditional biographer's goal of paying tribute to the subject of the biography. They present the elder as a role model, energetic and zestful, bright and productive in youth, and in senescence an exemplar of successful aging with dignity and grace, with wit and intelligence. These autobiographical narratives of aging are saturated with memories honoring elderly parents in their prime. Flashbacks that represent memories of the elderly parent's youth are juxtaposed poignantly to his or her current life and condition.

These wide-ranging memories enter the text in a variety of forms: they are transmitted from the parent to the child, who is the narrator, but are recast by the narrator as oft-repeated tales and anecdotes that take on the quality of family folklore or mythology; they are memories of the narrator from childhood and youth, affectionately recounted to reveal the parent's influence on the child and express the child's gratitude to the parent; and they are the memories of other family members conveyed through the filter of the narrator's perspective. Hence, readers have three different lenses—all of which are refracted in interesting ways by the narrator—through which to view the aged parent as well as the experience of aging, for both parent and child.

Two of these autobiographies of aging are the subject of this chapter, Madeleine L'Engle's *The Summer of the Great-Grandmother* (1974) and Philip Roth's *Patrimony* (1991). The daughter-mother and son-father dyads presented in the two texts offer interesting opportunities for comparison to uncover how gender influences the way one ages psychologically and philosophically and what role gender plays in elderly parent–adult child interactions. The different cultural contexts of the two dyads—L'Engle's Anglo-Saxon American with aristocratic Southern roots and Episcopalian beliefs compared to Roth's Jewish American, nonpracticing but warmly ethnic, with Northern and European roots—also flavor the interactions between the parent and child, influencing their musings on what constitutes a meaningful life and a "good death." Ethnicity helps to flavor the language that each author uses to convey personal feelings, dialogues with the parent, and the cultural mythology of senescence.

The language of the two autobiographies also reflects the novelistic techniques of both authors, although they write very different kinds of novels: L'Engle's more than forty novels for children and young adults, such as *A Wrinkle in Time, A Wind in the Door,* and *Swiftly Tilting Planet,* are steeped in fantasy and moral lessons, while Roth's, initially realistic and satirical (*When She Was Good, Goodbye, Columbus,* and *Portnoy's Complaint*), have more recently traversed the borders between fiction and autobiography and still bear a satirical cast (*The Counterlife, The Facts, Operation Shylock, The Ghost Writer*). Roth's skilled novelistic use of dialogue is apparent throughout *Patrimony,* whereas L'Engle's novelistic ability to evoke mystical scenes in human beings' lives is reflected in several passages of *The Summer of the Great-Grandmother.* Their novelistic skills increase the power of these autobiographical texts to engage readers in the lives of the elderly parents portrayed in them and vividly dramatize the issues facing children who take care of parents.

Madeleine L'Engle: Aging, Loss of Identity, and Community

The Summer of the Great-Grandmother focuses on the summer after the ninetieth birthday of Madeleine L'Engle's mother, a summer in which four generations of the author's family reunite at Crosswicks, the family farmhouse in Connecticut, a hundred miles north of New York City. These reunions at their beloved Crosswicks have occurred every summer for almost twenty-five years. In this family, there is little evidence of a "generation gap." The summer in which the narrative begins, however, marks what L'Engle calls the great-grandmother's "plunge into senility." It is a descent not unlike a toboggan ride—from the perspective of her daughter. The daughter's narrative point of view colors the entire portrait of the senior Madeleine L'Engle.

Readers are told from the beginning that this is not an "objective" sketch of the great-grandmother. L'Engle scrutinizes the issue of objectivity, claiming she can only be objective about the years of her mother's life before she herself was born. Yet even this objectivity is disputable because, as she acknowledges, "my objectivity is slanted by selectivity, my own, hers, and that of friends and relatives who told me stories which . . . Mother omitted from her repertoire" (105).

Recent biographical theory agrees with L'Engle, interrogating the idea of objectivity. Steeped in postmodern psychoanalytic, feminist, new historicist, and poststructuralist theories, biographical theory insists, as a basic premise, that objectivity is never possible in biographies. Biography "is commonly colored by the subjective world of the biographer" (Bell and Yalom, 3). What a biographer selects and how she or he interprets these materials is greatly influenced by the historical time and place in which the author writes, the author's psychological makeup, the author's many subject-positions (especially gender, ethnicity, class, and age), and the author's relationship(s) with the biographical subject. So a biography is quintessentially autobiographical in its promptings. Because the subject of L'Engle's text is her mother, flesh of her flesh, the author's "reading" of her subject is particularly personalized; her text records "my very subjective response to this woman who is, for me, always and irrevocably, first, Mother; and second, her own Madeleine" (105).

The subject of L'Engle's text is, of course, also herself, and that subject is also open to fictional construction, even as the author struggles to express truths about herself in what critics call the "autobiographical pact" between author and reader. Critic Paul John Eakin defines this pact: "the autobiographical pact is a form of contract between author and reader in which the autobiographer explicitly commits himself or herself not to some impossible historical exactitude but rather to the sincere effort to come to terms with and to understand his or her own life" (ix).

I would argue that there is a historicity and coherence to the author's portrait of her mother (she, for example, carefully researched letters and other primary documents and also spoke with family members about her mother's earlier years), but that this historicity is subjectively selected and assembled. I agree with the assertion of Bell and Yalom that in all autobiographies and biographies, a "referentiality [or] set of existential realities" connects the literary text to life, even though it may merely be the foundation "from which the author's imagination and interpretation may then take flight" (2). Grounded in referential reality, the auctorial imagination still has the opportunity to take flight since the very notion of identity is complex, and a neat unity of self is suspect in postmodern thinking. As Lejeune says, "a person is always *several* people when he is writing, even all alone, even his own life" (quoted in Eakin, xvii). Eakin adds, "How is it possible to honor the [author's] obligation to referential truth without determining first whose is the truth to be told?" (xix). Both the self in its multiplicity and the equally complex Other are constructed by the author in autobiographical and bio-graphical texts that traffic between fictionality and referentiality.

L'Engle's text, then, is a "truthful" narrative of her mother's earlier life and of her ninetieth summer, but it is also an imaginative construction of the personality of her mother, a woman with whom she strongly identifies. This imaginative construction of the biographical subject may blend aspects of her mother with aspects of herself. Biographers often become like the child of the subject they are depicting as a way of expressing their deference to the subject, even when their subjects are *not* their parents: "the subject provides a sanctioning parent for the biographer and . . . the biographer in turn vali-dates the life under scrutiny" (Bell and Yalom, 3). Furthermore, since L'Engle is a daughter, not a son, the identification with her mother is even more intense, as psychologist Carol Gilligan has observed in her work on female development: daughters "experience themselves as like their mothers, thus fusing the experience of attachment [between child and caretaker] with the process of identity formation" (8). Because L'Engle identifies so closely with her subject, it is not surprising that her impulse in this text is to validate her mother's life *and* justify her own, including her decisions regarding her mother's welfare.

Thus, the portrayal of her mother blends with L'Engle's personal medita-tions on how the great-grandmother's passage into senility and death affects the author herself in *her* body, spirit, and psyche: "I love her, and the change in her changes me, too" (5). *The Summer of the Great-Grandmother* aims to chart the changes in the author during this summer and to sort out L'Engle's feelings and ideas: about her mother and other family members, living and dead; about death and the possibilities of an afterlife; about God; about work; about what gives her life—or anyone's life—meaning.

L'Engle rightly claims that the adult child's experience of having an elderly parent become senile and then die is an increasingly universal experience, even though while enduring it the individual who is main caregiver may feel painfully isolated from others. She writes out of an impulse, not atypical in female biographers, to create a text that conveys a particular, personal ver-sion of this archetypal experience: "what I am experiencing this summer . . . is something I share with a great many other people. And I feel the need to reach out and say, 'This is how it is for me. How is it for you?'" (29). Communicating this experience to others counteracts the isolation and assuages the pain of watching her mother's deterioration and aberrant behavior. Writing this text also enables L'Engle to relive her memories of the wonderful mother she once knew, temporary respite from living with the intermittently deranged woman of ninety who in many ways has become a stranger to her. As the text revisits the past of her mother in flashbacks, L'Engle is underscoring the fact that her mother had a full and lucid old age through her eighty-ninth birthday. The narrative structure refuses to equate old age with senility.

Yet she does not deny the grim reality of this senility for Madeleine senior at ninety. Remembering and writing about the past are the author's own survival tactics, continuously renewing the old love that enables the author "to accept her [mother] as she is, now, for as long as this dwindling may take" (149). While she accepts her mother's senility, she refuses to be limited by the truth of senility, desiring to get to the "truth of love," her strongest feeling about her mother (181). In fact, what she does not acknowledge is that she *needs* to do some romanticizing of her mother—past and present—in order to fight her own depression about her mother's deterioration and to summon from readers positive feelings about her mother and the elderly in general. Writing this biography also gives her the opportunity to research, reconstruct, and interpret others' memories of the admirable woman she had never known—her mother before giving birth to the author at age forty. Recalling earlier, happier times gives her pleasure and motivates her to make it through each difficult day (181).

Writing this text, finally, allows the author to find answers to the question haunting her this final summer of her mother's life: "How do I reconcile my mother then and my mother now?" (34). How does L'Engle reconcile "the sedentary old woman with the mother [she] never knew? someone who rode donkeys across dangerous mountain passes?" (221). The question's subtext is more difficult to face: how is it possible to accept the difference, endure the loss of the vital mother, and maintain her devotion to the diminished old woman without succumbing to bitterness and embracing the nihilism that says existence is meaningless?

Many thoughtful passages in L'Engle's text fight these bouts of nihilism in herself and her cultural milieu as she seeks assurance, in the act of reassuring her own mother, that there is "a reasonable and loving power behind the creation of the universe" (62). The passages describe her intimations of another existence beyond the grave. She focuses in her writing on her mother's slow death as a transition into "a new birth, a new life," which L'Engle intuits. She writes to re-create and then extend a vision she experienced earlier "of something far more beautiful and strange than any of the great beauties I have seen on earth" (150–51). This vision is the underlying foundation of L'Engle's faith in God and an afterlife and enables her to endure the summer of the great-grandmother's deterioration and death.

These are some of the author's personal reasons for the book's existence. However, L'Engle also ventures into public, political issues about the elderly as well. Tacitly endorsing the feminist precept that the personal is political, she uses her mother's condition and the historical situations of her female ancestors to speculate on treatment of aging parents and ways of aging well. One issue focused on is family versus institutional caregiving for the elderly. L'Engle supports family care, would not isolate the elderly from the other generations (33), would reinforce the dignity and privacy of the old as much as possible by having them remain at home, despite the incursions of senility. Writing in the 1970s, she indicts our culture's climate of hostility toward elders, especially women who no longer have a useful position in the household or even a place by the younger generation's hearth. Such women, she argues, are less fortunate than earlier generations of elders, when an extra pair of hands were welcomed: "when grandmother or great-grandmother continued to live with the larger family, to be given meaning because she could at least stir the soup or rock the baby, the climate for growing old and dying was more healthy than it is today" (194). That the extended family is a thing of the past contributes to the alienation of the elderly in our culture. So does the fact that our youthful (and capitalistic) culture may assume, like their Victorian ancestors, that old age is a chronic disease preventing elders from being productive, that there is an "endpoint or *fixed period* of useful life" (Cole, 179, 207, 162).

L'Engle's position on home care for the elderly, given the historical moment in which she wrote, seems a nostalgic throwback to an earlier era. As I gaze backward twenty years from the 1990s, I recall the 1970s as entering a new phase of the women's movement, with the demand for *individual* women's recognition, power, and self-fulfillment. This goal of self-development (emphasis on the "self") may have been reinforced by the emergence of an attitude belonging to Tom Wolfe's "Me Generation," with its continual quest for individual gratification, its suspicion of team play and interdependence. In contrast, L'Engle seems a charming anachronism, with her insistence on the extended family structure as shelter for the elderly (she has the sheer numbers of four generations to support her in her decision of home care for the great-grandmother), on self-sacrifice (especially women's), and on the sharing of familial responsibility for eldercare. She wants her family to participate in the great-grandmother's care and be involved in the dying process. She makes a place for her mother in the family, refuses to isolate her from the grandchildren's blaring rock and roll, keeps her in the middle of the living room as much as possible: "[the great-grandmother] should not be isolated by the narrowing of old age" (33), even when she can no longer be a contributor to the life of the household.

L'Engle admits she has the financial resources—not available to everyone who must decide between home care and nursing home—to make this family participation in the great-grandmother's last months easier by hiring non-family members to assist in the care. She acknowledges that her family is "privileged," economically and logistically, to have this option of home care (28). L'Engle does the kind of work that allows her to remain at home to oversee this care. She can rise in the middle of the night to attend to her mother's nightmares without worrying about having to report to an office early the next morning, and when exhausted, she can turn her duties over temporarily to the hired caregivers.

In L'Engle's view, nursing homes for the old create isolation and undermine even healthy elders' usefulness. The author drily states that such institutions have not caused senility, but she suggests that they have both reflected and contributed to the marginalization and demoralization of the old (194). Her outrage at these institutions is not lost on me; she evokes memories of several visits I have made to nursing homes, most recently to the home where my father-in-law spent the last six months of his life. This nursing home seemed like a scene out of Dante's *Inferno,* with people sitting around in wheelchairs or lounge chairs in varying states of consciousness, some moaning, some dozing with heads drooping onto their shoulders, one man periodically shouting his dementia-driven protest against life; others did very little except watch television, eat, sleep, and bewail the slow passing of time. L'Engle's tone of outrage is bound to strike a chord in other readers who have been inside similar homes. She shares her aversion to these homes with

readers so they are more likely to approve of the decision-making process
the author and her family went through in choosing home care for the great-
grandmother during this summer.

The decision is made with the knowledge that this home care might place
a heavy burden on the rest of the family (45–46). Yet L'Engle's fundamental
belief is that "homes for the aged, nursing homes, are one of the horrors of
our time"; she cannot understand why some people think her mother
"should be put away. Put away. Everything in me revolts at the thought" (28).
I found L'Engle's argument impassioned and almost persuasive, but she did
not address the fact that some families have no other financial or medical
recourse except the nursing home for their frail or infirm elderly. Nor did she
consider that some nursing homes are respectful of elders' needs, providing a
homelike atmosphere that saves many from painful isolation.

As gerontologist Jaber Gubrium observes in his research on nursing home
residents in *Speaking of Life,* some residents move beyond the typically hostile
notion of the nursing home, the negative assumptions that staff are abusive
or indifferent and that "identity and self-worth become matters of institutional definition and management" (10). They are able to make a home for
themselves in the institution, to form relationships with kindly staff and
other residents, and to participate in the daily life of the residents. Gubrium
defines *home* as follows: "When home signifies nurturance, friendship, security, and shelter, what could be a more satisfying life than life at home?" Then
Gubrium demonstrates through interviews with residents that this kind of
life is possible for some individuals in a nursing home, especially those whose
past home lives had been dysfunctional (52, 37). The other residents can become their adoptive family. These individuals also can feel needed by trying
to help one another and by creating their own projects that keep them productive and give their lives meaning. Gubrium concludes that nursing home
"residents construct and live in worlds of their own making as much as they
participate in or forebear the official nursing home world and its roles" (180).
L'Engle never presents this perspective on nursing homes because her political and moral objectives are to interrogate institutional care, exposing its horrors. Moreover, her personal objective—and who can blame her?—is to seek
affirmation of her conduct as a good daughter (full marks as an only child),
one who protects her mother from the indignities of institutional aging.

Thus, Madeleine L'Engle can offer her mother the comfort of dying at home with the help of family and gentle young women neighbors hired to relieve some of the family's burden. Even though the great-grandmother's senility and incontinence rob her of much of her dignity, at least she need not endure institutional abuse over her loss of self-control; L'Engle even asks the young women caring for her mother to wake L'Engle up at night if the sheets are soiled because "I did not want anybody to witness the humiliation of my aristocratic mother" (42). L'Engle assumes that the nursing home is an institution that discounts the individual's dignity and robs the old person of power by playing on his or her bodily failings; incontinence is one such weakness "used against [the elderly]. . . . the idea of having her abused over a soiled bed is one of many reasons why putting her in a hospital or nursing home is still impossible to me" (43). Again, she assumes the worst about the behavior of nursing home staff, whereas Gubrium's interviews with residents uncover the fact that the quality of actual care is usually good, if standardized; most staff do their jobs efficiently but are more concerned about efficiency than about the quality of life for residents (184). L'Engle wishes to provide individualized, efficient care for her mother and a high quality of life, within the parameters of her mother's senility.

Even though her position against nursing homes is strong, the author herself acknowledges, finally, that this summer her "belief is being put to the test" (28). The narrative aims for unequivocally accurate referentiality on this issue. L'Engle makes readers appreciate the costs of the decision to care for the great-grandmother at home and share her dying by vividly describing first the physical and mental deterioration of Madeleine's mother and then the emotional reactions of family members (especially the author) to witnessing signs of this deterioration. There is no romanticizing of the daily struggles.

For example, the author contrasts her mother's almost daily incontinence to the soiled diapers of childhood: her two-year-old granddaughter Charlotte's diapers "have the still-innocuous odor of a baby's. As we grow older we, as well as our environment, become polluted. The smell of both urine and feces becomes yearly stronger" (42). The psychological deterioration is even more upsetting to L'Engle. When she, for example, sees her mother's confusion during their drive to Crosswicks, the author takes refuge in emotional numbness, so painful is it to see her mother disoriented (6–7). She is also wrenched by her mother's nightmares and free-floating fears that something is wrong, and she tries to mother her mother, to utter the "classic, maternal, instinctive words of reassurance" (20); she wants to comfort her and persuade her that "everything will be all right." Despite her own doubts this summer about the "all-rightness" of the universe, she must repeatedly try to calm her mother's anxiety, listen for her mother's nightmares at night as she had done for her own children. Her mother's nightmares disrupt the entire household, causing L'Engle anxiety and insomnia (22). Her mother's outbursts of rage are also unsettling until she begins to grasp its origins: "her atypical rage is an instinctive rebellion against her total inability to control what is going on in the arteries of her brain. . . . Surely Mother's outbursts of violence come from that part of her subconscious mind which still functions through the devouring of arteries by atherosclerosis. It is frustration which sparks the wild rage" (64).

Besides dealing with her mother's loss of physical and mental control, L'Engle must also contend with her own guilt, that she cannot be the perfect daughter meeting her mother's ever-increasing demands. One of several wise insights we can extrapolate from this book concerns L'Engle's distinction between guilt and false guilt in the parent-child relationship. False guilt is associated with the desire for perfection, control, and a martyr's role, which the author rejects for herself. She determines to unloosen the false guilt and accept the real guilt when she does wrong, which is inevitable, since, as she says emphatically, "we all, all of us without exception, have cause for guilt about our parents" (50). Such statements pull from readers a host of remembered occasions in which we did not participate in our parents' joys, sorrows, or struggles, neglected to celebrate a birthday with them, were too busy with work or lived too far away to visit them during an illness or on Mother's Day. Her intense introspection invites our own. Readers are likely to identify with L'Engle's efforts in her narrative to purge the false guilt and accept the "earned" guilt. Not the least of her guilt comes from her confession, when her mother threatens to throw her plate and refuses to eat, that she wants her mother to die (44).

Devoting this summer almost exclusively to the great-grandmother becomes one direct and healthy way of confronting her guilt and making productive, humane use of it. However, she learns in the course of the summer, by interrogating her position as martyred daughter to senile mother, that her own usefulness will diminish if she denies herself her other important outlets.

She needs time to work on her own writing, time away from the house in contemplation by a brook on the grounds of her home (46–47). So these activities, as well as her removal to another part of the house in order to sleep at night, become important acts of self-preservation for the adult child as caregiver. She does not try to elicit pity from readers about this summer's ordeal, for pity would reinforce the role of martyred daughter in this scenario. Instead, L'Engle gives her work of writing and her pleasure in nature appropriate space in her narrative so that she can demonstrate to readers that she does not seek their pity.

Yet there are moments in the story when I feel another kind of pity: pity for this daughter's loss of a good mother while the mother still lives, pity for the moments when she sees the major personality changes wrought by the great-grandmother's atherosclerosis. L'Engle alternately mourns and rages against these changes. I can well remember having similar feelings after my own mother suffered a stroke and turned from a witty, articulate, and dynamic woman to a dependent, linguistically hesitant, somehow blunted person. This past experience shapes my reading of L'Engle's text, makes my response even stronger as the text pulls from me these memories of my mother, impelling me to identify closely with L'Engle and her loss of her aristocratic mother.

Obscuring the real personality of L'Engle's mother are the incontinence, the confusion, the rages, the nightmares and generalized fears—fear of falling, fear of the future, fear of "leaving us to go into the unknown country of death" (62), fear of the violent struggle toward a new birth after the act of dying (72). In addition, the real Madeleine L'Engle senior has been banished through the loss of her own memory, the loss of a sense of time, and the fragmentation of her identity. These losses rob the great-grandmother of her freedom, imprisoning her in her body.

If we read paratactically, we can see how the author highlights these changes in her mother. That is, we can read this text not just as a linear narrative but as a series of juxtaposed passages and larger sections of text, and sometimes as juxtapositions within a passage, in which the great-grandmother's present senile self is contrasted to her younger incarnations. In the midst of carrying on in a fit of temper or fear, the great-grandmother will lucidly admit to feeling "so ashamed about everything" (43). The author quietly states that her mother would never have wished to exist in this way:

"It was the last thing she would have wanted, to live in this unliving, unloving manner" (44). When the great-grandmother threatens to throw her plate, the author recalls that "this is my mother, my rational, courteous, Southern gentlewoman mother, behaving in this irrational manner" (44). Hurt when her mother irrationally accuses L'Engle of treating her cruelly, L'Engle then reasons that the essence of her mother's identity is not hurling insults, her senility is: "the *ousia* of my mother could never say such a thing"; she remembers that this woman (in her right mind) would always love her daughter (63–64). Throughout the book, the author, confronted by her mother's senile behavior, seeks the contrasting *ousia* of her mother from her past. *Ousia,* from the Greek, means the essence, or central identity of a person.

Passages of her indignities and irrational rages are thus placed alongside passages describing the great-grandmother's recollections of her youthful experiences and younger selves, her joie de vivre and patrician elegance, her affectionate closeness with her daughter. These memories are transcribed by the author and colored by her own memories. A Bakhtinian dialogic imagination is at work here, creating the contesting voices of the author's senile old, young-old, middle-aged, and young mother, and mediating among them in the voice of the middle-aged daughter-narrator.

The four subdivisions of the book participate in these juxtapositions of the young and old mother of the author; the first and fourth sections focus mainly on the old senile mother ("Summer's Beginning" and "Summer's End"), while the two middle sections focus on the past of the author's mother and maternal ancestors ("The Mother I Knew" and "The Mother I Did Not Know") in the years after and before the author's birth. Even within each section, however, the past and the present confront each other, encouraging paratactic reading.

Past and present frequently converge in memories. The workings of memory in the narrator and her mother, as well as its failures, are major emphases of the narrative. L'Engle demonstrates how memory is a central facet of human identity and a means of orienting the individual to reality. She uses an underwater metaphor to describe the unconscious preserves of both memory and imagination and likens her own writing to going deep-sea diving to retrieve memories from her "enormous underwater treasure trove" (90). The reader-as-amateur-psychologist notes with interest what memories the author retrieves and what they tell about her needs, her psyche. They reveal, among other things, that L'Engle needs to escape from the senile stranger whom she cannot embrace as her mother and to return to the essence of her mother's personality so that she can sustain her love.

She must, for example, refresh her own memories of lingering over break-fast in long, delicious conversations with her mother about religion, litera-ture, and politics. In the past, her mother's dynamic intellect and articu-lateness made her dominant in such conversations and central to the author's life. As she reminisces about these intimate conversations, readers glimpse what gerontologists have long noted about elderly mother–adult daughter relationships: "The conventional wisdom in gerontology holds that the strongest bond of later life [in our culture] is between the aging mother and her daughters" (Gutmann, 168). Memories of this strong bond resurface in the text when L'Engle juxtaposes her mother at these breakfast tables to her mother now: "Our long conversations are over. . . . She is humped over; she does not even notice that the stockings are wrinkled on her still shapely legs. Our conversation wreathes about her like smoke; she notices it only to brush it away" (146). The great-grandmother is now on the far margins of the world of conversation and alienated from L'Engle.

But where is the great-grandmother, in terms of her imagination, her memories, and the meanderings of her mind? As readers outside the world of dementia, we wonder with the author where she dwells. Perhaps we feel somewhat alarmed by her mental state, so alien, inaccessible, and threaten-ing to our own sense of reality and mental stability. The author's efforts to explore the great-grandmother's mental condition, however, somewhat re-duce its alien and threatening aspects for me.

Extending her water metaphor, L'Engle says that the great-grandmother is no longer able to partake of pleasurable diving among her own memories: "Mother is like a sunken ship held at the bottom of the sea, with no choice as to the fishes who swim in and out of the interstices, the eels and turtles who make their homes in the remains" (90). She observes that if growing up is a journey to integration (especially of the self in relation to the "real" underwater world and the "real" daily world), then her mother is taking the opposite journey: "She is lost somewhere in the subterranean self; she can-not come up into the light of the day" (102–3). She also cannot complete the journey of life, a completion that Thomas Cole suggests older people in the late twentieth century increasingly desire; they seek integration as well

identity

memory

as "self-knowledge and conciliation with finitude" (244). Instead, L'Engle's mother experiences loss of self-consciousness and fragmented identity: her self is now "a dark shard broken and splintered" (103). Unable to control what is happening in her brain, unable to retrieve memories, there is not much personhood left in her, "only the rarest, briefest flashes of a person in this huddled, frightened, frightening, ancient woman" (64). This fright involves the great-grandmother's disorientation and fear of death; she is not lucid enough to achieve conciliation with finitude.

In the past, the author informs us, her mother, possessing a marvelous memory, had shared with her daughter much family history and memories of family experiences. The narrative contains several of her mother's vividly recalled episodes, as re-created by the author: the time when as newlyweds she and her husband made love among the pyramids near the haunt of a gang of bandits; her years in Jacksonville, Florida, and recollections of the great fire that destroyed the city; the story of Greatie (Susan Philippa Fatio), L'Engle's mother's great-grandmother, who had a friendship with an African princess. Because she does not have the "password" to release her mother's permanently locked memory, because her mother is trapped in the present (36), the author must re-create these memories from her own storehouse. Her mother's detailed knowledge of the complicated family tree is also inaccessible, and the author realizes with regret that she had not learned or recorded it because "somehow it never occurred to me that there might be a time like this, when she cannot tell me" (193).

The phrase "a time like this" seems meant to haunt readers, prompting us to seek out living relatives who can transmit family history to us, enabling us to record it for the next generation. L'Engle's sentence captures the regret of many who have felt the desire to do so—too late. Her descriptions of her mother's loss of memory capture the grim reality of senility, tempering what could have been merely romanticized, sentimental memories of her mother's youth. These sentences show readers how L'Engle schools herself to accept the great-grandmother's condition. In creating these family portraits, the author also suggests that she is not writing hagiography but is seeking "beacons to guide me" (196), again revealing how rudderless or without compass she herself feels now that her mother's knowledge of the family tree, her memory, and her selfhood are lost.

She speculates often on where her mother's self has gone because as a writer she knows she is herself often "lost" to the mundane, rational world, plumbing the depths of her "underwater" imagination, an elusive, intuitive world, "the mysterious country . . . the undiscovered world I grope for in my stories, and where I am seeking to understand death, especially the death of the mind as we are witnessing it this summer" (211). When recalling that the great-grandmother's family had always read aloud to one another and thus shared fine literature with great pleasure, L'Engle wonders, "Does Mother remember, somewhere deep inside her, any of these years of treasure?" (202). In asking this question, the author seems to leave a margin of hope that her mother's personhood still exists, buried though it may be under the waters of dementia. She draws readers into contemplating the mysterious depths of the human mind, beyond the mere physiology of the aging brain.

Still identifying with her mother, she compares the forgetfulness of her mother's senility to her own flawed capacity to remember, at once humanizing her portrait of senility, making elders less alien, bringing them in from the margins of society, and also reminding younger readers of everyone's susceptibility to mental deterioration. After her mother's death, she vows that she will never forget her; but the vow is made poignant by the statement that follows it: our memories are "so limited, so finite" (235). She also acknowledges that the memory often operates—or fails to operate—beyond our conscious will, even for a writer trained to remember: "Although a writer of stories works constantly to train an observant and accurate memory, remembering is not necessarily a conscious act; it is often something which happens to me, rather than something I do" (89). Once, in an interesting syntactic construct that mimics the language or process of remembering and how aging affects it, she catches herself forgetting in the middle of recounting the story of her mother and father's lovemaking among the pyramids: "I'm not sure how it was that they learned (I wish I could ask Mother: did I know once? does my memory, too, flag?) that a group of murderous bandits thought this love-making so charming that they watched benevolently" (218). If a middle-aged memory can be shown to fail occasionally, it seems to make elders' memory loss more understandable and less frightening.

Yet it is still an alarming loss to most people. The author pinpoints what makes this loss so threatening: "Her [mother's] loss of memory is the loss of her self, her uniqueness, and this frightens me, for myself, as well as for her" (37). The loss of memory, equivalent to the loss of self, requires that L'Engle mourn for her mother twice, the more painful mourning to be endured before her actual death. The author also identifies so closely with her mother that she fears her own loss of memory and entry into senility: "one of the hardest things for all of us is the fear that one day we will be like this. Because I am already a grandmother, this fear is acute in me" (66). L'Engle does not want her mother to live as "a travesty of a person" because she fears becoming a travesty of a person herself. With sentences like these, I revisit my own fears of what a stroke can do to the mind and personality, anxiously recalling my mother's loss of intellectual sharpness, wit, and strength after her stroke. Yet, L'Engle's narrative confession also prompts me to confront my fears, a good thing since naming them is the first step in conquering or managing them. Setting this fear out in print also acknowledges its reality and universalizes it, so that we readers may feel less alone in our fears. L'Engle's autobiography of aging thus has a referential reality: it enables readers to deal effectively with frightening aspects of their own and their parents' aging.

Another way in which readers experience the sensations of her mother's disintegrating mind, lack of orientation, and fading personality is in L'Engle's description of the great-grandmother's loss of a sense of time. Again, L'Engle contrasts her grandchildren to the great-grandmother to make her point. This is the toddlers' sense of time: "so long that it comes close to breaking time and becoming part of eternity"; this is the elder's disorganized apprehension of time: it "unravels, rather than knits up. It is as erratic as nightmare" (133). The erratic nature of the great-grandmother's sense of time makes her feel out of control and "deconstructive," gives her a sense of isolation from the family and increases her feeling of ill treatment: when did they last visit her or bring her food? The great-grandmother's daily existence assumes the aspect of nightmare; this, in turn, affects the daughter, as the great-grandmother hurls accusations of neglect and hurtful denunciations, even though the author knows that a common symptom of atherosclerosis is "this turning against the person you love most" (38). Her mother's rage and frustration come, in part, from her inability to intuit the orderly structure and passage of time.

The great-grandmother's disorientation about time becomes "one of the greatest deprivations of senility. Time is indeed out of joint" (133). Being without an orderly view of time places the great-grandmother perennially on the verge of catastrophe: "Time stretches like old, worn-out elastic," and this elastic is about to snap (133). Her loss of a sense of time imprisons her in a lonely, hostile present.

Witnessing the erosion of her mother's personality suggests to the author the fragile nature of identity and its ambiguity (such notions are explored in many biographies and autobiographies). She explores these ideas through an anecdote about an occasion when her elderly mother viewed L'Engle's husband Hugh on television (Hugh Franklin was an actor); the great-grandmother claimed that the person on the screen was pretending to be Hugh. This leads L'Engle to speculate: how does she know that the stranger questioning her husband's identity is her mother? She has an epiphany: "Suddenly the whole structure of human identity seems precarious" (61). Frequently she doubts that the irrational, shouting stranger in her living room is her mother, which is why she seeks her mother's *ousia* through memories, research, and the writing of this text: "Who is this cross old woman for whom I can do nothing right? I don't know her" (37). She reflects on the relationship between the act of writing the great-grandmother's biography through selective memories and the creation of her mother's identity out of her own needs: "Am I making Mother up as I remember her? Am I overcompensating?" (106). Such ideas about identity are posed frequently by literary critics studying biography and autobiography. Postmodern notions of identity as fluid and constructed from multiple subject-positions also complicate identity. Senile dementia problematizes the concept even further. That L'Engle acknowledges the fluidity and elusiveness of her mother's identity is hinted in her statement in the book's final section, "Summer's End": "Only death will give me back my mother" (225). Aging and senility have taken away the diverse incarnations of her mother, but death will release her to L'Engle whenever she remembers, writes her mother's life, and re-creates her multivocal identity in text.

The author's speculation about identity extends also to other metaphysical issues, such as how we construe reality: "There's something to learn from this strange, senile madness about the nature of reality," because the mother does not know "where she is, or who we are; or . . . *whether* we are" (106). We may, indeed, exist in different worlds, on differing levels of perception, and atherosclerosis may rearrange those worlds haphazardly for us. Readers exposed to these speculations develop more flexibility in their views of both reality and identity. L'Engle's book creates more space for elders in readers' notions of identity and teaches us how aging may change one's identity and grasp of reality.

The aging and deterioration of her mother raise not only these metaphysical questions about identity and aging but also some issues arising from the emotional exchange of parent-child subject-positions and the shift of power to the daughter. L'Engle explores the intense emotions released in her by this reversal of positions and considers the issue of how the adult daughter can use power justly to make decisions for the dependent parent's well-being. The predominant feeling in L'Engle seems to be anger, anger that she can no longer be a daughter because her mother can no longer be a mother to her; the language in which she expresses this reaction to the exchanged subject-positions is at once that of childish petulance and that of a mature person trying to school herself in a grim reality: "I want my mother to be my mother. And she is not. Not any more. Not ever again" (38). The repetition in the last two sentences of the quotation suggests that she is lecturing herself in order to assimilate the fact that the nature of their relationship has changed. Toward the middle of the book, the author's anger blends with a maternal, protective affection and nostalgia for the mother she had known, but these feelings do not dissipate that anger: "I am furious with Mother for not being my mother, and I am filled with an aching tenderness I have never known before" (92). L'Engle also suggests that for her it is frightening to be in a position of power and responsibility over her mother, as when she, for example, urges her against her wishes to eat or to walk around to keep her clogging arteries in circulation: "I do not want power over my mother. I am her child; I *want* to be her child. Instead, I have to be the mother" (67). Again the child's petulance blends with anger in her tone as she acknowledges their exchanged positions.

Mothering her mother, the author also experiences an immense emotional fatigue, a sense of being drained dry. In the past, even after she became a widow, L'Engle's mother had never been the "bloodsucker" who expected her daughter to stay home and take care of her; L'Engle was not destined to become like her "shriveled female cousins" who devoted their lives to parental care and then after the parents' death were "sucked dry and it [was] too late for living" (131). Yet L'Engle feels that her own creative energy is being siphoned off, that she cannot write, as she participates in her mother's dying process. She compares this enervation to a similar sensation during her pregnancies, when she wrote very little that was productive: "In a reverse way, sharing my mother's long, slow dying consumes my creative energy. . . . Watching her slowly being snuffed out is the opposite of pregnancy, depleting instead of fulfilling" (65). Her emotional exhaustion comes from internal conflicts: wishing for her mother's death while mourning the death of her "real" mother; being torn between love and anger; enduring decisions about caregiving that move her from guilt to resentment to love, and back.

Now that L'Engle has acquired power over her mother (the power to cajole her mother to eat and to implement medically intrusive force-feeding), she must consider the moral issues embedded in power. She comes up with a guiding principle to support her decision not to try these invasive measures, not to treat her mother like a baby, not to add the indignity of force-feeding to the other indignities of senility: "Do I have a right to make this decision? Perhaps not, but I make it because it is the decision I would want my children to make if I were in my mother's place" (68). Here L'Engle's moral guideline is the golden rule ("Do unto others as you would have them do unto you"), made more forceful because she identifies so closely with her own mother as "other."

Anger, fear, nostalgic tenderness, powerfulness, ethical exercise, conflict: the range of emotions L'Engle experiences this summer prepares her for her own "new birth" after her mother's death, her transition from the role of daughter (prioritized over her role as mother to her own children during this summer) into the role of grandmother. She explains these liminal changes through a dance metaphor: "The pattern has shifted: we have changed places in the dance. I am no longer anybody's child. I have become the Grandmother. It is going to take a while to get used to this unfamiliar role. . . . I don't want it, but I will have to accept it . . . as a change of pattern, the steps of the dance shifting" (243). Conceptualizing these changes as a dance implies that L'Engle sees aging as part of an orderly, cyclical life performance in which we all participate. It has prescribed steps that may be individually interpreted with grace or awkwardness, but that can be practiced and mastered by most, set to music, and enjoyed.

Despite some personal apprehensions about taking on the role of grandmother, L'Engle chooses language to suggest the rich new movements, harmonies, and rhythms of old age, especially for women, and the pleasures it can bring (if one is still able to participate; the great-grandmother could not, at the end). As David Gutmann writes in *Reclaimed Powers: Toward a New Psychology of Men and Women in Later Life,* older women, freed from the constraints of child rearing, often become assertive and energetic explorers of new paths in life (152); they create new roles for themselves to employ their increasing energies: "we see their surgent vitality cutting new channels in whatever settings they find themselves" (158). Gerontologists widely observe "the unofficial matriarchy of later life . . . a shift toward greater female dominance" (156). Gutmann could be speaking here about L'Engle in her new role of family matriarch after her mother's death.

Finally, watching her mother aging and dying as she mothers her, L'Engle holds a mirror up to her own old age and that of her husband, one that is not always easy to see and accept. Kathleen Woodward applies the Lacanian notion of the mirror stage to old age and describes its appearance in literature. She argues that it is the reflection in the mirror from which the gazer wishes to alienate herself: "In the mirror stage of old age, the narcissistic impulse directs itself *against* the mirror image as it is embodied literally and figuratively in the faces and bodies—the images—of old people" (68). L'Engle's mirror reflection, uncannily, is her mother, or herself in her mother. In this mirror reflection, a Doppelgänger effect, frightening portents of the author's own old age and death appear, and she resists them. While she acknowledges that this summer "is practice in dying for me as well as for my mother" (52), she declares, simply, that death is "the enemy, and I hate it" (52). This fear and loathing of death is widespread and, for many people, increases with age, as researchers such as Jaber Gubrium (19–35) and Erik Erikson and his colleagues (65–66) observe in elders.

Nevertheless, L'Engle tries to defuse her "primordial terror" (78) and hatred of death by lessening its strangeness: she argues that life contains many births and deaths over which we have some freedom and control, prior to the final physiological death, such as "the death of self-will, self-indulgence, self-deception, all those self-devices which, instead of making us more fully alive, make us less" (53). We obtain lots of practice in dying before the actual event—another way of saying that death is a part of life and winds its way through daily existence. L'Engle does not, however, underestimate the strength of death's influence. She often chooses a birth analogy to characterize death, which emphasizes the violence of giving birth for the mother and the desperate struggle of the child to be born. These qualities also describe the great-grandmother's struggle to die: "Perhaps the great-grandmother is as much afraid of the violence of a new birth as she is of the act of dying" (72).

This new birth to which she alludes is an aspect of L'Engle's continuing religious speculation, for she ponders the reassuring possibility of the great-grandmother's birth into a realm of existence after death, "of which I can know nothing, and which I cannot prove; a new life which may not be; but of which I have had enough intimations so that I cannot discount its possibility" (150). If there is life after death for the great-grandmother, Death, where is thy sting? Yet no glib answers to these age-old questions greet readers, which for me makes L'Engle's spiritual intuitions more credible and sincere.

L'Engle's text is a prime example of how the autobiography of aging is often driven by the author's desire to share a metaphysical insight gained through one's own aging and that of one's parents. L'Engle describes the premise of her insight, an almost hallucinatory moment during her previous travels in England when "the world unfolded, and I moved into an indescribable place of many dimensions where colors were more brilliant and more varied than those of the everyday world. . . . everything deepened and opened, and I glimpsed relationships in which the truth of love was fully revealed" (151). This radiant, noumenal vision of the truth of love is the central wisdom of her book, and it is continually impressed upon her as she tends her mother in her final illness.

With this insight, L'Engle becomes even more aware "that we are all as intricately and irrevocably connected as the strands of a fugue" (70). Not only are we connected, she suggests, but we define ourselves in terms of others. As Carol Gilligan has found, L'Engle's view is typical of females in our culture: males stress the truth of "the role of separation as it defines and empowers the self," and females stress the truth "of the ongoing process of attachment that creates and sustains the human community" (156). L'Engle's book depicts the human community of her family and the emotional sustenance they provide, softening the grimness of death. Death is horrible, but it is not unbearable, for the author concludes that "the refusal to love is the only unbearable thing" (244). Although each of us moves into death alone, death's sting may be lessened by these intuitions of beauty, love, and interconnectedness.

The love of her whole family helps to get the author through the summer. It also helps her and her family to provide the great-grandmother with the kind of death—at home, in her grandson Bion's arms—that few are fortunate enough to have today and that the entire family is proud to have experienced together (231). The closeness of the L'Engle family—belying the stereotype of white Anglo-Saxon Protestants as reserved and independent people—helps to define what a good death is for them: a death without non-family (medical) intrusions and in the presence of family.

L'Engle's contemplation of death's role in life, of her mother's *ousia* and the nature of identity, and of love as the central relationship of the human community are building blocks in her construction of a meaningful existence in all stages of life. Her ideas have much in common with the notion developed by Erikson and his colleagues of "vital involvement in old age" and throughout life's stages. Old age can be marked by mutuality and generativity. How readers respond to L'Engle's meditations depends in part on their stage of the life cycle. If they have elderly parents and are themselves middle-aged, it is quite possible that they will receive *The Summer of the Great-Grandmother* with gratitude for its sensitive treatment of senility and care-giving, for its intelligent questions about identity and the indignities to which aging subjects it, and for the courage and candor of its tentative answers. Younger readers are more likely to ask, "Why should I read this depressing narrative of aging, senility, and death if I don't have to deal with it for another twenty years?"

Writer Judith Viorst has a good answer to such a question. In a recent (16 July 1995) review of two autobiographies that focus on the loss of a loved one (this growing class of books has been labeled *thanatography*), Viorst praises Edie Clark's *The Place He Made*, which describes the death of the author's husband at age thirty-nine from cancer. She then considers why the book could, or should, appeal to a range of audiences: "If you've already been there, why would you possibly want to rerun that tape? If thus far you've been spared, why subject yourself to such painful previews? The answers can be found in something that must be called—I wish there were fresher words—the triumph of the human spirit. . . . It is a . . . powerfully instructive triumph, composed of love, work, humor, courage, [and] prayer" (15). I would apply the same words to L'Engle's instructive text. Its lessons in love's power to deal gently with the ravages of illness and old age are timely ones for people of any age.

The experience of reading *The Summer of the Great-Grandmother* is likely to change minds about how we can continue to perform the dance of life into old age. The author's lively portrait of her mother's life up to her ninetieth summer assures us that Madeleine L'Engle's mother danced her life with gusto for eighty-nine years before retiring to the sidelines.

Philip Roth: Aging and Mortality for Father and Son

Early in November 1991, I was reading Philip Roth's autobiographical narrative of his father Herman's final years and battle against a brain tumor while my own father, Oscar Frey, was dying. I did not know that my father was battling terminal cancer until one week after I had finished reading *Patrimony*. Roth's book became interwoven with my life and helped me to get through the three weeks of my father's hospitalization and his death. The book is affectionate, medically sophisticated, psychologically penetrating, philosophically energizing, and warmly Jewish. In it Roth unravels the complexity of his love and other strong feelings for his father. He describes spiritual moments of oneness with his father and explains his reasons for writing about them. He creates a lifelike characterization of Herman interacting with others, especially with the narrator, by reconstructing vivid dialogues with his father and conversations with other family and friends about his father. He analyzes the control and power issues of the father-son relationship, portraying the disturbing changes in its dynamics as a father enters frail old age.

Roth also offers unflinching descriptions of the aged body's deterioration and pains and of his own ordeal with major surgery in middle age. He gives an account of his anxious negotiations with the medical profession and his dealings with living wills. He deliberates, while surveying the history of his father's life, on what constitutes a meaningful existence and how one's work creates life's meaning. These are the outstanding elements of Philip Roth's portrait of Herman Roth and of himself as Herman's good son.

Roth's stoical probing into what one of his friends calls the "horrible" loss of a parent—in which "Half, or more, of life goes. You feel poorer" (127)—has strengthened me in my new poverty, as a person having lost her second parent, and helped me to sound the psychological and philosophical depths of what I and my family endured that November and December of 1991. This is the backdrop for my strongly felt response to Roth's text. *Patrimony* had extraordinary power over me at that time in my life. I knew I would eventually have to return to this text to write about it and about my intense, grateful embrace of it.

My psychological and historical situatedness in rereading *Patrimony* one year after Oscar Frey's death, so imbued with the experiences of mourning for my father, colors and determines my analysis of the text in this chapter. (My basic interpretation was written in 1992, but it has been refined over the past four years). I offer a reader-response interpretation to uncover why this text is, for me, a source of wisdom, comfort, and humor and to determine what it may have to offer other readers. I write as a middle-aged daughter of American-born Jewish parents and European grandparents who in many respects resembled Roth's immigrant father. As critic Wolfgang Iser would say, my "store of experience" participates in the actualization of the meanings of *Patrimony* (Selden, 114).

Yet even if I had not recently lost my father or if I were not Jewish, I believe that I, and many other readers, could identify with this text's depictions of affectionate rapprochements between middle-aged sons and elderly fathers. We readers might, with the cues of this text, readjust our foreboding and anxious expectations about illness and the coming of old age and death for our parents and ourselves, might reassess our views of elderly characters as passive and colorless. As critic Raman Selden says in discussing reader-oriented theories, "We hold in our minds certain expectations, based on our memory of characters and events, but the expectations are continually modified, and the memories transformed as we pass through a text" (112). Through the process of reading about elders and aging in Roth's book, we may well adjust our expectations and our consciousnesses as we receive new information that challenges the myths equating old age with withdrawal, pain, angst, and deterioration. Instead of accepting the notion of later-life disengagement, Roth offers a portrait of a man vitally involved in life, one who exhibits Erikson's traits of generativity and mutuality, one whose actions and decisions suggest a continuous and "total process of transition and reengagement" (Gutmann, 226).

New texts are rewriting earlier literature's stereotyping of elders as passive dozers by the fireside, or as mad and mean old hags like Dickens's Miss Havisham and crotchety, selfish old men like his Mr. Scrooge. In contemporary texts like Roth's are rich possibilities for change in attitudes toward senescence and social practice toward elders; again, Selden says: "the reader's own 'world-view' may be modified as a result of internalising, negotiating and realising the partially indeterminate elements of the text" (114). As readers work to grasp the partially indeterminate elements of Roth's text, the ambiguities and complexities of Herman's feelings about his illness, treatment, and prognosis as well as Roth's feelings about these things, they understand Herman more and thus lessen the distance between themselves and him. Because Herman is a witty, colorful, slightly rakish raconteur who endears himself to readers, they may stop thinking of other people in their eighties as withered, gray nonentities.

Such changes are even more likely to take place in the reader of *Patrimony* if the reader has a real psychological need to understand issues about aging parents—and a large number of baby boomers do—particularly issues related to the shifts in emotional alignments and distribution of power between the generations. Changes in attitude are also more likely if the reader feels ready to face his or her own mortality. For such a reader, the text's journey into middle age (Philip Roth's at fifty-six) and old-old age (Herman's at eighty-six) is compelling and fulfilling. Reader-oriented, subjective critics like David Bleich see reading as a process "which satisfies or at least depends upon the psychological needs of the reader" (Selden, 125). My needs, the subjective motivations of my critical response to Roth's narrative, are, first, my desire, at age forty-nine, to confront my own mortality and, second, my desire to complete what Freud called "the work of mourning" for my father through remembering and recording moments of our relationship, just as Roth does, by taking pen to paper and making art out of life. As Barbara Myerhoff observes, "full recovery from mourning may restore what has been lost, maintaining it through incorporation into the present. Full recollection and retention may be . . . vital to recovery and well-being" (239).

Writing is an integral part of Roth's experiencing and processing of his father's final illness and death. Some of this writing is retrospective. In the middle of accompanying his father through the difficult decisions about how to deal medically and psychologically with his brain tumor, Roth acknowledges in a conversation with a friend that, like L'Engle, he is having trouble writing, that he cannot concentrate, cannot think, cannot even focus on a baseball game, normally one of his favorite pastimes (129), so his sketch of Herman must have been filled in and shaded after Herman's death. Nevertheless, even while his father is dying, he has the desire to remember him through the act of writing about him. In the last period of Herman's life, Roth adjures himself to remember so that he will be able to write it all down later: "'I must remember accurately,' I told myself, 'remember everything accurately so that when he is gone I can re-create the father who created me'" (177). He is going to father his father through writing about him.

Hence, Roth lives self-consciously, literarily, as a writer, through specific episodes of this story of his father, aware, for example, that his straying into the cemetery where his mother is buried before going to tell his father about the neurologist's findings, which sound Herman's death knell, is an event that is "*narratively* right: paradoxically, it had the feel of an event *not* entirely random and unpredictable and, in that way at least, offered a sort of strange relief from the impact of all that was frighteningly unforeseen" (74). Art, he suggests here, imposes some kind of control and order upon the unpredictable course of an illness that makes its victims and their loved ones feel helpless. For Roth, constructing a narrative about the events of Herman's final illness takes some of the edge off the nightmarish, uncontrollable aspects of witnessing the death of his father.

He confesses his guiltiness about making art out of his father's life by describing a dream he has. In the dream, his father returns from the grave to rebuke him for inappropriately clothing his corpse in a shroud; Roth interprets Herman's rebuke to mean that making art out of the dying Herman's life was insensitive to his father: "in keeping with the unseemliness of my profession, I had been writing [this book] all the while he was ill and dying" (237). Yet he is willing to accept his father's criticism (and the world's?), to bear a guilty conscience after Herman's death, because of the primacy of his artistic and filial commitment to remember Herman through language. The last words of *Patrimony*, reprise of an earlier passage (177), reflect his commitment: "You must not forget anything" (238).

This son has been well tutored by his father, whose remarkably vivid and plentiful memories of his family's history and of the Jewish immigrant neighborhood in old Newark pervade the book, charming readers into engagement with Herman and Philip Roth; as the narrator says of Herman: "You mustn't forget anything—that's the inscription on his coat of arms. To be alive, to him, is to be made of memory—to him if a man's not made of memory, he's made of nothing" (124). Herman sees preservation of family history and "generational memories" (Tamara Hareven's term, quoted in Myerhoff, 232) as a sacred trust. Myerhoff writes about a group of Holocaust survivors and their efforts to preserve through reportage their memories of European Jewish culture, wiped out by the Nazis; but her words could also apply to Herman's desire to keep in memory and teach his sons about the immigrant Jewish world of his boyhood. Herman and Myerhoff's Holocaust survivors think of themselves as "carriers of a precious, unique cargo" (Myerhoff, 232). Preserving memories furthers their mission "of maintaining social continuity" (Gutmann, 228). Assuming the role of "culture-tenders" (Gutmann, 216) keeps them vitally engaged, gives them an important reason to live. Roth, as his book testifies, embraces his father's philosophy of remembering. He records for posterity his father's life, his family history, and the culture of his father's generation. His act of remembering through keenly felt writing inspires the receptive reader to confront the liminal experiences of losing a parent.

Roth uses several methods to make art out of life that especially encourage readers of diverse cultural backgrounds and ages to identify with Roth's narrator in his impending loss and in his quest for answers about parents, aging, and meaningful work; to develop a strong affection for the father; and to begin to grasp the complexity of parent-child relationships. One method is his disarming confessional tone of not having the answers to questions about himself vis-à-vis Herman: "nothing could have been clearer to me than how little I knew. It wasn't that I hadn't understood that the connection to him was convoluted and deep—what I hadn't known was how deep deep can be" (129). Passages such as this season the text, in which Roth acknowledges the intensity and complexity of his feelings for his father, tries to figure out Herman and his own feelings for Herman, or expresses surprise at the overturning of another of his expectations or assumptions about the father he had thought he knew. Since Roth's narrator does not claim unfailing expertise on the subject of his father, his writing becomes a pathway to discovery about Herman simultaneously for him and for readers.

For example, when Roth, Herman, and the first neurosurgeon, Dr. Meyerson, are consulting, Herman asks difficult questions about the recuperation process after the tumor surgery, especially one that Roth, in all his horrid imaginings about the operation, had not considered and that reinforces our growing sense of Herman's realistic outlook and courage: he asks if he will have to learn to walk again, to which the reply is "yes" (116). Like the son, we begin to see in Herman "the stoical father whom I had never admired more in his life" (116). His stoicism persists and surprises Roth a year later as Herman's condition worsens and Roth wants to broach the subject of a living will but fears his father's horrified reaction (or projects his own horror onto his father). He stalls, thinking it might be wrong "to force him to face the most bitter of all possibilities" (204). When he does finally begin his sales pitch to draw up the will, Herman readily assents to signing it, behaving like the realistic old life insurance salesman that he had been, comfortable with death contracts. Roth, bemused, scolds himself: "How could I have forgotten that I was dealing with somebody who'd spent a lifetime talking to people about the thing they least wanted to think about?" (205).

While Herman may be resigned ultimately to death, he does not readily lay down his burdens of life. Herman's strength amazes his son, a strength stemming from his resistance to death, his desire to live (123). This surprises his fifty-six-year-old son: the will to live of an increasingly frail, ill eighty-six-year-old may be fierce. It is well for adult children of elders and health-care professionals to remember this. Age and illness do not necessarily curb the will to live in human beings. I remember learning from my stepmother that after my father received his diagnosis of advanced cancer, on a Thursday, he planned a business appointment with an associate for the following Monday, intending to continue with the daily routine of his life. In Roth's text, this lust for life is part of what makes his father so human and so vulnerable, and it should, in turn, humanize our conceptualization of other elders. Most want to live as passionately as a person in midlife or youth, to continue to wage the "long, distinguished battle" for life against death (123). When learning of the tumor and the possibility of its being operable, Herman says it would be nice to have a few more years (89). He even tries to "bargain" with the neurosurgeon for them.

That Herman is not ready to lay down his earthly burdens, to relinquish his fatherly role, is also attested as Roth reports in the narrative the first visit he has with his father just after his own major heart surgery, news of which he had kept from his dying father until well into his own recovery. His father's distress and fury are reported by Roth in Herman's words, with Roth's gloss on them: "'I should have been there!' . . . He meant by my side at the hospital" (231). Herman is still very much the concerned father, desiring to nurture his son through major surgery three weeks before his own death. As David Gutmann observes, "older individuals become emeritus parents rather than former parents" (234). Roth, relinquishing his earlier belief in elders' gradual disengagement from life, expresses affectionate amazement at his father's love and paternal behavior, his courage, and his strong will to live.

Readers also feel greater intimacy with Herman when the filial narrator incorporates into the text dialogue and passages from Herman's own letters. We see his various ways of relating to other people when we can read Herman's letter to his other son, Sandy, and a letter to Lil, his lover after the death of his wife. In his letter to Sandy, his role as a person who cares deeply and works for those about whom he cares is clearly expressed; he defends himself as a *hocker,* a Yiddish word for one who keeps hounding people, by showing that his *hocking* is related to his real concern for helping those he loves (80–81). Until the very end of his life, as this letter reinforces, Herman is an activist and a pragmatist, passionately caring and working hard for his family and close friends. We see another side of the man when Roth quotes from several letters Herman sent to Lil daily while he was wintering in Florida and she was still working in New Jersey during the first two years of their relationship. The letters show Herman's flirtatious, romantic side and his sustained, affectionate sexuality. We learn through these letters that he is an untutored, unpretentious man with a joie de vivre and energy contagious to all those about whom he cares (75–77). The impassioned "force of blood bonds," his love of family, drives Herman, even though on the surface he may appear to be an unsentimental man who unceremoniously gives back the keepsakes family members give him (90–91).

Dialogue featuring Herman is very plentiful in *Patrimony.* The *heteroglossia* of this text is colorful and stimulating: Herman's and Philip's voices speak loudest, but we hear Sandy, Philip's wife Claire Bloom, Lil, Bessie, Herman's friend Bill Weber, Philip's friend Joanna Clark, several doctors, a nutty New York City cabdriver, and many others contending for expression of the text's realities. Yet the dialogue focuses mainly on Herman. We hear him bravely asking the neurosurgeon his list of questions about the operation on his head. His bullying of Lil is apparent in a conversation about how to open and heat a can of soup. His charm as a raconteur is evident as this "bard of Newark" (125) recites the history of his Jewish immigrant neighborhood in Newark, circa 1912. As he walks through his current neighborhood of Elizabeth with

Philip, we hear him sorrowfully reliving the last walk he took with his wife, Bessie, which exhausted her and may have precipitated her death. He talks about the Roth family's history, about Aunt Millie, who had died recently, and Uncle Ed, whom his father had had to beat to stop his marriage to "a worldly woman" (86). He reminisces about his years as a businessman working for Metropolitan Life Insurance Company. In sum, we hear the multiple voices of Herman that reflect his diverse subject-positions throughout his life.

Roth's well-established skills as a novelist are evident here; he fashions dialogue to make Herman a real person to readers by imagining his father from all these angles. Because Herman is both a real person and so realistically drawn, readers become attached to this quirky, honest, no-nonsense, endearing old man. A kind of transference takes place so that many readers will feel that he is their surrogate father (I certainly felt so) and experience a deep sense of loss after "attending" the funeral of Herman Roth.

The filial narrator also takes pains to present Herman from other people's perspectives. Readers can see the patient Lil's exasperation with the stubborn and at times stonily depressed Herman. A flashback to an earlier winter in Florida reveals his friend Bill Weber good-naturedly resisting Herman's officious but affectionate attempts to encourage him to date women, to rescue him from loneliness. Roth reports that a neighbor at the retirement condo in Florida says to him, "Your dad's a real human being—he's the one here who gives spirit to everybody else" (56). These "testimonials" of other characters in their own voices work together with the narrator's frequent flashbacks to Herman's younger days to make Herman as familiar to readers as a family member would be. In these flashbacks, Roth offers anecdotes about important events or activities in Herman's life: his years as a manager at Metropolitan Life, the night his office was robbed, his years in retirement, including his increasingly frequent Jewish activities, his hours at the "Y," his bossy supervision of his wife's kitchen business, and then the early period of his widowerhood, beginning six years before his illness. Through such dialogue and flashbacks to actual events of the past, readers acquire Herman's personal history as a family member might.

Through family history, dialogue, and some dramatic events, past and present in the narrative, Roth creates an appealing portrait of his father, paying graceful tribute to Herman, a common convention of biographies. Moreover, more than in L'Engle's book, *Patrimony* presents in Herman the disparity between the deteriorating body and the ever-sharp mind that retains a youthful self-image, that resists aging and illness, that remains vitally engaged with life. The book also has another important autobiographical impulse: it does Roth's work of mourning. *Patrimony* is about both Philip and Herman Roth: it expresses Roth's sense of loss as well as his continuing strong identification with his father, even after the older man's death. Rabbi Marc D. Angel, in his book on the adult orphan, notes that this identification is a common aspect of bereavement: "It is almost as if the children can feel the presence of their parents within them" (78). *Patrimony* often describes Roth's spiritual moments of oneness with his father in Roth's survey of Herman's life history. As he witnesses his father's dying, Roth also wrestles with what constitutes a meaningful existence for himself. Roth seasons his philosophical meditations and narrative history with descriptions of the aging body's deteriorations, trials, and occasional triumphs, his father's and his own. As he undergoes coronary bypass surgery during his father's final months, Roth's speculations about aging and life's meanings intensify.

This intensifying preoccupation with aging and death is common in middle-aged people, Kathleen Woodward observes. She notes that the middle-aged male experiences a reprise of the Oedipus complex: the boy avoids the pleasure of having the mother and the punishment of castration by identifying with the father; the middle-aged son identifies even more strongly with the father but feels "anxieties about aging," seeing his father's infirmity as a foreshadowing of his own castration in the future (Woodward, 36–37). Challenging Freud's view of old age as castration, however, Roth is empowered by his eighty-six-year-old father's robustness until the last months of Herman's life.

He dwells with relish, for example, on the large and "serviceable" appearance of Herman's penis as he observes him in the bathtub (177). Referring to an eighty-six-year-old male's penis in this way has a certain shock value (somewhat reminiscent of the old Roth's style when he described Portnoy's unusual means of masturbating); how many readers have ever thought about elderly men's genitals at all, let alone as large and serviceable apparatus? Roth meditates upon the paternal organ and revisits the Freudian primal scene, imagining Herman's organ giving his mother pleasure over the years (and Lil, more recently). He interrogates Freud's anxiety about aging by indicating his own positive identification with Herman's virility.

David Gutmann's research agrees with Roth that old men effectively obtain sensuous pleasures, but he locates these pleasures more in orality than
in genitality: "Time does take away from older men their edge, their genital
and phallic appetites for dominance, victory, and successful agency, but it
gives back an extended range of hitherto closeted pleasures, those of the table
and the community of *companions,* literally, those who take bread together"
(115). So Roth may be projecting onto Herman his middle-aged male's need
to affirm his own genitality. Nevertheless, Roth's genital identification with
his father makes the prospect of old age less frightening for the son. He revises one of our cultural paradigms that characterizes old age as asexual and
physically weak—an instance of his text's efforts to transform ageist attitudes.

Roth may decrease his own and readers' anxieties about old age by portraying in *Patrimony* Herman's vitality and virility, but he does not avoid the
work of mourning occasioned by Herman's eventual weakness unto death.
He mourns by rekindling memories that help him contrast—like L'Engle—
the brave, tough, but deteriorating old man in the present with the man
of vigor in his prime. His narrative focuses, for comparative purposes, on a
photograph of Herman Roth the patriarch taken with his two sons, the male
line, at ages four, nine, and thirty-six; a copy of the photo adorns the book's
dust jacket. This photo captures a moment in time that Roth remembers as
if it were yesterday and helps him as well as readers to place the young,
strong, happy Herman beside the shrunken, frail, almost broken old man at
the end of his life. The old Herman becomes even more human and appealing if we recognize the youthful Herman at his core.

The narrator describes his immense imaginative effort to merge the two
Hermans into one image of his father, which he calls "a bewildering, even
hellish job" (231). In fact, while the photo may be one means of accomplishing
the job, the act of writing this book is the overarching effort to connect the
robust, cheerful, stubborn Herman with the ailing old man. The hesitant
language he uses in parentheses to describe the merging effort in this passage
suggests how difficult an act of imagination it has been to perform this task:
"I suddenly did feel (or made myself feel) that I could perfectly well remember (or make myself think I remembered) the very moment when that picture had been taken, over half a century before. . . . that I was as much back
in Bradley with him towering over me as here in Elizabeth with him all but
broken at my feet" (231). Performing such an imaginative task is required

of adult children who write biographies of their elderly parents, as noted in L'Engle's positioning of her gracious, intelligent, and cultured Southern mother beside the angry, senile old woman. To remember their parents' prime is a way for adult children to negotiate daily their parents' shocking metamorphoses in old age and to reaffirm their parents' humanness despite these changes. Moreover, comprehending the sweep of a parent's life history, from youth to prime to senescence, helps an adult child perform the work of mourning after the parent's life story reaches closure.

While his son struggles to accept Herman-as-old-man, Herman, on the other hand, imagines himself to be like a man of forty until the last months of his life. I observed this phenomenon in my own father-in-law, who, until age eighty-nine when a heart condition and mini-strokes made him frail, spoke with disdain of the dilapidated bodies and old attitudes of other old folks in his senior citizens' apartment building; they were old, he was not. And such an outlook is in itself rejuvenating. This youthfulness in both my father-in-law and Herman Roth contributes to the ability to maintain control over one's own life. Especially since retirement, Herman can structure his days, use his leisure time for activities he had pursued only sporadically in his middle years when he was busy working to support his family. Gerontologists who subscribe to the continuity theory of aging would surmise that Herman is aging successfully. He visits the "Y" regularly, attends synagogue services, and travels to Florida in the winters, socializing with the widows, going to concerts, going out to dinner. Herman is a doer and a gregarious person, which may surprise younger readers who associate old age with passivity and loneliness. Herman fights both conditions by conducting a long-term affair with his neighbor Lillian. Well into his eighties, Herman Roth maintains an unstudied, unpretentious virility that his son admires and aspires to. Even after taking the blow of the news of his tumor and moping about it for several days, he convinces himself that he has to start living again. Roth the narrator constantly marvels at his father's strength and resilience, regularly questioning his own stereotypical association of old age with rigidity and frailty, taking hope for his own old age from his mirror reflection in Herman.

When control is increasingly threatened by bodily breakdown, however, when Herman cannot see due to his cataracts, and when he cannot navigate because his tumor undermines his equilibrium and subjects him to falling, he is depressed, angry, demoralized. As Woodward puts it, "In old age, . . . the psyche and the body are inevitably incongruent. The psyche longs for youth, and the body is an insult and an impediment" (188). Roth's narrator-self mourns these changes in his father by reminding readers of what Herman had been. In his earlier years, he had been a doer and a controller, a forceful manager at Metropolitan Life Insurance. Now he wrestles to regain some power over his usurping body. While he cannot control the presence of the tumor and its influence on his future, Herman figures out he can control or cure his blindness by undergoing cataract surgery. His thinking is clear on this issue: what he wants is a temporary reprieve from incapacitating old age: he wants to regain a modicum of control over his life, to be independent enough to "go to the bank, . . . go to the dentist, I wouldn't need anybody" (197). Although later in this passage he accepts the reality that he *will* need help, Herman is still energized by the restoration of his sight after the cataract surgery, which gives him more autonomy and improves the quality of the final year of his life. Again, Roth learns from his father about how to age successfully and pays tribute to Herman's wisdom.

Besides teaching his son about aging well, Herman also instructs him in the management of one's dying. Herman invents a way to "domesticate his terror" about dying (71). Hearing a prediction of one's imminent death and departure from this earth while the rest of the world is to stay and live is a supremely isolating event, but Herman figures out how to contextualize the news to alleviate his isolation: he reminisces about other family members' illnesses and deaths. Through direct dialogue, Roth has Herman speak these reminiscences to Philip. Then the narrator analyzes the motive for Herman's recollections: they ease his isolation by placing his terminal illness "in a context where he was no longer someone alone with an affliction peculiarly and horribly his own but a member of a clan whose trials he . . . had no choice but to share" (71). Here Herman names his kinship with dead family members, and he does the same thing later by naming friends who are dying, like him, from a variety of ailments (109). Memories of these friends and family members are a resource, a saving force that brings him back from the alien margins of the universe. Roth again recognizes the vitalizing capacities of memory for his father, memories of his family and friends and of himself in earlier stages of his life.

Revisiting his memories is a way for Herman to assert that he is alive despite his terminal illness, and that his own identity will not be extinguished even after death. Barbara Myerhoff observes that remembering one's past allows for "the integration with earlier states of being [which] . . . provides the sense of continuity and completeness that may be counted as an essential developmental task in old age" (239). Herman performs this developmental task assiduously. Roth further assures his family's continuity through the book he writes to preserve his memories of Herman's identity for posterity.

Herman thus demonstrates effective survival techniques worth learning: this wresting of psychological and philosophical control and self-assertion out of the isolation and victimizations inflicted by old age and illness, and this declaration of connection, through memory, with others of the human family, living and dead. It has an almost mystical dimension to it, implying a conviction of an animating force connecting people on earth to those beyond the grave. *Patrimony* offers a sampling of what Thomas Cole urges us to seek in the last stage of life, "renewed sources of social and cosmic connection" (239). Roth's dedication on the frontispiece to his book, "For our family, the living and the dead," suggests his own belief in connection, in the aliveness of his father, whose judgments influenced him when he wrote the book and follow him in his daily life. As Rabbi Marc Angel puts it, "There is a mysterious connection between the world of the dead [parent] and the world of the living [adult child]. It is almost as if there is a shared community" (86). Herman's influence remains a presence in Roth's mind and in the books he writes.

Despite these meditations on Herman's inspiriting survival and eternal presence, however, Roth returns often in his narrative, like L'Engle, to the material horrors of old age. The narrator instructs readers in these horrors. Herman cannot rely on his body for locomotion or to perform the normal bodily functions. His tumor is joined by his failing eyes, drooping face, rotting teeth, and bleeding bowels in Roth's description of the elderly father's body (170). More demoralizing still is that Herman, with his tumor as apt emblem of all the engulfing, wasting, corrupting effects of old age and illness, must endure the sense of his body as his enemy, as the prison that has trapped him and will ultimately kill him. L'Engle's mother, in her senility, is spared this consciousness of entrapment and betrayal by the body.

Roth's bodily descriptions express Kathleen Woodward's "phantasm of the fragmenting body unto death," an imagining of the deteriorating body as it moves from life to death (183–84). Roth imagines Herman's powerlessness and entrapment within his treacherous body: "he was utterly isolated within a body that had become a terrifying escape-proof enclosure, the holding pen in a slaughterhouse" (171). Here Roth also vividly presents what Woodward has called the "*psychic* body" of the aged, a sensation of how the body of the old person might feel "phantasmatically," a rendering of the elder's "body-in-space, ... the interior of the body, and ... the body-in-parts" (169). Age and illness imprison people within their own poisonous bodies and gradually break down the harmonious linkages between elements of those bodies. Roth concludes that at the end of life there is no exit from the body, no choice except to die. Roth is determined to present unvarnished realities of old age. Recording the concrete physical details of his father's deterioration leading to death may also contribute to the work of mourning undertaken by the author, the acceptance of Herman's physical extinction.

Roth's role of support with his father and his rehearsal of his own mortality enable him, like L'Engle, to raise philosophical questions about suffering and dying and to frame some speculative answers. One ethical question arises about choosing medical treatment for the tumor. Roth places this decision about medical intervention in the context of Herman's long life. Herman is already scarred by struggles bravely fought, and Roth decides it is too much to ask his father to endure ten hours of brain surgery. His next question becomes: "Isn't there a limit?"—a limit to the degree and extent of suffering anyone must endure. His answer is a cynical no (115). He realizes with the bitter wisdom of an existential philosopher that there is no limit to the suffering Herman, or anyone else, may expect in a hostile universe. Yet, there is a suggestion once again of the spiritual and even the mystical in Roth. While he is recovering from his heart surgery, he prays silently to Herman not to die; he feels a telepathy with his father: "I believe now that he understood what it was I was silently asking of him" (229). If he believes in anything, it is in the intense linkage between him and his father. Herman's presence is not just in Roth's memories of him; it is more palpable, more influential, almost like the belief of some African religions that the "undead" ancestors dwell among the living.

Such a belief or intuition provides a tentative answer to another question Roth raises, or rather, that he imagines Herman asking the neurosurgeon as he bargains with the doctor for a few more years of life: "'Why,' he would ask him, 'should a man die at all?' And of course, he would have been right to ask. It's a good question" (134). Roth's answer to this question, in his mystical moments, might be that a man does not die at all; although in the grave, he dwells with his family. Such a belief, even if held only intermittently, would mitigate some of the pain of losing his father. The loss is not irrevocable if Herman's presence is felt, even more keenly after his death. Roth's sense of his father's presence may, realistically, derive from the intensification of his own memory and from his psychological need—"wish fulfillment"; but Roth also intimates that it is a surreal presence. In creating a book that focuses on Herman Roth, Philip Roth must surely have felt his uncanny, almost corporeal, presence. And I, in rereading *Patrimony* and responding to it here, also experience the presence of my father, whose death so closely followed upon the literary death of Herman Roth.

It is possible for readers vicariously experiencing the eternal presence of Herman Roth and of Madeleine L'Engle's mother to lose their foreboding about the coming of age and death, for their own parents and for themselves. They may re-imagine the nature of elderly identities, extending elders' identities beyond the corporeal and beyond time. Roth's and L'Engle's strong texts about elders and old age will change many readers' assumptions, challenging the myths of old age and undermining earlier literature's stereotypes of elders. As Woodward says, the literature of aging can change attitudes or expand "horizons of expectations," by enabling readers to project themselves imaginatively into their own old age: "Our reading can help shape the unacknowledged possibilities of our future experience in that largely unexplored realm of our cultural imagination—old age" (14). Both Roth and L'Engle open windows upon this unexplored realm and implant important elements of old age in our cultural imagination.

Discuss in terms of autobios.

2

The Passage to Seventy

WHEN I WAS NINETEEN, my maternal grandfather died suddenly, in the middle of a busy New York City train station, en route to Philadelphia with my grandmother to visit their younger daughter. My grandfather was seventy. Since he was, in my experience, the first member of my close-knit family to die, I was shocked, unprepared for the gap in our family, seeking ways to respond to the loss, wanting to make sense of it. My grandfather had seemed so full of life, so forward looking. Was he too young to die at seventy? Was I to associate seventy with imminent death? I remember at the time that my mother, trying to reconcile herself to the loss of her father, reflected on the idea that, according to Jewish tradition, as written in the Hebrew Scriptures, we are allotted "three score and ten years" of life; anything beyond that is a bonus. This "fact" seemed to comfort her and the rest of us. My grandfather had lived out his promised years on earth. Thus, attaining seventy, for many people raised within the Judeo-Christian tradition, suggests not being cheated out of a long life, having the opportunity for a full life of love, work, and the experiences to acquire wisdom. Perhaps these biblical associations with seventy are what prompt writers May Sarton and Doris

Grumbach to contemplate the attainment of their seventieth year in autobiographies. Other associations with seventy have also evolved in our culture and in the two writers' personal lives that I explore in this chapter.

I began this chapter about Sarton's and Grumbach's texts on the seventieth year with this personal memory because it may have a resonance for other readers thinking about the human life span. It leads me to a brief glance at Psalm 90, the source of comfort to my family thirty years ago when my seventy-year-old grandfather was taken from us.

Psalm 90 is a "Prayer of Moses, the man of God." Moses is seen throughout the Hebrew Scriptures (Jewish Publication Society of America translation) as a man of spiritual wisdom, a leader of his people, teaching others how to live wisely. In the second stanza, Moses says,

> The days of our years are three-score years and ten,
> Or even by reason of strength four-score years;
> Yet is their pride but travail and vanity;
> For it is speedily gone, and we fly away.
>
> . . . .
>
> So teach us to number our days,
> That we may get us a heart of wisdom.

We are allotted seventy years, eighty if we are fortunate enough to be strong and healthy, but these years pass quickly, so we need to make each day count. If we use our time well, we can attain the wisdom that earns elders the respect of the younger generation. The notion of respect for elders is thus linked to a positive view of aging, as Sheldon Isenberg argues in his essay on aging and Judaism: "long life brings with it a wisdom born of experience" (153).

How we might number our days to become a wise elder is a subject worth contemplating, which Moses does. So do Sarton and Grumbach. Barbara Myerhoff was also drawn to this subject and the lines of the psalm when she named her study of elderly Jewish Holocaust survivors *Number Our Days*. In interviews with her subjects, she sought their views on the ways in which they wanted to make their lives count before they died. As subsequent stanzas of the psalm indicate, Moses prays for the attainment of several goals in life, several ways to number his days: "to get us a heart of wisdom"; to "rejoice and be glad" because of our faith in God and God's mercy; and to find and do "the work of our hands" that God has established for us. For the

Holocaust survivors, the work of their hands became their desire to pass along to the next generation the European Jewish culture that the Nazis had virtually destroyed. Sarton and Grumbach describe their own ways to make their days count.

Sarton, who died in July 1995 at age eighty-three, had a full career as novelist, poet, journalist, and speaker at colleges and literary gathering places all over the United States. Belgian by birth, New Englander by choice, she published nineteen books of poetry, including *A Grain of Mustard Seed* and *Halfway to Silence,* nineteen novels, including *As We Are Now* and *Kinds of Love,* eleven journals, from *Journal of a Solitude* to *Endgame* and beyond, and two children's books, including *Punch's Secret.* As she aged, her reputation grew. In her seventies she finally began to receive critical praise, years after achieving popularity with many devoted "lay" readers. Yet her almost daily journal of her seventieth year seriously reflects upon the extent to which she has numbered the days of her life. The journal is filled with entries in which she tries to uncover what she has become through living seventy years, to observe how her priorities and goals in life have evolved, to reconsider what makes her happy. Love, friendships, her work as a writer, and her avocation of gardening not surprisingly fill her pages as they fill her life and give it purpose. She has the help of role models, ancient women whose marvelous energy, passion, and resilience help Sarton and readers to redefine senescence.

As my response to her journal shows, Sarton seems well on her way to attaining a heart of wisdom. Yet her journal indicates that the process of living, learning, and growing does not stop at seventy; she does not have all the answers to what makes her happy, has not fully defined who she is. As Harry J. Berman notes, "perhaps the central product . . . of Sarton's creative efforts has been the creation of her self" (1992, 186). This self is continually evolving. Reinventing the self is to Sarton "a sacred duty" (79). Self-analytical, self-examining, painstakingly honest and perceptive all her life, Sarton seems peculiarly equipped in this journal to explain for readers what being seventy can signify. She interrogates the myths of seventy-ness and reinscribes this age with multiple meanings out of her own experiences and subject-positions as woman, daughter, friend, European American, writer, gardener, lesbian, and elder.

Grumbach has also had a distinguished career as literary critic, literary editor of the *New Republic,* teacher, novelist, and radio book reviewer. Her novels include *Chamber Music* and *The Magician's Girl*. In her memoir, Grumbach, like Sarton, traces her year chronologically, but in contrast, she divides it up into chapters by months. She too seeks to understand the personal meanings of being seventy, the concept of being old in relation to her own multivocal senses of herself. She reconsiders her career as a writer, reviews her married life, her later homosexual love relationships, her relationships with her children, and her friendships. She too rejects conventional definitions of seventy-ness as she articulates her evolving philosophy. Her narrative reveals her own developing heart of wisdom, her openness to love and change.

The ambiguity of her title, *Coming into the End Zone,* as applied to the age seventy, suggests there is more than one way to be seventy: you may at times feel that seventy marks the approach to or beginning of the end of the game of life, the running out of the allotted "time clock" in the end zone. Or seventy may be the ticket for gaining entry into the zone of victory or triumph, the touchdown zone of football, the space in which hard work brings rewards but not closure, as the game still goes forward. Like Sarton's autobiographical expression of seventy-ness, Grumbach's is no swan song. Moreover, her use of the masculine language of football to describe her later life seems to suggest the new potency that she develops over her seventieth year; she fits the description of the "virile older woman" that David Gutmann observes as a transcultural and transhistorical phenomenon (155–84). Although Grumbach's seventieth year begins with a surge of despair as she contemplates her physical limitations, closer proximity to death, anxiety about the short time remaining for her, and questions about the meaning of her life, the narrative gradually shifts mood as she undergoes changes and she again finds a sense of purpose. Readers will be struck by the energy, optimism, and future orientation of Grumbach as she, like Sarton, comes to celebrate being seventy.

The Journal and the Memoir as Genres

Before investigating Sarton's and Grumbach's approaches to seventy, I want to pause and consider briefly the genres in which they couch their observations of being seventy because these genres also influence my reaction to their observations. I have certain expectations or assumptions about the almost daily diary or journal form in which Sarton writes; I expect it to be meticulously observant, "realistic," "sincere," but, frankly, somewhat slight. I do not expect it to be elaborately wrought or profound and intense: the form is too unsustained, diffuse, and fragmented, as compared to a novel or a sustained autobiography (the "chaptered" kind), to achieve intensity or complex thinking on important issues—or so went my preconceptions. In comparison to Sarton's journal, Grumbach's memoir is divided into more sustained chapters, but it still is marked by fragmented entries within each month's chapters. The diary is generally an undervalued medium, neglected by literary critics; I think of Dorothy Wordsworth's *Grasmere Journals* in contrast to her brother William's *Prelude* and their respective places in literary history, or even in the sophomore survey of British literature. Later I came to appreciate the journal keeper's opportunities to create poetic gems and flashes of philosophical insight in those fragmented entries.

Critic Shari Benstock agrees that diaries and journals have been underappreciated. In the introduction to her book *The Private Self: Theory and Practice of Women's Autobiographical Writings*, she says that autobiographical forms, especially diaries, memoirs, and journals, "have traditionally been considered illegitimate" (2). That is, they are not seen as artistic literature; they are not belles-lettres. These genres, Jane Marcus further notes, have usually been associated with women precisely because of their lowly status within literary history, in contrast to epic poetry, plays, or novels: "Because autobiography was a 'lesser' form, requiring from its author keen observation rather than divine creativity, men were less likely to criticize women for engaging in a harmless activity that required only talent, not genius"; the form echoed female conversation's intimacy, "retaining sincerity and a certain naive realism" (120). Thus, candor, descriptive accuracy, and unpretentious lack of artifice (or artistry) are assumed characteristics of journals and memoirs.

Yet the truthfulness of autobiography is, as I mentioned briefly in the introduction, quite problematic. French theorist of autobiography Philippe Lejeune explains that readers of autobiography expect the truth from autobiographers; reader and author construct an assumed "autobiographical pact" in which author and subject of the autobiographical text are identical, in which the "I" or the proper name of the author is "both textual and referential" (19–21). Reader and autobiographer also subscribe to "the referential pact," wherein the author works to convey a reality outside the text; the autobiographer strives for more than "simple verisimilitude" and follows the for-mula, "'I swear to tell the truth, the whole truth, and nothing but the truth'. . . . such as it appears to me, inasmuch as I can know it" (22). However, as a postmodern critic, I distrust these assumptions about truthfulness in autobiography, even in journals, diaries, and memoirs, and question any to-talizing representations of truth, identity, or "claims [of] a stable reference to reality" (Marcus, 114).

I interrogate these texts even when Sarton disarmingly lets her readers in on a "trade secret" that seems to absolve her of total allegiance to the autobiographical contract's pledge of authenticity and accuracy while doing obeisance to the pact's rule of candor. She confesses: "There is always some sleight of hand going on in writing autobiography. So much has to be left out, especially things that might hurt or dismay people" (224). The gaps in autobiography often occur precisely because readers expect honesty from the genre. Sometimes the truth is too unpalatable; desiring, nevertheless, to remain committed to truth, autobiographers swerve from lies by practicing omission of the truth, the lesser of evils, a way of technically keeping the pact with readers. Cathy Davidson's words about the nineteenth-century diary of one Ethan Allen Greenwood can illuminate the passage I quoted from Sar-ton: "even in a diary, even within this supposed realm of the entirely personal and private, there is a fictionalizing, a quasi-literary shaping of everyday life into narrative patterns. Ethan Allen Greenwood not only exercises artistic control—self-censorship—but also is aware that he is doing so: he is telling that he is not telling even though he is not telling what he is not telling. . . . Greenwood assumes the role of narrator . . . of his own diary" (1070). Sarton is, like Greenwood, narrator of *At Seventy,* practicing sleight of hand to make elements of her life disappear, censoring some events and relationships while foregrounding others. Besides confessing to gaps in the journal, Sarton char-acterizes the journal writer's tools, words, as "elusive, sometimes damaged, often ambivalent" (50), further suggesting the limited reliability of the journal.

The issue of believing truths about the self in autobiography is also com-plicated by postmodernists' conceptions of selfhood as multivalent. While "coming-to-knowledge of the self" may be the trigger of autobiographical writing and its goal (Benstock, 11), that goal may be undermined by the ques-tion of just how knowable the self is, and just how cohesive or unified (15,

18–19). Each of us inhabits many subject-positions. Writers of journals and memoirs seem especially drawn to depicting fragments or prismatic facets of the self as well as instances of the self in conflict with the self. Readers learn, for example, that what is "true" about Grumbach the literary critic may not be applicable to Grumbach the lover or mother.

Equally unreliable may be the memories of a seventy-year-lifetime as retrieved and described by Grumbach or Sarton. There are discontinuities between memories and our feelings about these memories that change over time. There are, additionally, limitations in the ability of language to recapture these memories and articulate the feelings associated with the remembered experiences (Benstock, 18–19).

With this problematizing of the genre, how can readers trust in the heart of wisdom of the seventy-year-old autobiographer and in her ability to convey the essence of being seventy according to her individual experience? My trust in the authority of journal writers and diarists of aging derives from the same assumptions I have about the essential truths within fables, allegories, biblical texts, or classical myths. I understand that although narratives of elders may omit or otherwise distort, enough intense and insightful material remains that I will be able to extrapolate the "truth" about these elders' feelings and their wisdom about ways to number our days fully. As Susan Groag Bell and Marilyn Yalom point out, autobiography combines "historicity and textuality" to create the appealing mythology of a human being (2). The same view leads Lejeune to declare that "autobiography is 'one of the most fascinating aspects of one of the great myths of modern occidental civilization, the myth of the *self*'" (162). My responses to Sarton's journal and Grumbach's memoir are fueled by the assumption that myths or fictions of the older self may offer readers some home truths about senescence and also questions about purported truths and stereotypes.

May Sarton: Work, Love, and the Eternal Moment

With these attitudes about the genre of autobiography as well as my personal and familial associations with age seventy as the factors coloring my readings, I turn first to May Sarton's journal. Of interest to me as reader are her analytical remarks about the nature of aging, especially the essence of sev-

Journaling as
sacred

enty as a stage of development or rite of passage; the physiological dimensions; the impact of aging on one's identity, self-knowledge, and creativity; the reconceptualizing of time and the passage of time; the reprioritizing of what is now important in one's life; the unfolding of a philosophy of life and a spiritual outlook. She discusses these concerns directly, as addressed later in the chapter, and in two additional contexts.

The first context involves her meditations about the act of keeping a journal. For Sarton, the daily act of journal writing underscores the sacredness of daily existence; the act of observing, analyzing, and distilling the essences of daily experiences through language creates what she calls "the sacramentalization of ordinary life" in *After the Stroke* (164). Writing about her life improves its quality by intensifying it. She is compelled by the daily (or almost daily) entries to slow down the present and think about what she is experiencing. She influences readers to slow down, too, so they can analyze the rhythms and special moments of twenty-four-hour chunks of time in their lives. Since the present has a way of slipping rapidly into the past, the journal "written on the pulse" concentrates on the present, "must be concerned with the immediate, looking back only when the past suddenly becomes relevant in the light of the present moment" (183). Despite the incessant demands of daily existence, journal keeping nurtures the "inner life, [which] must be kept going under all the clutter" (204).

This journal, because it makes contact with the inner life, becomes a way for Sarton to sort through the clutter, to find threads of meaning, and to reemphasize what is meaningful in her existence: "Keeping a journal again validates and clarifies" (50). Journal keeping crystallizes the priorities and goals of Sarton's life. The journal-keeping segment of her day, finally, brings her a joyous sense of being at home, in the world and in her own skin, because when she names the elements of her surroundings in her journal, she can enjoy the beauty of her environment and take pleasure in being alive.

Journal writing, then, serves an important function for the individual whose writing has been a lifetime habit. The underlying assumption is how do I know what I mean—and who I am—until I write it down? We write to discover the meanings, to catch up with ourselves, to figure out who we are at seventy. "[T]hat self is the real goal" for Sarton, as for most autobiographers (86).

She does, however, complain that this journal, far from being the "peaceful, reflective" record of her seventieth year, charts the race of "a runner who never catches up with herself" (86). Although she sounds out of breath at the relentlessness of her life and her inability to keep pace with its marathon demands, I read this passage as an indicator that the author is resisting inertia and the desire for rest, associated by Freud and Western culture with the death instinct, which often gains ascendency over eros in old age (Woodward, 49). If she did catch up with herself, it might signal the encroachment of death and the extinction of self. Not courting death, this journal is rooted in a fluent present, exhibiting energy in motion, robust self-centeredness, and the continual self-fashioning of the seventy-year-old Sarton's life.

The second context in which Sarton investigates being seventy is that of her many friendships with other women and, in particular, with older women. Octogenarian friends teach her about her relative youth and instruct her in the aging process. She also examines friendships with younger women, who look at her as "old." These friendships show the workings of Woodward's theory of the mirror stage of old age, which she contrasts to Lacan's mirror stage of infancy. One aspect of Woodward's theory is that the individual is informed, with a shock of recognition, of her own old age through the mirror reflection of others (especially others who are her peers and whom she must observe to have aged), even more than she is taught aging through bodily ills and physical limitations. That is, a person recognizes herself as old by identifying her "mirror image of old age as reflected in the eyes of others, the social world" (Woodward, 103). If her social world sees her as old and treats her as old, she is, on one level, old. The reverse is also possible: an octogenarian friend will not perceive or treat Sarton as old. Sarton's text plays with mirror reflections in her conceptualizing of seventy-ness, both literal reflections and the metaphorical reflections of the social world of her friends. Playing with the mirror revises her construction of her own identity and helps Sarton to understand the fluidity of the category of old age.

Early in the journal, for example, Sarton raises the issue of what constitutes old age by placing herself on a kind of continuum with her friends. She considers that she has always welcomed the prospect of her own old age because she has had wonderful older role models or trailblazers, such as Jean Dominique and Eva Le Gallienne (11–12); about the latter, who made a triumphant acting comeback in her eighties, she says, "She is proof that one can be eighty-three and still young. She too is a great gardener, so perhaps a good old age has to do with being still a friend of the earth" (12). Sarton, herself an avid gardener, seeks to reassure herself that she is following a paradigm of successful aging by maintaining her hobby, like Eva and another gardening friend in her eighties, Eleanor Blair (12). Many of Sarton's journal entries are studded with observations about flowers from her youthful gardener's eyes.

She also names an elderly friend, Camille Mayran, who in her nineties authors a book that Sarton praises highly, and who claims to see "no change in herself except for a 'slight slowing down'" (12). To Sarton, Camille represents "old age at its most splendid" (62). Finally, the example of Elizabeth Roget, a writer friend, reassures her that the eighties are filled with potential for creativity and happiness; Elizabeth at eighty-three had recently finished her second novel, is a keen observer of the life around her, is direct, strong, and realistic, and is content to be her age; Sarton comments on her: "It is a pleasure to be with someone who says that the eighties are her happiest years. . . . I admire her resilience and toughness. She is very realistic and not afraid to be blunt" (74–75). Robert Kastenbaum, writing about creativity in late life, would see Elizabeth Roget as an example of those vital elders who maintain their creativity across the life span by imaginatively facing the challenges of aging: "Aging tests the creative spirit in a way that might be compared with the ordeal of a saint. . . . The triumph of the creative spirit in old age . . . would be cherished by a more perceptive society as perceptive people now cherish a glowing sunset at the end of a long and eventful day" (304).

Sarton, one of the perceptive people to whom Kastenbaum refers, admires the "glowing sunset" of Roget's longstanding creativity and her joie de vivre, the way she has actively made "her peace with life and enjoys everything so much" (76). Having creative, vital, and generous-spirited older role models is quite useful, as Erik Erikson and colleagues point out: "Striving to emulate such ideals [of other elders] seems to give a kind of strength, to counterbalance old age's uncertainty about how to behave now, in order to be true to the past as well as to prepare for what may come next" (60).

When Sarton contemplates the coming birthdays of cherished friends Eleanor (age eighty-eight), Marguerite (age ninety), and Laurie (age ninety-one), "three great women all in full possession of their powers," she concludes that "seventy is not old, after all, and if I can be like them at the end of two more decades I shall have reason to be happy" (136). What Sarton observes in her older female friends is supported by gerontological research on older women. David Gutmann describes the "protean energy of the older woman" in American culture and cross-culturally; he also notes that "the same liveliness extends beyond the young-old to include the old-old American woman," even the institutionalized old-old (158). Sarton, a good student-observer of these lively elders, lived thirteen years after writing about them in *At Seventy,* and in many respects her life reflected their existential fullness.

From these role models she extrapolates a secret of successful aging that contributes to her own philosophy at seventy: "Perhaps the answer is . . . to be deeply involved in something, is to be attached. I am attached in a thousand ways" (12). Like Gutmann, Sarton would discredit the theory of later-life disengagement from work and relationships (Gutmann, 222, 226). Gutmann observes that aging elders participate in a continuous and "total process of transition and re-engagement" (226). Sarton reassures herself that she is aging well by asserting her myriad engagements—some newly forming—to people, her work, her gardening, nature. Her journal keeping tries to prioritize these attachments.

Connecting with close friends is her highest priority at seventy, followed by her work and then her garden (92). Sarton's friendships are a major source of happiness. She reaffirms this in the context of her seventieth birthday year: "What better way in fact to celebrate a seventieth year than with a feast of friends?" (136). Throughout her journal writing life, Sarton has experienced a tension between the desire for the solitude in which to reflect and write and the desire to be encircled by her friends, "the tension between attachment and separateness is the conflict over what is owed to others versus what is owed to oneself" (Berman 1989, 18–19). In *At Seventy,* however, she continually celebrates her friendships more than her work.

Although, as she indicates early in the journal, her life is no longer centered by one intensely beloved person, all her friends act as her extended family so that she sees herself as "a centipede heart, so full of love it beats very fast and can race around" (15). She explains that she is grateful to have friends with whom to share the good things that happen to her, especially the recognition she achieves for her work, because as she poignantly says, "it is then that I long for my parents to know and sometimes feel rather an orphan" (163). Such sentences are bound to strike a resonant chord in many readers; I think of sharing my happiness over publication of my work or my children's achievements with my husband and friends, while I still long to reach beyond the grave to tell my mother and father my good news. As we age, most of us inevitably come to orphanhood, as I discuss in relation to Philip Roth's and Madeleine L'Engle's works in chapter 1. Rabbi Marc Angel comments in *The Orphaned Adult* that "we are a society of orphans" (153). Sarton touches readers of middle age and old age as she describes the orphan's loneliness. Yet she is convinced that friendships can assuage this loneliness, and her cheerful reportage of gatherings with friends persuades readers to value their own friendships as they age; I think of how my family and I spend our Thanksgivings with our friends in town, who have become like family, creating new traditions and shared memories. For familial losses there is some recompense.

Another perspective on aging comes to Sarton from her relationships with younger friends. Sarton may not be old in relation to Elizabeth Blair or Camille Mayran, but she is in relation to Karen Saum and Betsy Swart. An especially interesting concept emerges from her analysis of her relationship with Betsy Swart, a woman forty years Sarton's junior, who after reading some of Sarton's novels decided abruptly to write her dissertation on them and to abandon another thesis half finished. Such an act marks Betsy as young, to Sarton; it is the act of an "adventurer," an act of "such spontaneous combustion, grand and courageous," that contrasts with Sarton's conduct of her life now: "I feel my age when I am with such a young person, not because I feel old but because, in the forty years that separate us, I have deeply grooved my life in one direction" (67). The grooves of her life were formed by her devotion to writing, her love of music and nature, her choice of solitude as a lifestyle, and her pursuit of gardening. The things that bring joy to her life are consistent: "They do not change. Flowers, the morning and evening light, music, poetry, silence, the goldfinches darting about" (17). Sarton also admires Karen Saum's decision to change her life by entering the St. Francis Community to do "formidable and imaginative work among the very poor" (26). Sarton sees herself, at seventy, as unlikely to make such major lifestyle changes although she still looks forward to life's daily surprises (10).

Do these examples imply that Sarton thinks only the young have the flexibility and courage to change their lives radically? It becomes a pivotal question of Doris Grumbach's memoir as well. Underlying this question is a polarization common to our culture: age/rigidity and youth/change. Sarton implicitly reinforces the bipolarity here but questions it in other passages.

She challenges the polarization, for example, when she names the exciting new activities of Elizabeth Roget (writing another novel, etc.) and of her other eighty- to -ninety-year-old friends. She also encourages readers to think of the people they know who have undertaken changes and new adventures in later life. I think of my family and friends in their sixties and seventies who have traveled across the country and beyond, moved, become painters, taken on new volunteer activities or learned a foreign language, found new careers or new loves. Elders who have changed their lives may provide an impetus to change our own "grooved" lives and teach us that later life need not equate with rigidity or conservatism.

In fact, in the journal's more direct statements about what being seventy means to Sarton, receptivity to change figures prominently. What seventy feels like to Sarton is what our culture normally associates with youthfulness. She describes the relativity of the concept of age, what Berman has called the idea of "'felt age,' one's subjective sense of feeling old or feeling young" (1992, 15). This "felt age" corresponds more to events in one's career and private life than to chronology or a biological condition. Sarton declares, "I realize that seventy must seem extremely old to my young friends, but I actually feel much younger than I did . . . when I wrote the poem 'Gestalt at Sixty'" (37). She gives two reasons for feeling so young: the achievement of recognition for her writing (Berman 1992, 5), which eases her anxieties about the future, and her development of internal response mechanisms that give her both flexibility and a sense of control over her life. About the latter she says, "I am far better able to cope at seventy than I was at fifty. I think that is partly because I have learned to glide instead of to force myself at moments of tension" (37). Because she is more fully centered in herself, she has dispelled many of the inner conflicts that once sapped her powers (10). She can glide through the vicissitudes and crises of her life because she feels less vulnerable to potential hurts and losses, less subject to anger or anxiety.

I responded to Sarton's reflection about seventy versus fifty by reflecting upon my own maturing process, comparing myself at forty-nine to my younger incarnation at twenty-nine; like Sarton, I feel less subject to conflict, anger, anxiety, and self-doubts, more able to meet changes with equanimity and confidence. In fact, I am proud of changes I have made, of taking new ventures: learning to ride a bicycle at forty, moving into a new house at forty-eight, "autobiographizing" my scholarly style of writing, and undertaking in my forties the collaborative writing of a couple of essays with two English department colleagues. Change is possible, irrespective of age, and exhilarating when implemented. Maturity, moreover, helps us adjust to change more skillfully. Sarton's journal reminds us of our potential for change throughout life.

Sarton's attitude toward time, particularly toward the future and the present, is also changing in her seventieth year. She notes that she is more hopeful, less anxious about the future. In fact, she is receptive to the future's unexpectedness, distinguishing her attitude of fluidity and progression from that of the truly old: "I suppose real old age begins when one looks backward rather than forward, but I look forward with joy to the years ahead" (10). Ongoing self-development, enthusiasm, active questing for spontaneous, intense experiences, and a future orientation are some distinguishing traits of the young (or young mentality) in our culture. Sarton co-opts this language for herself, accepts the dichotomy of youth/future/progress versus age/past/stasis, but she claims for herself at seventy the youthful pole or declares her membership in another category often described by gerontologists as "the young old." The young old (active people in their sixties and seventies), like the young, often embrace life as an adventure; says Sarton, "I feel . . . in a constant state of expectation before each day. . . . Who knows what may happen? I am ready to be connected with whatever does" (305).

In some respects, elders may be more receptive to change than adolescents just beginning to fashion who they are; last year I was struck by my then fourteen-year-old daughter's resistance to our family's move into our new house, while I sought the change to gain more space and sunlight and adjusted with an alacrity that surprised myself. Yet I need not have been surprised. I knew who I was and what I needed and wanted more than my teenage daughter did. So the move was my active choice, whereas it was not her choice at all. Also, I had experienced several moves in my life, knew the process, knew how to minimize the inevitable stress and sense of dislocation better than she; it was her first move ever. Age and experience can make many of us more open to change, not less, more seasoned in how to adapt to new circumstances. Sarton certainly wishes to reclaim the language of adaptability and adventurousness for later life.

A woman of language, Sarton is also concerned about a common metaphor of our culture that places her in the autumn of her life, the time often associated with saying farewell and winding down. So she reinscribes that stereotypical metaphor with another meaning of autumn: its association with youth and the energizing beginning of a new school year, the time for reunions and saying hello (161). She reiterates in the autumn passage her alert appreciation for the present, her sense of countless opportunities and plans, professional and personal, for the future. Her enthusiasm and spontaneity have the ring of youth about them, counteracting the earlier passage in which she saw her life as deeply grooved compared with Betsy Swarts's life.

While in another entry Sarton distinguishes the "genius of youth" from the "subtler and gentler, so much wiser" genius of old age, she immediately thereafter blurs the distinction or, more accurately, extends the borders of youth by arguing that "it is possible to keep the genius of youth into old age, the curiosity, the intense interest in everything from a bird to a book to a dog" (76). Unlike youth, the seventy-year-old has an extensive past, which gives her "food to grow on"; the past does not imprison her (10) but does bolster her confidence to meet challenges in the present. The present offers more pleasures and intensity: "I live more completely in the moment these days . . . and am far more detached from the areas of pain, the loss of love, the struggle to get the work completed, the fear of death" (37).

In other words, seventy for Sarton means less waste of energy on frustrations and self-doubts, more receptivity to the unpredictable evolutions of her life, more practiced navigation of her life's twists and turns. Because, as she indicates at the end of the journal, she feels herself "coming into a period of inner calm" in which her life's work is reaching fruition, her friends are with her, and she can continue to work when alone, she is contented: "Who could ask for more?" (334). Erikson has observed this phenomenon of coming "into one's own" in old age (180–81).

Even as she tries to claim a youthful outlook and conduct of life in some entries, however, in others Sarton insists upon clear differences between a youth and a person having lived seventy years. Sometimes she assumes the mantle of the aged sage by virtue of what the years have taught her. She argues that there are big differences between a forty-year-old and a seventy-year-old because of "what life itself does to force us to maturity" (181). Surely other readers will respond to such a statement as I did by remembering some of the difficult problems and experiences in their lives that have educated them, claimed their innocence, and compelled them to grow up: deaths of parents, disappointments and dashed ambitions, confrontations with one's own limitations, regrets for one's insensitive behavior or bad decisions, shocked lessons about other people's malevolence or selfishness. Sarton at seventy knows what a woman of forty might not yet have learned: "what such a life costs" (76). This bald and restrained phrase suggests the painful effects of the pivotal decisions and daily choices that lead to sacrifices and losses, the endlessly delayed gratifications, the denial of whole areas of pleasure and self-affirmation. No one knows how difficult life is better than an older person.

Sarton's journal offers no whitewashing of the life experienced by a woman of seventy. Yet meeting the challenges of a lifetime and paying the costs of living do precipitate changes in elders, do give them a new kind of wisdom. Many of the elders Erikson studied talked to him about this wiser condition: "These people describe both themselves and their aged contemporaries as more tolerant, more patient, more open-minded, more understanding, more compassionate, and less critical than they were in younger years" (60). Sarton's introspection reveals similar changes in herself, a deepening of insight and widening of tolerance.

Another difference in Sarton from having lived seventy years is her intermittent sense that despite her intense life in the present and her anticipation of the future, little future time remains. This negative fact is balanced by the growing wealth of her memory bank: "I sometimes feel old these days when I am suddenly made aware of the little time *ahead*. . . . I have at most ten or fifteen springs! . . . On the other side though, what I do have is seventy springs in my head, and they flow back with all their riches now" (50–51). Sarton accurately estimates the time remaining to her: thirteen springs until her death at eighty-three; she is in tune with the temporal rhythms of her body. Yet she confesses to having a "compulsive sense of time passing" (76–77), a compulsion that is with her in her journals before *At Seventy,* but not quite as persistently. She observes that only her subjective perception of time's forward speed distinguishes seventy from sixty-five: "I don't see much difference, except that time accelerates. The days go by with frightful rapidity, and so do the years. . . . time does not stand still in old age" (286). There is a note of dismay in this observation, a desire to slow the passage of time.

This dismay at time's fleeting may be what prompts Sarton to shift in some passages from conceptualizing time as a limited quotidian commodity to considering time spiritually. Dwelling in spiritual time means placing her-self in an eternal present where she passionately experiences each moment: "To live in eternity means to live in the moment, the moment unalloyed—to allow feeling to the limit of what can be felt"(190; cf. 37). To live each moment intensely is to transcend time, to bathe in "eternity's light" (190). Sarton makes years out of her days. To live in the center of the moment is the best way to number our days.

To live intensely in the moment and to continue to write her poetry allay Sarton's panic about time's acceleration. Intense living also enriches her writing and transforms her identity. In her introduction to *Aging and Gender in Literature*, Anne Wyatt-Brown observes this transformation in many writers: "[Writers'] late-life writing . . . suggests that even the threat of imminent death can inspire writers to new creativity. Time may be short, but for many [poets and novelists] their later writing marks a new beginning, a bold attempt to re-create their identities for the remainder of their lives" (13). Robert Kastenbaum also articulates the idea of artists' innovative "late style" as a response to "a sense of time urgency . . . an outcome—or casualty—of the aging individual's confrontation with the prospect of cessation and the hope of renewal" (301–2).

Throughout these journal entries on Sarton's "felt sense" of being seventy, then, she wrestles with the notion that our culture may deem the septuagenarian as elderly and no longer productive or creative, but she rejects the epithet of "old" and celebrates a sense of her deepening complexities as she ages. She also regularly acknowledges deep internal differences between forty and seventy wrought by experiences over the years. She happily describes the wisdom and memories acquired, the self-assurance and calm.

Yet for every generalization I make about Sarton's attitude toward the state of being seventy, I can find a passage that challenges that generalization. For example, Sarton may in some entries write about the seventy-year-old as wise, self-assured, and calm, while at other times she will bemoan the evidence of her own aging, show distress at her changed physical appearance. In fact, a passage in which she "writes the body"—or, more precisely, the face—of the seventy-year-old woman reveals much about her own ambivalence toward aging, about the inadequacy of words to describe her conflicted feelings, and about the influence of our culture's negative messages about old women. She questions her culture's and her own preoccupation with wrinkles, claiming that the spirit of a person shines through the wrinkles and that the wrinkles are emblems of a life fully and intensely experienced; she describes her friend Lotte Jacobi's face as an example. Still, she confesses to using a night cream regularly and to "mourn[ing] one's young face sometimes" (61). In the next sentence she reverses her position again and declares that she likes her face better now, that it has improved, "because I am a far more complete and richer person than I was at twenty-five" (61). She emblematizes her new integrity and self-acceptance in this mirror gaze at her face: "Now I wear the inside person outside and am more comfortable with my self" (61).

Interestingly, she ends the passage on her wrinkled face by applying verbal skin cream to it, by claiming a new kind of youthfulness born of experiences that enable her to be candid and to let her defenses down: "In some ways I am younger because I can admit vulnerability and more innocent because I do not have to pretend" (61). The youthful innocence and candor are antidotes to the wrinkles. This passage registers dismay, but also pride in her own lined face. She reproaches herself for her obeisance to our culture's negative assessment of elders' appearance.

Sarton's attempts to create signification for seventy-ness are most illuminating when she tries to analyze what is important to her at seventy, what brings her happiness. We leave *At Seventy* with a dawning awareness of how to reprioritize our own lives. Her thoughts focus, not surprisingly, on the two areas Freud would emphasize as potential sources of pleasure (and hence pain) in life: work and love. Writing poetry, for Sarton at seventy, takes precedence even over the pursuit of love: with gratitude that "the amazing gift of poems" still exists for her, Sarton clarifies her values: "A love affair at this point is not in the cards, but poetry is here, and that is all that matters" (190). She wishes for solitude to write her poems (193, 334), taking time out only to visit with close friends and tend her garden (in an earlier entry, page 92, she actually put friends before poetry in her priorities, although friendship is not equivalent to the love that she discusses here). She is convinced, after all her years of self-doubt about her writing, that she has achieved some mastery of her craft and is "worthy of being esteemed" (180–81).

This is not to say that she leaves love behind her at seventy, or that love is not in some significant way connected to her work; during her career, sexual love has centered Sarton's life and acted as muse to her writing, especially

*change in sexual importance of
passion in old age*

during the fifteen years of her relationship with Judy Matlack. It is simply
that for her at seventy, love is redefined to exclude an obsessive sexual
element (192–93), the love affair's enslaving passions, its animal-like consequences, the "rousing of the daimon . . . out of its lair" (193). Such a redefini-
tion of love to avoid sexual passion's unsettling complications, which she no
longer "feel[s] up to," is a distinguishing characteristic of age for Sarton: "So
there are some changes at seventy that mean old age" (193). Doris Lessing
has also written of sexuality's enslaving qualities, and the middle-aged protagonist of her novel *The Summer before the Dark,* Kate Brown, discovers that
shedding her sexuality or disregarding her culture's prescribed traits of sexual
attractiveness for women (no longer dyeing her hair, wearing clothing that
clings to her body, or swinging her hips as she walks) becomes powerfully liberating.

For Sarton, the entry dated 13 November describes a new love relationship
without sexuality: "I am happy because there is someone to focus the world
for me again and to hold time still" (192); love enables her to live in the eternal
moment, to stop the accelerated passage of time. This new love also enables
her to write with facility once more, fertilizes the soil of her creativity: "And
what is it that suddenly opens the door into poetry? A face, a voice, two
hours of rich communion and the world has changed" (192–93; cf. 225). This
new love rejects sexual consummation, and Sarton accepts the reality "that
this time it will not be a love affair. Circumstances preclude that consummation, and I sense that there the guardian angel has been wise" (193).

Sarton specifically says that she does not mind the lack of this sexual element and that it is a prudent decision to avoid sexuality's tumultuous consequences at this stage of her life. Yet I hear a note of regret or nostalgia for
past affairs' sexual tumult in her characterization of this relationship's more
detached quality. Interestingly, a later entry that alludes to her receipt of a
letter signaling the end of this relationship describes her feelings as hardly
calm ("I boiled like a kettle on the stove," 233); moreover, after the relationship ends, she feels "bereft," and the flow of poetry ceases (256). These allusions suggest the continuing intensity of Sarton in love, with or without the
ingredient of sexuality in her relationships. Although elsewhere in the journal, as she responds to her reading of Alyse Gregory's journal, Sarton declares
herself glad to be "free of passion . . . , [since] it is a great blessing not to be
in its thrall" (109), she still seems committed to love, erotic and platonic, as

one of life's primary adventures. Early in her journal she quotes from the birthday greetings sent to her by her adopted brother, Charles Feldstein: "you taught those who love you that despite chronology, adventure is there for those who remain open to love" (15). Sarton remains open to love in many forms at seventy.

Perhaps by suggesting that love need not involve sexual consummation, Sarton aims to extend the possible significations of love and to claim it for elders as well as for the young. She challenges our culture's association of impassioned love with the young, but she continues to subscribe to the hegemonic belief that love has enormous energizing, restorative, or inspirational powers. She can, indeed, sound like an old-fashioned romantic, as when she describes Judy as "the precious only love with whom I lived for years, the only one" (213) and explains why she must visit with the now senile Judy (because "[t]rue love does not die" 147), or when she describes "that special kind of love," the passionate attachment to one person that acts like the muse to summon poetry and that "brings more life, that makes life sparkle if only for a month or two" (218). While sexual consummation of these passionate attachments may no longer be likely for Sarton, she still feels "violently attached" to individuals (217) from time to time, buffeted by the storminess of romantic love, and she cites similar propensities in her eighty-seven-year-old friend Lotte Jacobi. Both women are "the living proof that love is always possible" (218), a central point in Sarton's portrayal of herself at seventy.

Both love and work enable Sarton "to live in eternity" and place Sarton squarely in the center of the eternal moment, intensifying her experiencing of time and slowing its movement (190). Early in the journal, Sarton says, "I have always believed that one must live as though one were dying—and we all are, of course—because then the priorities become clear" (44). This philosophy is crystallized for her as she turns seventy: she makes clear that writing poetry, love, and friendships are the centerpieces of her life as they are of her text, At Seventy. These activities, Sarton states repeatedly, continue unabated and gather greater force during her seventieth year. Unlike Freud, who feared old age because he perceived it "as a period not of simple decline but of regression . . . referring to his life in work" (Woodward, 42), Sarton sees seventy as fertile field for work *and* love.

One essential piece of wisdom I distill for my own life from my reading of *At Seventy*, then, is to strive, through whatever activities are most important,

challenging, and stimulating, to intensify the experiencing of time, to sacra-
mentalize each day, and to remove obstacles, internal and external, to that
intensity. It may be that we cannot remove the internal obstacles until we
have lived seventy summers and know both the costs and the payoffs of living. This gives us much to anticipate.

Doris Grumbach: Seventy as Re-creation of One's Life

I was not as familiar with the novels of Doris Grumbach as I had been with
Sarton's fiction and poetry when I began reading *Coming into the End Zone*. All
I knew of Grumbach was her work as literary editor of the *New Republic* and
as guest book reviewer on National Public Radio. In fact, I first heard of her
book when it was featured on *All Things Considered*. But I was intrigued by
the fact that she is a friend of May Sarton's; her visits to Sarton's home are
recorded in Sarton's journals, and Grumbach refers to one visit in *End Zone*.
I have no doubt that Grumbach has read and been influenced by these journals, especially *At Seventy*, in the writing of her own, albeit very different,
memoir. An intertextuality of nonfiction on aging is operating with these
aging autobiographers.

I am also influenced by this intertextuality as reader in my response to
Grumbach's memoir; having read *At Seventy* (and several of Sarton's other
journals) before *End Zone*, I constantly compare and contrast them, at one
time taken aback by the more negative cast Grumbach gives in most of her
text to the aging body and the effects of being seventy on one's life. To Grumbach, seventy is old, and she shows readers why repeatedly. This harsh dose
of reality and Grumbach's complaints about old age helped me to trust her
observations and believe in the gradual changes in her attitude about being
seventy (and seventy-one), which the memoir traces. *End Zone* is, by the conclusion of the book's literal and metaphysical journey, almost as optimistic a
depiction of being seventy as Sarton's journal. *End Zone*, finally, celebrates the
seventy-year-old author's capacity for love and friendship, for adaptability to
change, for re-creating her life, for tapping into new spirituality. In so doing,
Grumbach surely gives younger readers cause to redefine what being seventy
means. Readers in the author's age cohort will applaud this corroboration of
their young-oldness.

Unlike Sarton at seventy, Grumbach unswervingly sees herself as old, calls herself elderly, portrays herself as frail, increasingly less mobile, vulnerable to falls and city crime. (Sarton at seventy-four in *After the Stroke* and at seventy-nine in *Endgame* sounds more like Grumbach.) *End Zone* begins as a rather dark book, with the author dreading "the terrible Twelfth" of July, her seventieth birthday, and bemoaning the mental and physical incapacitations of her years. Yet she seeks, without too much hope of finding, "a positive value to living so long, some glory to survival" (12). Berman sees in the memoir's dark earlier passages the recording of losses, especially losses "of the internal anchoring of her life, losses of faith, optimism, physical pleasure, and great expectations" (1992, 103). Readers may also see in Grumbach's dark language the guilt of the elderly survivor, many of her friends having recently died young of AIDS (12; cf. 137).

Grumbach's narrator first lays out our culture's typically negative assumptions about being seventy: "This should be the age of settled decorum, stability, even sedentary acceptance of what one has or is left with" (147). She characterizes old age as set in its ways and resistant to life's flux. Then she overturns these outdated stereotypes.

She reassesses what it means to be old, challenges her own thinking: "Growing old means abandoning the established rituals of one's life, not hardening into them" (26). She discovers that "it is [not] too late . . . for [her] to live in a new place" at age seventy (25). By the end of the book she no longer perceives age as "loss of the enjoyment of leaving home" (25). She also rejects the myth that seventy is "too old to be something else" (156). A person may continue to remake herself in late life.

This overturning of her stereotypical thinking takes place over the course of a narrative that details her return journey, after many years, to the ancient Mayan cities of Mexico, as well as the process by which she and her companion, Sybil, decide to leave Washington, D.C., buy a home in Maine, and relocate their bookstore business there. Despite the questions, doubts, and fears that her text honestly raises, she declares with optimism, "now it seemed the older one grew, the less realistic one was about the future" (146)—which suggests the less willing to accept physiological and mental signs that limit us and hint that we will not live forever, the more apt to keep planning for a full future.

As the book's epigraph, a quotation from Winston Churchill, implies,

Grumbach sees this time of her life as a transition from the end of its beginning to a new phase, the beginning of the end. She closes her book with a reference to the epigraph in the firm statement, "I am ready to begin the end" (252). This readiness grows out of her move to Maine and her meditations upon her age, beliefs, and lifestyle over the year traced in her book. So the book moves from darkness to light, ends with quiet celebration of life, love, and work, revealing good cause and determination "to turn up the lights on what remains of my life" (252).

Is the recording process of this change, however, an honest one—honest to her readers and to herself? Grumbach raises this very question self-reflexively as she considers how her reading of other authors' memoirs and journals makes her aware of the autobiographer's dilemma of truth versus fictionalization of a life. As with Sarton, so with Grumbach, an intertextuality of autobiographical texts about aging influences her own text. She wonders "how much truth ought to be included here" (159). Even if she tries to articulate what she thinks is the truth of her life, "will not the very process of putting it into words and setting it down fictionalize it?" (159). In fact, by phrasing as a rhetorical question this notion of the narrated life story as a fictionalizing process, she further problematizes the autobiographical pact and the referential pact between reader and autobiographer. Moreover, like Sarton, she candidly acknowledges her unwillingness to tell all, "the natural reluctance to open all the sores and secret miseries of one's life, the misdoings and meannesses" (159).

Yet acknowledging that the autobiographical narrative must be one of omissions as well as inclusions reassures readers that Grumbach is honest about what she does include in her text. This honesty is underscored when readers recall her confessions of selfish behavior in her relationship with Sybil. Finally, her candor in confessing that "[i]n print, I would prefer to appear better than I am" (159) and that although her intentions have been to use her materials and present the people that are a part of them fairly, she knows she has not done so, disarms readers and helps us to trust in her version of the seventieth year. This "sincere" version is, nevertheless, carefully crafted.

Grumbach's memoir of this year is a distillation and a self-consciously creative vision: "dredging up masses of personal history in the hope of producing a modicum of literature" (101). To me it is more literary than Sarton's

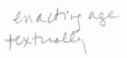
enacting age textually

quotidian journal. She even refers to her structure as that of a literary work. It forms an annual cycle, divided into monthly chapters, beginning with July, her birthday. The penultimate chapter, May, describes the move to Maine, and the final chapter conflates June and July in Maine. A brief "Afterwords" condenses some events of the years between the writing and publication of the memoir in her seventy-third year. She acknowledges the book's literary structure even as she says that with the afterword she is consciously unsettling "the symmetry of the book, or what Aristotle called one of the essential unities of a literary work" (253).

Is this unsettling of the symmetry or stepping outside the structure in the afterword a warranty of the author's authenticity *despite* her work's literariness, or is it simply further testimony to the memoir's literariness? Or does it testify to both? In her avoidance of labeled daily entries except in one episode (her fall and subsequent rescue by a homeless elderly street lady), Grumbach underscores the literary aims of her text: "If something is worth recording, I have always thought, it ought to be general enough to be free of dull, diurnal notation" (108). Her narrative feels unified and constructed, like that of a novel. This does not, for me, threaten the truthfulness of its content; rather, I respond more deeply to the "felt sense of age" she artfully enacts for readers than I might to a daily journal.

One way Grumbach artfully enacts the state of being seventy is, like Sarton, through her "mirror stage" interactions with other elders in her life and with those who preceded her in death. For example, the book opens with Grumbach's memories of her mother's death at fifty-nine and her guilt at surpassing her mother's life span when she turned sixty. She also dwells upon having outlived her younger sister by eighteen years (at the time of writing). As Woodward has pointed out (50), Freud was acutely aware of the ages at which his father, mother, and brother had died, especially as he grew older. Many of us tacitly assume that the ages of parents at death are a kind of legacy; they gauge the likeliness of our own death at either of those ages, but more likely that of the same-sex parent. My sister and I have confessed to each other our anxiety about turning age forty-eight, the age at which our mother suffered a major stroke; age fifty-three evokes a similar dread in our minds, when a second stroke claimed our mother's life.

Grumbach also reflects on the lives of several elderly friends and colleagues, sometimes heartened, like Sarton, by their prodigious energy and activities until almost the end, other times aware of age's constraining power. Brenda Ueland, a serious swimmer and walker who lived to ninety and wrote a book on writing as well as an autobiography, inspires Grumbach (173–74). She also tells the story of the oldest inhabitant of Clark Island, Massachusetts, a woman in her nineties who on her birthday rows a boat twice around the island (184).

Readers also become acquainted with Grumbach's English professor at New York University, Margaret Schlauch, who remained intellectually productive well into her eighties, enthusiastic about writing, reading, and research. Grumbach calls her "intellectually ageless" (87). Schlauch at thirty-seven took seventeen-year-old Grumbach to Mexico and watched her climb to the top of the Temple of the Dwarf. Grumbach does the same thing fifty years later, watching from below as her daughter ascends the 365 steps to the top. This is a graphic image of the aging of the generations and of how age imposes limitations. It becomes a touchstone of Grumbach's narrative.

Finally, there is 103-year-old Aunt Bet (Elizabeth Luther), confined to a wheelchair in a nursing home but still alert and reading after successful cataract surgery. That age has not entirely curbed her is evident in the fact that she still smokes and takes her occasional nip of brandy. Her animation is evident to Grumbach each time she visits Aunt Bet. She is another paradigm of successful aging. Grumbach attempts through these portraits to overturn the signification of extreme old age as the surrender of mobility, activity, mental acuity, and choices. These stories of active elders create a mythology of old age that counters our culture's negative stereotypes.

End Zone is not without its depictions of the toll aging takes on people's lives, however. The portraits of Ueland and the woman from Clark Island contrast to Grumbach's visits with sick friends like Sarton and Barbara Probst. Probst is confined to bed with crushed vertebrae from osteoporosis, a common disease of elderly women. A sign of her own age is Grumbach's query to herself, which will resonate with thousands of readers: "will much of the rest of my life be spent visiting the sick of my generation? A preferable alternative to being sick myself, I suppose" (44). Although she is pleased by Probst's "wry but cheerful" determination to overcome her osteoporosis, Grumbach uses Probst's condition to describe her own sense of frailty as an elder and to speculate on the bodily breakdowns of the aged: "What infinitely fragile creatures we elderly are. Falls, turns, failures of sight and hearing and

Mirror images in
Laurence, Lessing,
Grumbach

mental acuity, we deteriorate almost without noticing it" (46). Grumbach is forcing us, with her pen, to notice these deteriorations in ourselves and others, to take heed of aging's realities.

From this engagement with Probst and Grumbach's subsequent reflections about the deteriorations brought by age, the narrative turns the author's gaze to Grumbach's own mirror and to concrete events that demonstrate her own sensory losses, losses of strength, mobility, and stability. In one such event, which her narrative emphasizes as endemic to old age, she falls and injures her shoulder in New York City's Central Park.

The mirror examination of the aging body, fittingly, takes place on the Terrible Twelfth, her birthday. Such scenes have become an important convention of the literature of aging. Herman Roth and Audre Lorde gaze at their wounded bodies in the mirror (see chapters 1 and 3). Novels such as Margaret Laurence's *The Stone Angel* and Doris Lessing's *The Diaries of Jane Somers* use these mirror-gazing moments at crisis points in the life of the aging protagonist to signal the shock of recognition at having aged. This is the moment when an individual disabuses herself of the illusion that she has not changed, that she is immortal. The mirror's reflection and the reflection of the faces of one's now elderly peers offer physical evidence that the mind's eye can no longer dismiss.

Grumbach acknowledges that since her youth she has avoided looking in the mirror, "believing it would be better not to know the truth about change and decline. In my memory of my body nothing had changed" (52). The ostrich syndrome has clearly been operating in Grumbach. In her inventory at seventy, however, she finally is ready to attend to the sagging breasts and buttocks, the shrinking of flesh against bone, the softening of muscles, the wrinkling, age-spotted skin of neck and face (52–53, 71). She records her dismayed reaction, as influenced by America's youth-loving culture: "There is nothing lovely about the sight of me. I have been taught that firm and unlined is beautiful. Shall I try to learn to love what I am left with?" (53).

Although I think she implies here that she ought to learn to embrace and even love her aged body (like Lorde when she sees her chest after her mastectomy; see chapter 3), elsewhere Grumbach goes to some lengths to gather repugnant physical images and metaphors of the old, suggesting both the difficulty of transforming self-disgust to self-acceptance and also the firmness of her cultural embeddedness (cf. 124). For example, she examines the idiom "to turn seventy" and associates it with "what happens to wine when it be-comes vinegar" (48). There is a sourness to her outlook on turning seventy; she associates it with images of loss, deterioration, and death, with spoilt wine, wilting, unfragrant flowers, stale pies, as well as her own diminished hearing, crooked vision, and slowed, stumbling gait (54).

Grumbach obsessively gathers metaphors for death and associates them with seventy-ness: a dead cicada and a rigid butterfly (35), a dying refrigerator and other failing machinery (23–24), the prematurely "senile" American elm tree outside her study window (74), a memory of a pile of dead horseshoe crabs in Maine (35) and of moribund old lions in a cage in Florida. She com-pares her old body to the lions' cage, her life at seventy to theirs, describing a feeling of entrapment in her aging body and a foreclosure of possibilities for transforming her life: "What remains of their lives is a dirty joke. . . . What remains of mine is not much more elevated: There are too few years left to make another life. My age is my cage; only death can free me" (56). She sees her aging anatomy as her destiny, reflecting an essentialist tendency of much literature on aging. Although Grumbach acknowledges that old age is better than death and that if she is, for example, losing her hearing, there is compensation in her ability to tune out some of the multiplying unpleasant noises of her life, readers can readily hear the dark, depressed, ageist tone of the narrator at this early stage of the memoir. Her mind is stuck in what Woodward has identified as a common literary "phantasm of the fragment-ing body" (182–83).

Convinced that the fountain of youth ought still to be sought (37), Grum-bach expresses anger and frustration at her inability to act youthful: she can no longer move at her former pace without help, she cannot "sail by the ash breeze" (a nautical term, 160). Her pace "is determined by failing limbs, weak ankles, loss of confidence" (160). These failing limbs make her fearful of young criminals in her neighborhood (76, 106) and susceptible to falling. She describes well the sensation of being unable to control her limbs, of her bo-dy's unpredictability, as she gets up from the park bench: "I finish my coffee, stand up to walk to the trash container, and, inexplicably, fall on my face. There is pain in my right ankle that turned and caused me to fall, and greater pain in my left shoulder. . . . I try to think of a strategy that will get me on my feet, but without the use of my left arm and hand nothing works" (109–

Erikson: Mental disability as losing the last vestige of autonomy

10). The unnerving unreliability of her companionate body is conveyed especially well in the word *inexplicably* here.

Elsewhere she supplies the historical facts that she has broken her ankle
twice and strained it several times, her back aches, her teeth, no longer firmly
anchored in her gums, are unreliable chewers, her arms are weak and struggle to lift her body out of chairs. Her summation: "I have little sense that my
body is any longer a good servant that will obey my orders. . . .I am always
in fear of slipping, stumbling, and being hurt when I fall" (80–81). This fear
and distrust of her body, formerly an ally but now at times a foe, is substanti-
ated by the episode in Central Park. Ever the realist, Grumbach concludes
dolorously, "My once-firm, reliable body, quick to command and as quick to
respond, now moves in slow motion, dry to the touch, weary, lax, unresponsive" (81).

As readers learn in several passages, Grumbach is also plagued by an unreliable memory. Early in the memoir she assesses the gradual deterioration
since age fifty of her once-superb memory. She compares her mind to "a hard
disk that suddenly fails to deliver what has been stored there"; extending
the analogy, she confesses that she functions with difficulty since the entire
"storage system of my personal computer is often down" (23). Then she
switches to an organic metaphor no less derogatory about her fading mental
powers, essentially describing her mind as rotting: a "ripe, aging compost
heap . . . is my mind" (23). While compost may provide fertilizer for future
growth, it is itself, alas, decaying matter, not a pretty thought when it is your
gray matter decaying.

Grumbach also refers to her habit of repeating her favorite stories to the
same people, a common tendency in the elderly that she attributes to forgetfulness (125). She fights against her continuous misplacing of things like her
keys, with "aging's forgetfulness" as the enemy (17). Like Grumbach, many
of us fear the mental deterioration that may accompany age; as Erikson observes, "physiological disability can be compensated for or denied in the
service of willful autonomy. But a disabled mind can neither deny nor compensate. . . . mental disability seems to loom as a shameful helplessness that
will permit no vestiges of autonomy" (200).

Fearing such a loss of autonomy in old age, my first readerly response to
these catalogs of deterioration and vulnerability, to what the narrator ac-

Effects on reader of age narratives.

knowledges as her "dolorous thinking" (237) about being seventy, is a matching dolorousness. Yet I am glad of the chance to acquire an almost visceral preview of seventy's physical limitations and of the frustration and mourning over these losses of physical control. I also admit to a desire to escape from the grimness of Grumbach's realistic depiction, as if menacingly caught in the age cage described in the passage about the old lions. I think, "So this is how it is! I always wondered what it felt like to be old and it *is* as bad as I had imagined. So take me away from this and into the literary world of a young ingenue or at least of a middle-aged, ripening, confident woman, instead of subjecting me to a crotchety, complaining, decaying old crone!" There is an undeniable onerousness in reading and absorbing this negative language of aging. It does, nevertheless, set most readers up for anticipation of change, primes them to welcome the methods that Grumbach invents to compensate for the ills and limitations of senescence. It also makes the compensations more believable since Grumbach from the beginning of the book refuses to soft-pedal the difficulties of being seventy.

For example, she may be forgetful about the location of her possessions, but Grumbach has found a way to outsmart her unreliable memory: she mentally retraces her steps and her activities leading up to her desire for the lost object. When she thereby remembers where her keys are, she rather playfully says, "They are found, *I* am found, in possession of my possessions, not because I looked everywhere, but because I thought about it. A double triumph over aging's forgetfulness" (17). Not only is she in possession of her possessions, but this language suggests that Grumbach is in possession of her faculties, using her reasoning and wit to assist the less-functioning memory, and hence diminishing the inroads of old age. In another example, although she has more trouble getting around at seventy, she derives pleasure from using the gift of a carved ash cane from her friend Richard Lucas. Still another compensation: she may need hearing aids, but like a telephone message machine, she can use them to screen out what intrudes upon and irritates her (21).

Moreover, while she repeatedly describes the unreliability and unresponsive heaviness of her limbs and the limits of her mobility, she also creates a wonderful passage in which she describes her body in the water and her enthusiastic swimming: "I return to the state of my youth. I move without fear. . . . I turn fast, acquire some speed, advance, retreat, rest, and start again

Age as a "Subjective Construct"

without effort" (81). Grumbach at seventy taking to the water and reclaiming speed, grace, and control, becomes, for me, a crystallizing metaphor for the adaptations that she makes at this age in order to continue to live fully. It suggests possibilities that exist to compensate for age's incapacitations, a contrast to the passages about no longer being able to climb the Temple of the Dwarf's steps.

Beyond the physical context, while she reads more slowly now, she reads more deeply and appreciatively. She is entering upon "a new age of self-indulgence," reading only what truly interests her, doing what she wants to do (42). As Berman persuasively argues, such behavior is not a shift to selfishness; it is actually "less saturated with self [since] what is essential to the inner person comes to coincide with what is of enduring beauty in the outside world" (1992, 110). As she becomes more aware of enduring beauty in daily life, her relationship with time changes. The time remaining to her is shrinking, but she no longer passes through time unawares as she had done for too many years: "Now, I am aware of every moment of every day, especially of the summer days" (48).

Like Sarton, Grumbach is increasingly living in the center of each moment and contacting eternal moments. There is greater intensity and richness to her life at seventy, which her narrative increasingly acknowledges. If at the beginning of the book she grumblingly declares, "I'd be surprised if anything of interest happens. . . . youth . . . is everlastingly expectant, and old age . . . has almost given up on expectation" (17), toward the end she doggedly embraces the future with less realism and more optimism (146), with relish for life's surprises, with receptivity to the richness and beauty of her environment.

The point is—as I sigh with relief—that "seventy" is in large measure a subjective construct. A quotation from baseball great Satchel Paige about age and mental outlook, which Grumbach put on the broadside she made for Aunt Bet's birthday, becomes the humorous but meaningful shibboleth of the book: "How old would you be if you didn't know how old you was?" (205, 238). If we do not know, or we discount, our chronological age, we can be as young or old as we ourselves determine. If we reject the notion that we are beyond further productivity, if we contend that we still have work to do, as Grumbach concludes once she has moved to Maine, then our lives will go on, intensely, toward the future: "we die only when our work is done. I would like to think that is true. I have work still to do, I think" (238). Indeed, she has continued to write, publishing a sequel to *End Zone* whose title switches from football to baseball: *Extra Innings*. Her philosophy of work in late life is that of the astonishingly energetic Maine elders she meets: "When I rest, I rust" (235).

In this point Grumbach echoes Sarton and, as chapter 4 shows, Donald Hall, too. Our work, especially when it is creative work taking us off into new directions, keeps us youthful, motivated, and forward-thinking. The last part of her memoir is, indeed, a "paean to the possibility of beginning successful new enterprises late in life" (Berman 1994, 107).

Grumbach professes no need yet for a "swan costume" at seventy although she is ready to *begin* the end of her life. She feels less obsessed by her age as the year after her seventieth birthday closes and less alarmed by the imminence of death: "I seem not to have grown older in the year, but more content with whatever age it is I am" (251). At the end of the memoir, Grumbach returns to the metaphor of the steps up the Temple of the Dwarf at Chichén Itzá, this time to indicate her contentedness with her age and capacities for living: "the certainty that I shall never again climb them [the steps] no longer disturbs me" (251). The satisfying nature of the memoir's literary constructedness is apparent in her return to this touchstone image of the Mexican ruins as they trace Grumbach's changed attitude toward aging and dying. Grumbach's earlier resentment at being unable to climb the steps (77), her fearful sense of mortality before the Temple of the Dwarf, the Temple of the Warriors, the Governor's Palace, and other ancient structures on the Great Plain, her throat-constricting sensation of being threatened by "the stone eternities" (166), make way at the end of the book for her deepening inner peace.

Her perspective has gradually lightened and expanded over this seventieth year, committing Grumbach "to turn up the lights on what remains of my life," to emphasize what is important *to her,* and to consider that death may simply be "a horizon, and a horizon is only the limit of our sight" (239). As her sight continues to expand, she suggests, it may even lead her beyond the horizon of death into another dimension or state of clearer vision and wisdom.

Writing her memoir enables Grumbach, then, to sort out what is important in her life at the crossroads of seventy and frail old age. Being seventy has its perquisites, especially if one is a middle-class professional woman. It affords her the luxury, the leisure, the incentive to pursue psychologically and philosophically fruitful self-examination and productivity as a writer. She acknowledges at the outset that this self-examination begins with few preconceived principles and beliefs, that "taking stock" is a difficult task with her "bits and pieces" view of her life (59), that formulation of a ruling philosophy for her life is not possible for her (70), that her sense of her own identity and her life's meaning is not clear (70). She will use the language of questions as the appropriate rhetorical mode for her psychological and philosophical questing (68).

This rhetorical stance—not claiming to have all the answers (like Philip Roth about his father), articulating a postmodern skepticism about obtaining "all" the answers, and questioning just how useful and lasting some of these answers may be—disarms readers like me who harbor their own skepticism or anxieties about receiving the meanings of being seventy. In fact, Grumbach tests the serious aims and optimistic energy of the elderly writer's questing memoir when she explores Ezra Pound's contention that in the end of one's life, "Nothing really matters"; Grumbach's gloss on Pound follows: "Today I understand this. At the end, or close to the end, or closer to the end than the beginning, the value of what we once thought mattered is lost to us. Even survival, once so important, money, food, family, country, accomplishment, recognition, fame, even: Pound was right" (50). In this reflection, Grumbach seems to express the elder's impulse to dismiss many of the beliefs, values, goals, and activities that formerly mattered and the inclination not to replace these too quickly with other beliefs and values.

Refreshed by this minimalist tendency of Grumbach's, I become more receptive to the modest philosophical and psychological discoveries and tentative formulations that Grumbach does gradually unfold for the reader. If, as Norman K. Denzin has theorized, the (auto)biographical method uses materials that "describe turning-point moments in an individual's life" (69) and presents epiphanies, "interactional moments and experiences which leave marks on people's lives . . . alter[ing] the fundamental meaning structures in a person's life" (70), Grumbach's memoir does not subscribe to this rule. Her text resists focusing on the major and minor epiphanies, dramatic breakthroughs in her relationships, and sweeping interpretations of events in her life. She prefers instead to look at the "cumulative or *representative event,* which signifies eruptions or reactions to experiences which have been going on for a long period of time" (Denzin, 71). This perspective makes more sense for a woman of seventy years, one who is looking to construct a larger picture of who she is and what her life means.

One cumulative event of her life of primary importance to Grumbach, as already implied, is her writing career. Like Sarton, she puts this above reading in her life, quoting Marina Tsvetayeva, "whatever I need, I shall write myself" (68). In several passages Grumbach considers why writing is important to her. The need for fame and recognition has diminished; she believes that the craving for fame invariably poisons a writer's creative wellsprings (40). She ponders writers' compulsive struggle to write (114) and considers why older writers continue to make writing central to their lives when it is so difficult to do. Perhaps writers' commitment has to do with "the mystery of having been moved by words" (245), a phrase she uses to describe her own early reaction to Dylan Thomas's language.

Grumbach increasingly associates this mysterious power of words and her creative work with the divine presence, with God. God as a creative force also becomes increasingly important in her life; she approvingly quotes sculptor Lenore Straus:

> O God,
> hold my hand
> that
> holds the tool. (133)

She further celebrates the late-life artist's emphasis on her art by assenting to the words of Louise Nevelson, "In the end, as you grow older, your life is your art, and you are alone with it" (134). She seeks the quiet, isolation, and peace of her new home in Maine to be alone with her art and the divine presence that drives it.

This does not mean that Grumbach's spiritual epiphanies direct her to complete withdrawal from the world into a self-absorbed cocoon of work. In fact, another growing impulse of hers is to move beyond solipsism, to look outward more, to "empty my glutted interior self, and fill it with the beauty of a world that is not the self, and never has been" (207). Such an impulse is reflected in her desire to maintain close contact with the ocean. In her youth, swimming in the ocean enabled her to believe in God (80). In recent years, it consoled her for her losses of loved ones and her losses of "faith, optimism, physical pleasure, great expectations," easing the burden of her own mortality (27). Now, her closeness to the water in her new home in Maine underscores her deepening appreciation of the beauty surrounding her and a commitment to cultivating the spirituality of her life.

In the description of growing old with grace that Grumbach writes to honor the birthday of Aunt Bet, she articulates this impulse toward outwardness in relation to the physical world: "we wake with pleasure to enjoy the music, poetry, and glory of the natural world" (204). Her reverent communion with water resembles Sarton's passion for her flower garden. Both authors show the possibilities in later life for spiritual intensity through interactions with the natural world, a recurring theme in many autobiographies of aging. (See, for example, the discussion of Howell Raines's work in chapter 4.)

This outwardness also applies to interactions with other people. Achieving an inner contentedness, the gracefully aging elder relinquishes vanity, conquers self-centeredness and self-seeking, and loves others out of a recognition of the divine presence in them: "We sense the spiritual in our friends. We suspect God is in them, and in us" (204). Elsewhere she meditates upon Katherine Mansfield's notion that love is important, regardless of the object of that love. On the contrary, Grumbach argues that it is important what and whom we choose to love (159), underscoring her belief about the divine presence in specific individuals. Woven through Grumbach's memoir is evidence that she has been selective in the objects of her love and that she holds her close relationships as sacred.

Her friendship with her partner Sybil is a stable, sanctified presence in the text. Sybil is portrayed as a wise woman. She influences their major decision to leave Washington and settle in Maine, and she tactfully downplays Grumbach's anxious celebration of her seventieth birthday. Unlike Sarton at seventy, Grumbach has a central person in her life who makes the prospect of frail old age less frightening, one in whom, for her, the divine presence shines. Moreover, even as she apologizes for her own egocentrism in their love relationship (187), she portrays the relationship as a sustaining and comforting focus of her life. A typical omission of private material in autobiographies is apparent in her faint allusion to the sexual nature of the relationship; one time she mentions the double bed that they sleep in, but in that one allusion is enough information to elicit my admiration for the courage she must have had to leave her husband of many years, the father of her three grown daughters, and enter into a lesbian marriage with Sybil. Hers is another example of late-life courage in nonconformity.

Other relationships also claim prominent space in the memoir. Her friend Richard, whom she loses midtext to AIDS, is cherished and remembered through the ash cane. Author Kay Boyle has been a source of inspiration for her courageous survival of several illnesses and her unselfish devotion to other people and causes. Margaret Schlauch, her English professor and mentor, is honored as her role model of an active, fervent, intellectual elder. And Grumbach's daughters are her friends; she even describes with enthusiasm her travels to Paris with Jane and her husband. Grumbach seems less pressured by her relationships than Sarton, does not construe them as making excessive demands on her work time, and is more able to extract unalloyed pleasures from them. Her efforts to be more outward in interactions with her friends create this growing reservoir of pleasure during her seventieth year.

Work, love, and friendship: Grumbach and Sarton affirm the importance and need of all three pursuits for happiness, into the seventieth year and beyond. Grumbach adds the element of spirituality, which she associates with the other three pursuits, and also expresses through her active participation in a small Episcopal church communion in Maine. She, like Sarton, strives to foster the intensification of time through work, love, friendship, and passionate attention to the natural world's offerings. A reader may thus leave Grumbach's meditative memoir feeling nurtured and with a sense of the author's having quested successfully for a richer, more light-filled existence, abounding in eternal moments.

The afterword, which Grumbach adds to the memoir in her seventy-third year, reaffirms that she has found contentment in Maine and that life is a natural cycle of births (including that of her new grandchild) as well as deaths (she records the passing of Mary McCarthy, about whom she had years before written a biography). She indicates that she is still committed to her Episcopal communion, evidence of her spiritual pursuits in later life. Finally, she reports with pleasure that Aunt Bet, her paradigm of vital engagement with life at 103, is still "bright, cheerful, and quite well," able to read and enjoy her apricot brandy (256).

Indeed, *Coming into the End Zone* can act like a heady nip of brandy for readers who might have initially thought it a diatribe against the stagnation, deterioration, losses, and limitations of being seventy. Grumbach has made changes in her life that give her spiritual and emotional contentment as well as the context in which to continue her productivity as a writer. Because of books like Grumbach's, being seventy can also begin to mean intoxicating opportunities for others in our culture.

3

Women Warriors against
Racism and Ageism

IN THE SECOND HALF of the twentieth century, race and ethnicity still exert a powerful influence on identity and on one's position in American society. So dominant are they, so persistently shaping, distorting, and complicating of a person's sense of self, that it is difficult to find a text by an author of color that focuses primarily on the subject-position of the elder, that examines the identity factor of age. Even when elders of color write autobiographically, they usually focus on race as significantly shaping their lives.

For example, W. E. B. Du Bois, an eminent political activist, sociologist, and author trained at Harvard, wrote in *In Battle for Peace: The Story of My 83rd Birthday* (1952) about the need to work for world peace in order to end the race problem, about his work with the Council on African Affairs, about using his birthday and the republication of his writings as a fund-raiser for these political causes, and about the U.S. government's indictment against him for his peace activism, which they called the criminal work of an "agent for a foreign principal" against the government. There is scant mention of his own advanced age in this narrative of Du Bois's eighty-third year. In one passage he describes himself as "not only getting older, but now passing the limits which folkloric custom had long allotted to human existence" (62), living to an age that has required him to endure the loss of his wife and many boyhood friends. Yet, as gerontologists concerned with issues of engagement and disengagement in old age might observe, he does not stop to meditate on his old age as a new stage or condition of his life. Old age is simply a continuation of his life's movement toward the future.

In fact, this passage on his age precedes his matter-of-fact reporting of his engagement and marriage to Shirley Graham—a continuation of his usual domestic lifestyle. Du Bois dovetails this matrimonial activity with discussion of his work for the Peace Information Center and related pan-African causes. He truly exemplifies Erik Erikson's concept of generativity in old age, guiding the younger generation of African Americans in its political work. Although once he alludes to the drawback of running at his age for U.S. senator on the American Labor Party ticket (43), he does run, nevertheless, and records his surprisingly large vote count (205,729) with a remark not about his age but about his race: the votes were "from men and women of courage, without the prejudice against color which I always expect and usually experience" (50). Age could not hold Du Bois back when he contended over a lifetime with the constraints of race in America's racist society. In this country, age can only rarely be foregrounded over race as a marginalizing, predominant subject-position.

Later in his narrative, when he describes his criminal trial (for his "treasonous" socialist beliefs), Du Bois notes that "most Negros are sent to jail by persons who hate or despise them" (119). There is no mention of his age except when Du Bois notes that his old age does not evoke sympathy in the jury. He does not see his age as a disadvantage either. During jury selection, the prosecution had asked potential jurors "if they had any prejudice against convicting a person of advanced years" (120), and none had said they did. Clearly an eighty-three-year-old black man is merely a "boy" (in Richard Wright's insulting sense of the term) in the eyes of racist America in 1951, three years before the Supreme Court's *Brown vs. The Board of Education* decision that launched the Civil Rights movement. He is not accorded the respect usually given elderly whites (especially males) before the youth-worshipping 1960s, during which the "Age of Aquarius" *Hair* generation promoted intensely ageist attitudes. Aware of the respect given old white men in the culture of 1951, Du Bois clearly feels the shame and injustice of his indictment as a black man more keenly because he is eighty-three: "never in any single year has the frustration and paradox of life stood out so clearly as in this year when, having finished 83 years of my life in decency and honor, with something done and something planning, I stepped into the 84th year with handcuffs on my wrists" (179). Racial oppression forces the loss of respect due him for his years and his accomplishments. He is only constrained by his age in that it has mistakenly led him to expect more honorable treatment than his race allows him to have in America in the 1950s. A reader in 1998 sees that the marginalization Du Bois experiences and the frustrations of his life have to do not with ageism but with his treatment as a black in the United States in 1951.

Ageism may not be uppermost in Du Bois's thoughts when he writes, but at the end of his *Autobiography* (1968), written at age ninety-one, Du Bois expresses—a little more than in his book at age eighty-three—his awareness of the significance of age as a factor in his life. He describes the experience of traveling into his tenth decade against the backdrop of a cultural assumption about work: "it characterized my day that most men thought their work would be about done at 60 and they would be dead or practically dead at 70" (13). Du Bois explains that he never subscribed to this assumption and accepted demanding jobs throughout his life, "eager to work and work continuously" (13). He refuses to see age as an obstacle to work or to worry about preparations for an old age in which productivity would cease, and he acknowledges that this outlook is atypical: "That neglect to worry about my old age was peculiar and contradicted my complete surroundings. . . . the first worry of the average citizen was for provision for his old age" (13). Du Bois does not consider himself an average citizen (the middle-class white male fits that label), and also atypically, he does not seem to think of himself as old until he reaches his tenth decade, as described in the final chapter of his *Autobiography*.

Then he assumes the role of elder statesman or wise old man, one who, as David Gutmann says, "stay[s] in place, add[s] [his] accrued experience to the general knowledge store, and . . . build[s] culture" (216). The elder statesman acts as one of "the interpreters and administrators of the moral sector of society" (226). In his public addresses, which he excerpts in this chapter of his autobiography, Du Bois is continually dispensing wisdom and preaching moral choices, begging the indulgence of younger folks by citing his advanced age. He advises his great-grandson, whom he addresses in a speech on his ninetieth birthday, to seek work that he loves and work that the world needs, noting that "great-grandparents are supposed usually to inflict [advice] on the helpless young" (398). He modestly tenders his advice to the African political leader Nkrumah about the future of Ghana and Africa because he knows that nation's ruler, but also "because of the fact that I am now entering the 90th year of my life" (399). In another speech, delivered for him at Accra by his wife (his travels having exhausted him, Du Bois was resting in a Soviet sanitarium), he places his ideas about socialism in the context of "advice from one who has lived long" (402).

But Du Bois does not even accept this elder statesman role when in China at an official celebration of his ninety-first birthday. There he rejects the authority that age or education or anything else might give him and speaks only with the authority of a person who owns his own soul, emphasizing not age but the race issue in this ownership: "One thing alone I own and that is my own soul. Ownership of that I have even while in my own country for near a century I have been nothing but a 'nigger.' On this basis and this alone I dare speak, I dare advise" (405). Once again, race preempts age in shaping Du Bois's identity and frame of reference for communicating the wealth of his accumulated wisdom.

Du Bois's postlude to his *Autobiography* suggests that he is still engaged in his life's work. Only in relation to work does he gauge the meaning of age and contemplate his own advanced age. He acknowledges that his great age forces him to plan his work differently because he cannot claim a long future and because he is physically weaker: "I plan my work, but plan less for shorter periods. I live from year to year and day to day. I expect snatches of pain and discomfort to come and go" (422). Time shrinks, work is truncated, and physical stamina diminishes; Du Bois finally acknowledges these attributes of aging at age ninety-one. He has epitomized the elder with the youthful outlook.

In the postlude, he also recognizes the ageism of American culture, which releases people from their work at a certain age and puts them at risk of starvation. About the young political leaders who promote compulsory retirement and other ageist policies, Du Bois has this to say: "I have lived to an age of life which is increasingly distasteful to this nation . . . if [a man] is foolish enough to survive until 90, he is often regarded as a freak. This is because in the face of human experience the United States has discovered that Youth knows more than Age" (414). His ironic tone here suggests that "Age" has the right to claim the wisdom earned through experience, but that our youth-worshipping culture fails to recognize this right. There is mild anger here about America's ageism, but Du Bois saves his real wrath for American racism, ending his autobiography with an impassioned plea to Americans in 1968 not to "stew in this Evil—the Evil of South Africa, the Evil of Mississippi. . . . this is a wonderful America, which the founding fathers dreamed until their sons drowned it in the blood of slavery" (422). About racism Du Bois speaks passionately, from the core of his soul. His parting words at the end of his life story are to urge Americans to end racism and rebuild the egalitarian dream of our nation's founders.

Du Bois's texts are apt representatives of what researchers on the literature of aging by authors of color are likely to find. As Kwame Anthony Appiah has pointed out in his essay on race in literary study, because there is a long history of ridicule or at least neglect of black writing in this country, inevitably "the major proportion of the published writing of Afro-Americans, even when not directed to countering racist mythology, has been concerned thematically with issues of race" (286). Because writers influenced by issues of color either de-emphasize age or approach aging obliquely as they underscore race, literary critics must study texts in which age is embedded in a constellation of other identity-determining factors, themes, and issues. We extrapolate from these constellations what it means to be an *older* African American, considering how ageism and racism, interlocking forms of oppression, constrain African-American elders. For although race is a dominant subject-position for African-American writers who have endured racial oppression, it is not the only influential one, and we need not reductively read texts by African Americans only for the racial issues implicit in them. I agree with the argument of Henry Louis Gates Jr. for the complexity of black literature and culture vis-à-vis white culture in America: "Black literature . . . can no longer simply name 'the margin.' Close readings . . . [reveal] the depth and range of cultural details far beyond the economic [and social and political] exploitation of blacks by whites" (20).

So the literary critic interested in the interplay between race and age in

autobiographies by African Americans has a legitimate aim, that of complicating and enriching our readings of African-American autobiographies. But
to fulfill that aim, the critic often examines conceptualizations of identity—
characterizations—in which age is not foregrounded. With this in mind, I
examine portraits of the older African American that come from the pen of
African-American writer Lucille Clifton.

Clifton, a poet and author of children's books, also has written an autobiographical piece in response to the death of her father. Her response is in
many respects similar to those articulated in Madeleine L'Engle's *The Summer
of the Great-Grandmother* and Philip Roth's *Patrimony:* the old age and death of
a parent, especially the second parent, creates the yearning to study and record the lives and personalities of one's parents, the entire family's history,
and relationships between oneself and one's parents (see chapter 1). These
become translated into a memoir that is a tribal-historical treasure-house of
language. Such is Clifton's approach in *Generations: A Memoir* (1976). Unlike
L'Engle and Roth, however, Clifton, in unlocking the family's historical
treasure-house and sketching portraits of her father and mother, also creates
a narrative of African cultural pride (mingling with pride in African *woman-
hood*) and of American racial exclusion in association with economic
barriers.

Another context that enables readers to encounter age meshed with race
is that of a serious illness suffered by an aging author of color. Breast cancer is
the occasion for middle-aged, African-American, lesbian, and feminist author
Audre Lorde to compose *The Cancer Journals* (1980), in which she records her
physical struggles with the disease, her battles with the (white male) medical
establishment, her confrontation with death, and her reprioritizing of her
life's activities.

Lorde is more conscious in her writing than Du Bois that age is a significant factor shaping identity and that ageism is prevalent in America. Lorde
speaks out against ageism in an essay from *Sister Outsider* titled "Age, Race,
Class, and Sex: Women Redefining Difference." She sees ageism as "another
distortion of relationship which interferes without vision" (116–17). In fact,
She says that ageism, like other forms of oppression, badly distorts an individual's vision of people. Lorde, furthermore, denounces the generation gap—
prompted by the younger generation's disdain for the older—"as an important social tool for any repressive society" (116–17); she explains that the

younger generation of women needs to reject the shibboleth that people over thirty cannot be trusted in order to become more receptive to the lessons that older women can pass along to them. Vilifying older women means the young will not be able to receive older women's memories and knowledge about life in the past, creating a "historical amnesia" that denies the young some already proven tactics, tools, and methods for overcoming oppression. She celebrates diversity among women—black/white, young/old—when she argues that in order to foster social change we must extirpate the ageism and other oppressive practices of the patriarchy that women have internalized; we must also appreciate our differences and use them in imaginative ways "to enrich our visions and our joint struggles" (122). Ageism may have a more negative impact on African-American females than it does on African-American males because our culture, in general, requires an attractive, youthful appearance of its women, more than it does of its men. Lorde argues that age marginalizes women in America, that young women even use it to oppress older women, and that older African-American women are triply oppressed in our culture.

Since "the master's tools will never dismantle the master's house," Lorde argues (123), women need to reject patriarchy's tools and forge their own to fight all forms of oppression in our culture. Writers and literary critics must create imaginative texts as tools to scrutinize the dynamics of oppression and battle their effects. However, age frequently recedes before the more overt constraints of race, as we observe in Clifton's and Lorde's works. Gender oppression is also present in their works, although, like age, it sometimes pales before the destruction wrought by racism. This fact has been noted by other African-American autobiographers, including 101-year-old Bessie Delany (recently deceased), who observes in her popular autobiographical book, *Having Our Say* (coauthored with her sister Sadie and writer Amy Hill Hearth): "As a woman dentist, I faced sexual harassment—that's what they call it today—but to me, racism was always a bigger problem" (10). Like *Having Our Say,* Clifton's and Lorde's autobiographical works are cultural texts of racism, with issues of gender and age occasionally intensifying the virulence of racism.

This chapter extensively analyzes Clifton's and Lorde's texts and then turns briefly, for comparison, to autobiographical essays by Maya Angelou and to an autobiographically framed tribal tale narrated by Native American writer Velma Wallis.

WOMEN WARRIORS AGAINST RACISM AND AGEISM

Lucille Clifton: A Tribute to Her Father—and Mother

Clifton begins *Generations* with a dedication to her father,

> for
> samuel louis sayles, sr.
> daddy
> 1902–1969
> who is somewhere,
> being a man (223)

With these words she suggests that, for her, Samuel Sayles has not died: he is somewhere, he exists in her memories, in her deeds, in the words of this memoir. The dedication also implies, in my view, that for her Samuel Sayles is the epitome of manhood; he is, eternally, being a man, just as he will always be her Daddy. The dedication and the poem resist the "black boy" tactics of racist America by stressing Samuel's manhood. This memoir is a tribute to the man, the whole man: in the prime of his life, in his old age, after his death, in his eternal presence.

It is also a tribute to the line of Dahomey women from whom Samuel sprang, a reassertion of the lessons of "faith, dignity, intelligence, and integrity" (Peppers, 57) handed down from her great-great-grandmother Caroline Donald (Mammy Ca'line). Retelling the story of these Dahomey women is a way to celebrate notions of tribal community and racial continuity that transcend aloneness and death. Clifton's narrative refers repeatedly to Dahomey, the West African kingdom of her family's origins, a culture rich in native arts such as carved wooden masks, bronze sculpture, and tapestries, as well as music and dance (*Encyclopaedia Britannica Micropaedia* 1988, 2:102–3, under "Benin"; 3:848, under "Dahomey"). Dahomey prospered through slave trading with Europe and through the export of palm oil in the eighteenth and nineteenth centuries. The French colonized Dahomey from 1892 until 1960. In 1975, it became the People's Republic of Benin. As critic Carol Muske says, "*Generations* is more than an elegy or a personal memoir. It is an attempt . . . to retrieve, and lyrically to celebrate, her Afro-American heritage" (111).

Embracing her African heritage helps Clifton mourn Samuel's death and celebrate his life as she celebrates her whole family's survival despite the ordeals history had dealt them. Doing this work of mourning and celebration,

Clifton evolves her optimistic philosophy: "our lives are more than the days in them, our lives are our line and we go on" (276). Using individual and collective family memories to move beyond quotidian time, Clifton identifies an eternal present, a continuity rooted in family. Barbara Myerhoff describes a similar feeling of continuity and integrity in the Holocaust survivors with whom she worked as they recalled the European Jewish culture they left behind: "Time is abolished . . . by memory, for remembering the past fully and well retains it. . . . Simultaneity replaces sequence, and a sense of oneness with all that has been one's history is achieved. . . . The integration with earlier states of being . . . provides [a] sense of continuity and completeness" (238–39). Clifton's affectionate portrayal of this timelessness-through-family will persuade many readers not to see the death of a parent as irreconcilable loss. It helped me to see my parents' continuing presence in me and in my memories.

Clifton's orphaned state and her difficulty in accepting the reality of her father's death prompt her chronicle, tribute, and philosophizing. Orphanhood can elicit new, uncommon behaviors; the narrator records Samuel's observation about his early-orphaned father, Genie: "No he wasn't crazy. He was just somebody whose Mama and Daddy was dead" (251). The orphan is not quite hinged, not well rooted in reality. There is both an external and internal vacuum even in the adult orphan's life, as L'Engle and Roth have shown and as I experienced in my own life after the death of my second parent, my father. One's identity is somehow threatened as the adult orphan loses his or her parental "anchors," those originary threads tying them to material existence. The newly orphaned Clifton is quite dislocated. The phone call from her sister announcing Samuel's death and her trip to Samuel's Buffalo home for the funeral seem surreal. She travels filled with disbelief, trying to absorb the reality of her anchorless existence.

Clifton's language moves from reportage, with reader as audience, to direct address of her "dead" father as she denies his death with angry repetition of the phrase: "I didn't believe." In an incantatory manner she repeats the word "Daddy," as if to summon him to her side to belie his death: "I hung up the phone. . . . I didn't believe Mr. Sayles Lord was dead. . . . I didn't believe you were dead Daddy. You said you stayed on here because we had feet of clay. I didn't believe you could die Daddy. I didn't believe you would. I didn't want you to die Daddy. You always said you would haunt us if you did"

(229). In the narrative of her journey to the funeral, Clifton's memories of him and his whole family line tumble out of her; he *is* haunting her—just as Herman had haunted Philip Roth. Samuel's palpable presence for the whole family at their home in Buffalo underscores this haunting. His "ghost" also invites and dares Clifton to construct the reality of his death.

His death could have been better anticipated had Clifton not been geographically removed from her father; she might have more readily absorbed the reality of her father's old age and the health problems he had endured in recent years. This I readily understand as a daughter who lived in the South during the last fifteen years of my father's life in New York. Clifton's mission in her narrative is to resurrect and reassemble these facts and, with the help of her Buffalo relatives, to fill in some of the gaps of her knowledge about the aging, ailing Samuel. Readers learn about the trials of the aging father's body through the narrative's flashbacks to events reported by her siblings, to his emphysema, seizures, and operation for a brain tumor, to the amputation of his leg, to the hospital battles fought with negligent (racist?) nurses by Clifton's sisters (241, 255).

In retrospect, the narrator marvels at her family's denial of Samuel's decline and at his self-denial. With irony she remembers that they saw no deterioration in him through the ordeal of the tumor: "he was up and out of the hospital in a matter of weeks. And just the same. We saw no difference in him" (255). Denial of the toll taken by brushes with death seems a common reaction among families, death being one of our strongest cultural taboos. As Anne Wyatt-Brown points out (1993), old age and its infirmities are a similarly forbidden topic: "we suffer from a pervasive but almost completely repressed fear of death. Given our ability to avoid reminders of unpleasant truths, it is not surprising that old age became a cultural taboo" (3). My own family also avoided acknowledging both topics. My siblings and I have remarked many times on the ostrich-like attitude of my father and stepmother that must have blinded both of them to the symptoms of my father's cancer, a slow-growing variety that he probably had for five years before it killed him.

Samuel's denial of his vulnerability to death extends to the bare place where his leg had been. Clifton lets us glimpse Samuel's rock-like strength and humor about his amputation: "Yeah, they got my leg but they didn't get me, he would boast" (255). The rock becomes a recurring image in the narrative associated with Samuel's steadiness, strength, and ageless quality. Perhaps strength and the will to live must be accompanied by this denial of ills and a willed ignorance of death in order to sustain optimism. We may need to move through each day as though we were not beset by our mortality. Perhaps my maternal grandmother's philosophy that one must live as if one were going to live forever (the opposite of the Psalms' message that we should number the limited days allotted us; see chapter 2) diminishes the power of mortality to terrorize and paralyze our efforts to plan for the future.

Despite the braggadocio of the "ageless" man and his reality-denying children, however, Samuel does age, and his wife Thel tells Lucille "he's getting old" after he buys the house in New York. He buys the house even though his children are almost grown because he says every man must do three things in his life: buy a house, plant a tree, and have a son. Emphasizing his identity as an aging man whose time is beginning to run out, he accomplishes all three, as proof of his mature manhood (249). His emphasis on the mature man as homeowner means he has bought into the (white) American Dream and sees fulfillment of that dream as a way to challenge his status as black boy in white America. So age *and* race prompt Samuel to buy the house, no easy feat, even up north in New York in those days. There he lives out the rest of his days. Only Clifton, moving away from New York, does not see the aging of Samuel until she views his corpse.

Seeing his body, Clifton finally faces his death unblinkingly. I admired Clifton's act; seeing a dead parent's body requires enormous courage that many of us (myself included) would be unable to summon because it is a strong dose of reality, a chilling mirror reflection of one's mortality. From the viewing she learns that he does not, as the others insist, look good; that he does have a missing leg (which the undertaker sought to hide in his positioning of the body); that he *is* dead. His rock-like strength has turned to a stony demeanor that she cannot deny: "My father had become an old man and I didn't even know it. This old man in a box was my father. Daddy had been an old man" (238). Note how in repeating the phrase "old man" Clifton purposefully uses language to create and absorb the reality that Samuel, in old age, has died. (Some are old at age sixty-seven.) When describing her father's burial, Clifton repeats the reference to rocks to underscore how his identity or substance has been materially transformed in death: "My father bumped against the earth. Like a rock" (261). From a man of rock-like strength he has changed into the inertness of stone.

Spending the night before the funeral in Samuel's house also imposes reality on Clifton. The empty spaces that exist beside haunting presences in Samuel's house tell her of her orphanhood, yet also of her parents' continuing influence in her life: "I lay and listened to the house. My Daddy and Mama were dead and their house was full of them" (243). Aging is an ambiguous concept since Clifton believes in a notion widespread among diverse African cultures and African-American communities: the active presence of dead ancestors. Mama, Daddy, and the Dahomey women that birthed the Sayles line still live with Lucille. Yet she mourns their inability to converse: "My father was lowered into the ground. . . . I wanted to tell him something, my insides screamed. I remember everything. I believe" (261). Her words bear an uncanny resemblance to Roth's recurring phrase in *Patrimony*, "You must not forget anything." Memory must serve Clifton instead of living dialogue, however, and recording memories in written words becomes a way to negotiate the psychological distance between her and her parents. As Reynolds Price observes in a review of *Generations*, Clifton's memoir has as its aim "perpetuation and celebration" of her parents (110). Like Roth, Clifton promises, at her father's grave and after, to remember everything—for herself and the continuing line of Dahomey women. Even the myths, the "lies" of these family histories, are true and worthy of preservation (245), for they capture the values, the vision, the strong human wills, and interconnections of her family across time and space.

As Roth, when he learns of Herman's terminal illness, strays literally, psychologically, and narratively into the cemetery where his mother is buried, so Clifton after her father's death also turns her narrative to recollections about her mother, Thel, who died at age forty-four. Recollections of Thel wind through the chapters, ending with Samuel's funeral, after which Thelma gets her own chapter. It is the final and fullest chapter of the memoir, the one that most completely details her loving, self-sacrificing life amongst the lives of the other Sayles. Samuel was a widower for ten years after Thel's death, and although he took Thel's friend as a lover and housekeeper and made a new life for himself, he "missed her every day" (252). Clifton's narrative imaginatively constructs the ways in which Thel's presence is felt in the house for those ten years: by Samuel's girlfriend when she rose daily to get Samuel's breakfast and by Samuel as he returned daily from work and saw Thel "get up from the chair by the window and walk to the front door to meet him" (239, 252). The narrator, remembering some of Samuel's tales of Thel's continuing presence in his life, surmises that through his mind's effort to fill the empty space greeting him in the house and through his heart's belief in the presence of the dead, "he could hear somebody soft saying Samuel" (252). Through such lines readers glimpse the bittersweet life of the widower and Thel's influence beyond the grave. Thel's strength and love for Samuel are recorded in Clifton's recurring fragments of reminiscence, shards of Samuel's stories about how Thel haunted the house in Buffalo.

Clifton herself recalls the "magic wisdom" of her mother, a woman who possessed magical transformative skills: "Oh she was magic. If there were locks that were locked tight, she could get a little thing and open them. She could take old bent hangers and rags and make curtains and hang drapes" (273). You can hear the admiration of the author in these lines' tribute to her mother's skills. Of her loving nature the narrator recalls, "She . . . made cakes every week and everybody loved her. Everybody" (273). Thel's traditional selfless devotion to her husband and resigned acceptance of Samuel's infidelities are recorded nonjudgmentally by the more feminist Clifton (Price, 110). Through these fragments, readers obtain sketches of the poet's mother and father that reveal the special aura surrounding them in the author's memory.

Recalling a mother long gone helps Clifton come to grips with a father newly buried, but also underscores the painfulness of being alone in the world without a parental advocate. Acknowledging both parents' enduring presence in her life, nevertheless, gives Clifton a comforting companionship as she ages, and also enables her to analyze and understand the formation of her own identity.

The quotations from Walt Whitman's *Song of Myself* that appear on the title page of each chapter in the memoir seek answers to questions about identity: "What is a man anyhow? what am I? what are you?" (247). They also suggest the idea of the interconnectedness of all earthly things: "For every atom belonging to me as good belongs to you" (225). This enmeshment, represented by Clifton as her continuing family line, counteracts the power of death. Whitman describes an eternal essence of life in two passages excerpted by Clifton: "All goes onward and outward, nothing collapses, / And to die is different from what any one supposed, and luckier" (257); and, "They are alive and well somewhere, / The smallest sprout shows there is really no death" (263). To these words of Whitman, Clifton, mother of six, continuer

of the line of Dahomey women, adds words that echo the African writer
Chinua Achebe: "Things don't fall apart. Things hold. Lines connect in thin
ways that last and last and lives become generations made out of pictures
and words just kept" (275). The fact that Clifton's daughter was born one
month after Thel's death illustrates this philosophy of continuity.

The racial element in this vision of coherence that shepherds the Sayles
family through old age and beyond death is repeatedly underscored by the
narrator's references to Mammy Ca'line and the other Dahomey women. It
may strike readers as curious that an autobiographical tribute to the author's
father also becomes a feminist celebration of sisterhood with the women
who are her ancestors. Again, however, the driving force here seems to be
race and Afrocentrism more than gender. Gender does *also* provide a source
of pride for Clifton, nonetheless. She readily identifies with the women of
her clan, and she wishes to pass on the wisdom of her female elders as it
has shaped *her;* the autobiographical element of Clifton's biographical text is
foregrounded in this way. Her narrative's final statement of coherence, of
things holding, places Clifton in the maternal subject-position when she
proudly presents her six children as free folk of free folk, sloughing off the
skin of slavery, transcending any negative moral effects of slavery. One line
from her father recurs throughout the narrative, and she returns to it near
the end of the memoir, "slavery was terrible but we fooled them old people.
We [blacks] come out of it better than they [whites] did" (260, 275). As political theorists, including Paulo Freire, have noted, oppression dehumanizes the
oppressor as well as the victim (Freire, 30). Oppressors may become more
tainted than the oppressed by their acts, and the oppressed may rise up above
their oppressed condition. The Dahomey women have transcended their
oppressors.

Anecdotes from her family's triumphant past reinforce this assertion.
Grandma Lucy killed the white man who fathered her male child and was
hanged, but the line flourished. Blacks did not own dining room sets in those
days, but "his great-grandmother was a Dahomey woman and he could have
anything he wanted," so Clifton's father was the first black in Depew, New
York, to own a dining room set (266). Pride in the family's African ancestry
energizes Samuel and his family to seek what they need and want in life,
giving them a sense of entitlement. Samuel bought a home. Lucille went to
college. The narrator recites this litany of historical facts to report the fam-

ily's struggle against racial oppression throughout the narrative. This triumphant family history is backdrop to Clifton's reminiscence and confrontation
with Samuel's old age and death.

By reviewing his life in the context of his family's history, Clifton creates
an intimacy between her father and her readers. She also eternalizes Samuel
Sayles through language, at the same time emphasizing the whole family's
continuity. Her narrative, finally, reveals some ways in which race, age, and
gender intersect, with race still being the overdetermining factor. Readers
can glimpse a black man's old age through his middle-aged daughter's eyes, a
view not commonly represented in literature.

Although *Generations* is not overtly an exploration of old age among African Americans, readers can extrapolate Clifton's notions on this subject.
From her portrait of Samuel Sayles, I learned that to grow old and die may be
"luckier" (Whitman's term) if you are born of Dahomey women, but living to
a ripe old age as an African-American male requires meeting more challenges
than the common struggles against weakening body, loss of family and
friends, and increasing alienation from the youthful world. Longevity requires a tough will, fighting skills to confront a localized racism, and intense
nurturant love—the likes of Mammy Ca'line—to resist "a world of wrongs"
(Baughman, 133). So say the Sayles family's elders.

Despite having to live in a world of racist and ageist wrongs, these elders
teach that you can will yourself to live happily into old age. Clifton has
learned their lesson, fashioning for herself an optimistic philosophy. In a 1990
interview with Betty Parry, she acknowledges that she is a celebrant of life:
"Celebrating life is just a matter of the kind of human I've decided I want to
be" (24). Her father, Samuel, and all the Dahomey women would be proud
to hear her say so.

Audre Lorde: Illness and Confrontation
with Mortality in Middle Age

Six months after undergoing a modified radical mastectomy for breast cancer, writer Audre Lorde undertook to articulate the impact of this experience
on her identity and to analyze the changes it made in her life in *The Cancer
Journals*. This philosophical and politically activist memoir describes how

Lorde's experience with cancer creates in her a new self-consciousness in all she decides and does, and a new, positive perspective on time's limits. Her courageous narrative describes, furthermore, her growing appreciation of living. Confronting breast cancer and mortality at age forty-six catapults Lorde into a world of issues usually faced by older people and transforms her into a wise and aged philosopher. Cancer also transforms her view of herself as Other, beset by loneliness and oppression, "outsider in every group [she's] a part of" (12). She learns that community with other women offers her a chance for salvation, and she commits herself to building and sustaining this community.

Her illness also redirects Lorde's uses of language and reaffirms the centrality of language in her life. As with many older artists, Lorde's bout with cancer elicits from her a new consciousness of death that influences her work; as Wyatt-Brown notes, aging artists often respond to "a sense of time urgency" and to "worries about 'decay' and 'deterioration'" with the creation of a new "late style" or a new focus in their professional work (Wyatt-Brown 1993, 7–8). Lorde creates a highly politicized, gendered style in which to discuss her illness, mortality, her close relationships, and her work. Addressing women of all backgrounds and ages who understand as Lorde does that maintaining silence about any aspects of women's lives becomes "a tool for separation and powerlessness" (Lorde, 9), Lorde breaks silence and offers word gifts about the ordeal of her cancer. She argues for the good that may come of such word gifts, inscribing language that she hopes will "underline the possibilities of self-healing and the richness of living for all women" (10).

Lorde's introduction clearly acknowledges the transformative power of language. She intends to use it tellingly in these journals for several reasons: language can offer the opportunity for "painful reassessment" and self-analysis sought by many breast cancer patients (10); it can lessen the isolation and can lift one from depression and feelings of helplessness and victimization; it can create female community; it has the energy to resist patriarchal pressures on women to conform to men's expectations of female bodily image; it can galvanize the writer to make changes in her own life and in the world.

Lorde's paean to language as the wellspring of women's liberation resembles that of French feminist Hélène Cixous, who in her groundbreaking linguistic call to arms, "The Laugh of the Medusa," urged women to write themselves, to write through their bodies and inscribe their sexuality in order to force a "shattering entry into history" (284). Innovative language must declare woman's existence. Women writing can revolutionize the world, "bring about a mutation in human relations, in thought, in all praxis" (286). Inventing a womanist language (Alice Walker's term, xi) can change society. It can "wreck partitions, classes, and rhetorics, regulations and codes" because such writing is like "insurrectionary dough kneading itself" (Cixous, 290, 293). Lorde's view of language has a similar militancy to it. In the introduction, she describes a dream she has about language: in the dream, she is in training to change her life and at the same time is eager "to study the formation and crack and composure of words" (14); the activities of writing and radical self-transformation are juxtaposed and equated in the dream. The writer's greatest act of creativity may be self-creation through language (Berman 1994, 186).

In addition to praising language, the introduction establishes the psychological, philosophical, and political emphases of the journal. As she sorts through her moods of sadness, despair, and rage at the world's cruel indifference to her plight (12), Lorde admits to self-absorption in her journal, but contends self-analysis is the beginning of the external revolutionary act: "And yes I am completely self-referenced right now . . . and I do believe not until every woman traces her weave back strand by bloody self-referenced strand, will we begin to alter the whole pattern" (1 March 1979, 11). Here she echoes the feminist shibboleth that the personal is political, that the personal is the basis for political change and global activism. Her commitment to change is also feminist: "The enormity of our task, to turn the world around. It feels like turning my life around, inside out" (16 April, 11). Through personal growth, widespread political change is possible. Holding to this personal-public dyad of change, Lorde reveals her still youthful feminist optimism; the conservatism and complacency traditionally associated with middle age are not her traits.

Not all older African-American women share her optimism, of course. For example, centenarian Bessie Delany, in *Having Our Say*, contends that her long life taught her the difficulty of changing the world: "I thought I could change the world. It took me a hundred years to figure out I *can't* change the world. I can only change Bessie. And, honey, that ain't easy, either" (115); Sadie, her only slightly more optimistic elder sister, adds, "Or maybe change the world a little bit, just by changing me" (118). The Delanys' saga is filled with anecdotes about people who refuse to change their attitudes, especially about racial issues. Change is never easy, but Lorde persists in the effort.

As a critic, I join Lorde in affirming the power of the personal response or outcry to transform oppressive societal attitudes and to allay fears about aging and illness. The "personal is political" principle motivates me to inject my personal life into my literary analyses of aging and death here. My reading of Lorde's journals is interfused with my own fears about breast cancer and informed by my knowledge of family, friends, and former students— women of the same age as Lorde or younger—who have had brushes with this killer. So I read with more than mild "objective" interest, wanting to learn how the author could recast this nightmarish experience in positive psychological terms and change my mind about breast cancer, one of the common horrors awaiting women as they age.

The philosophical impulse coexists with the political and psychological in Lorde's mission to examine the role of death in our lives. Psychological gerontologist Harry J. Berman has written about the quest for "existential meaning" in autobiographies of later life; as he says, "In telling their life stories, people are drawn into consideration of the meaning of their lives" (1994, xxi–xxii). Lorde's confrontation with death compels her to consider the meanings of her life in relation to others' lives and to reconsider what makes her life meaningful. She observes, first, that people have erased her from their midst because they fear one who has been brushed by death (we see in chapter 4 that Donald Hall writes about the same cruel phenomenon): "I am not supposed to exist. I carry death around in my body like a condemnation. But I do live" (13). That Lorde's condition makes her a nonentity reflects our culture's designation of death as a cultural taboo. Her philosophical mission is to fight this erasure: "There must be some way to integrate death into living, neither ignoring it nor giving in to it" (13). One way of integrating death into life, she speculates, is to use time and make life's decisions with the unceasing consciousness of death's presence: "Living a self-conscious life, under the pressure of time, I work with the consciousness of death at my shoulder" (16). She shares with May Sarton this consciousness of death while making life choices (see chapter 2). Such a consciousness, psychological and philosophical, moves her beyond merely mourning for lost time. It directs her use of language and her ability to love, sharpens her vision and purpose,

What makes a person spiritual is her relationship to others.

increases the intensity of her joy in living, and makes her victorious in her daily battles against despair (16).

Also apparent from her daily struggles with despair is Lorde's central commitment to continuing the work of writing and maintaining the love of women. The two are closely linked, as Lorde says: "In the recognition of the existence of love lies the answer to despair. Work is that recognition given voice and name" (13). Writing converts her destructive fear and anger at her physical problems into creative, loving endeavors, and as Wyatt-Brown has observed about many late-life writers, Lorde's "art is enriched by [her] battle against despair" (Wyatt-Brown 1993, 12). Continuing to write relieves her temporarily of the isolation, the debilitating effects of her illness, and her anxieties about dying (12). Language, her role as "black woman warrior poet," transforms her from a breast cancer casualty into the radical lesbian soldier who will no longer accept the tyrannies imposed on her daily (21). Writing channels her fear and anger into political activism, into protests against, for example, government sanctioning of carcinogenic hormones in cattle feed (16). Writing also enables her to network with women, both to resist the patriarchy and to experience a sustaining love.

By writing, Lorde can discover where to place her confrontation with mortality and recognition of her own aging in "the larger tapestry of [her] work as a Black woman" (17). Stressing feminism as a factor in her work, she fits her writing into a feminist project of reclamation: reclaiming the earth and women's power. The black woman, by writing, transforms silence into language and action, makes herself visible and whole, better able to resist the invisibility wrought by racism. Gender and race shape Lorde's identity and her agenda; her writing mainly articulates these subject-positions. Yet illness forces Lorde to recognize age as another important element shaping her life, limiting her time, and increasing the urgency of her desire to root out oppression.

Chapter 1, "The Transformation of Silence into Language and Action," continues to argue for language as potent challenger of death, "the final silence" (20). There Lorde notes how facing her own mortality compels her to endure "an involuntary reorganization of [her] entire life" (20). Writing helps in this reorganization, helps her to realize her desires. Both the mortal illness and the writing that emerges out of her (altered) body enable her to see that what she has regretted most in her life are the tyrannical silences, the missed opportunities to express herself and to speak out against oppression.

In the centerpiece, the second chapter of *The Cancer Journals*, "Breast Cancer: A Black Lesbian Feminist Experience," the title itself reveals that the narrative will consider four subject-positions as they inflect Lorde's experience of having breast cancer: African American, woman, lesbian, and feminist. I would add "middle-aged" to this title, as it underscores the unexpectedness, unjustness, and prematurity of experiencing breast cancer at forty-six, which Lorde expresses, and it accentuates her rage at having to confront death at a young age as well as her power struggle against death. The chapter unfolds a psychological and philosophical journey, charts an important series of changes in Lorde's outlook on life and in her behavior. The chapter also writes the middle-aged woman's body in the throes of breast cancer through a language of intimacy and details that would make many women initially squirm with discomfort, anxiety, and a desire to escape: the ostrich syndrome. The language might, on the other hand, evoke in the curious a fascination with the medical protocols and physical sensations of the ordeal (for the E.R. and *Chicago Hope* devotees). In either case, Lorde's writing is likely to disrupt readers' complacency.

Early in this chapter, Lorde begins to work on the ostriches among readers, raising again the important issue of integrating death into her life, of ending the struggle against its presence; she asks in this quotation from her December 1978 journal entry: "What is there possibly left for us to be afraid of, after we have dealt face to face with death and not embraced it? Once I accept the existence of dying, as a life process, who can ever have power over me again?" (25). This pair of rhetorical questions indicates Lorde's overarching aim of placing death on a continuum with life and constructing life's meaning in relation to mortality. Conceptualizing death as meshed with life, she claims, has a liberating and empowering effect, releasing her from the fear that would subjugate her to other people, enabling her to move on to metaphysical questions of being and meaning: ontology, ethics, epistemology. Lorde cultivates the kind of existential thinking about aging and death that Thomas Cole argues is critically important in our aging society; we need to develop "our culture's ability to sustain morally compelling social practices and existentially vital ideals of aging" (230).

The rest of Lorde's second chapter acts as commentary upon this 1978 journal entry. She creates a Bakhtinian *heteroglossia* of women's voices, using several linguistic forms and methods to seek meanings in life and construct ways to face the traumas of aging (Bakhtin, 263, 272–73). She begins with voices representing aspects of herself from the recent past. Her narrative flashes back one year to the initial discovery of a breast tumor (three weeks later determined to be benign), her first confrontation with mortality, and the consequential crystallization of how she wanted to live: "with a determination and freedom to speak as I needed, and to enjoy and live my life as I needed to for my own meaning" (26). That meaning does not fully unfold until after her actual ordeal with breast cancer the next year. Yet she does understand as early as her dealings with the benign tumor that accepting the reality of her own death in the future has an energizing effect on her life.

The effect is ultimately energizing because she is compelled to construct and construe this experience without reliance on previous role models: "I have cancer. I'm a black lesbian feminist poet, how am I going to do this now? What are the models for what I'm supposed to be in this situation?" (28–29). Her construction sites of meaning will be these four subject-positions—although her age of forty-six years is the fifth subject-position that jolts her into a new conceptualization of death. Besides these subject-positions, there are other contending "voices" of Lorde in this chapter—fragments of the *heteroglossia*—presented as she reconstructs the days between her biopsy and the mastectomy and revisits the strife within her.

The strife derives from the necessity to decide between whether to have a mastectomy or to pursue alternative holistic medical treatments. One example of the *heteroglossia* appears when a practical voice counseling sleep to heal her body vies with an insomnious voice of despair and denial shouting that this has just been a bad dream, while another Audre Lorde detaches a parodic self from the whole nightmare, as she says: "Another part of me flew like a big bird to the ceiling of whatever place I was in, observing my actions and providing a running commentary, complete with suggestions of factors forgotten . . . and ribald remarks" (31). These voices, facets of her identity, form a continual concert in her head, sometimes a discordant one, making tranquil meditation hard and revealing her intermittent states of shock, confusion, and numbness (31). The voices also "converse" with diverse imagined readers, increasing the complexity of the *heteroglossia*.

As I am doing here, Marc Kaminsky uses Bakhtin's ideas to uncover a similar complexity in the dialogue with elders created by Barbara Myerhoff in her ethnographic text, *Number Our Days:* "[the] ethnographic text . . . is itself construed in Bakhtinian terms as a creative event, a realm of dialogic relations among author, content, and reader" (71). Lorde's dialogic relations with her subject of breast cancer and with me her reader are even more complicated and creative because Lorde's authorial-narratorial voices are multiple and change over time.

As a woman reading through Lorde's multiple, fragmented dialogue with "herselves," I now understand viscerally the need to detach part of oneself from the horror and pain of contemplating separation from one's breast. Lorde describes powerfully the wrenching psychic pain of this separation, apart from the physical experience, likening it to the sharp pain of separation from her mother (26). I grasp her self-protective desire for numbness and the rage mingled with denial; Lorde speaks directly to women readers whose worst fears for themselves she is describing. These pages are excruciating to read, threatening the core of one's femaleness. Given the primal terror that her strong text evokes, it is all the more impressive to readers like me that Lorde is able to tame her fears and heal her psychic fragmentation as she seeks a meaningful life and a way through her ordeal. Her successful pathfinding is quite comforting to middle-aged readers like myself. (I note that at this writing I am two years older than Lorde during her first bout with breast cancer; she died of it in 1992 at the age of 59.)

Competing with the other voices in the narration of this scene within Lorde's mind is the strong sage's voice, acting as "voice-over." It is a voice guided by retrospection, shaped by having endured and survived the experience itself. This voice analyzes how the dissonances can be resolved, how the contending identities may be reconciled, by naming these necessities: "what I really felt and wanted . . . was to live and to love and to do my work, as hard as I could and for as long as I could" (32). Lorde adapts and radicalizes Freud's recipe for happiness through love and work. To live and love: as a black lesbian feminist; to work: as a poet energized by the other three dominant dimensions of her being. Such a crystallization of her life's essential elements and purposes directs her decision to have the surgery as the safest way to fulfill her desires. She safeguards her life through the high price of her breast (33).

Deciding to have the mastectomy does not completely allay Lorde's fears that she will not survive the surgery or buy "enough" time to complete her work. Is there ever enough time for completion? Such a question is bound to assail and unsettle many readers, as it did me. But the mastectomy seems to maximize the possibility of increasing Lorde's reinscribed time frame. After the surgery, the contending voices calm down "into their melded quieter places" as the conscious part of self resurfaces to confront the losses of time and anatomy (38). She realizes she must adapt "to a new body, a new time span, a possible early death"—difficult physical, philosophical, and psychic grappling (38). Zalman Schachter-Shalomi and Ronald S. Miller, in their book on "spiritual eldering," *From Age-ing to Sage-ing,* note that the elder dwells "at the intersection between time and eternity . . . [and] the elder asks, 'What is the meaning of my life? What have I contributed to the world that makes a difference?'" (140). When time is reconfigured for Lorde by cancer at age forty-six, she becomes an elder, asking existential questions about her life, her relationships with others, her work.

Besides wrenching psychological and philosophical self-analysis, there is in this chapter extraordinary vividness in Lorde's physical writing of her body and the relationship she has with this body: the mingled love, hate, and feeling of betrayal by her flesh. The intimacy with her own breasts is portrayed through a maternal analogy of the child's attachment to the mother. Such close, trusting tenderness vies with the anger that she recalls feeling after her first biopsy, rage at the breast's treachery "because I felt as if it [the breast] had in some unexpected way . . . become already separate from me and had turned against me by creating this tumor"(33). Then she quotes her journal entry just before the mastectomy, in which she had recorded her sense of reconciliation with that breast and her gladness at having enjoyed both of them (34). She has weighed the choice between her breast, with all the erotic pleasures it can give, and her life. Her life must unquestionably win, despite the deep sadness and loss (35).

In a self-affirming linguistic act, Lorde connects her contemplated loss to an African tradition: the Amazon warriors of Dahomey had their right breasts cut off as young women to make themselves better archers, an activity to which they were deeply committed. Similarly, Lorde believes in the rightness of her life and the work she must do as an African-American feminist lesbian poet; the courage of the Dahomey women, which revives Clifton and the Sayles family, also sustains Lorde as she opts for surgery. Connecting to her African ancestors' ritual, Lorde, like Clifton, Roth, and L'Engle, experiences a feeling of continuity that transcends the limited span of her individual life.

As another way to prepare psychically for her impending bodily change, Lorde also recalls making love in her nineteenth year with Eudora Garrett, a forty-seven-year-old woman who had had a mastectomy, reseeing and retouching in her thoughts the "deeply scarred hollow under [Eudora's] right shoulder and across her chest"; she makes this recollection a prelude to her own scarred emptiness after the surgery (35). In her conversations with Lorde, Garrett never emphasized her impending death but dwelt on her work; Lorde recommits to the centrality of her own work now by recalling Garrett. She also dreams of Garrett the night before the surgery, and Garrett holds her hand. She derives comfort from remembering their intimacy and wonders if she had comforted Garrett. She also thinks of the dream, perhaps, as a promise that she herself will live to make love again, one of the requisite elements of her meaningful existence. She continues to write the physical language of her desire, undaunted by cancer.

Lorde also takes us bodily through the surgery, the anesthesia, the recovery room, the sites of pain and numbness, the bandages, the immobility, the initial euphoria of being alive. The thickness of the bandages, which she touches and views in the mirror, prevents her from fully experiencing the loss of her breast at first. The physical pain must be faced, however, and her language compels both the writer herself and her readers to witness it. Besides the stabbing and burning pain in her chest wall, back, and right shoulder, there is the pain at the site of the lost breast, forever to remind her of its absence: "My breast which was no longer there would hurt as if it were being squeezed in a vise . . . [the worst] suffering [was] in a part of me which was no longer there" (38). The repetition of the phrase "which was no longer there" is the language of the author's dawning realization or reinforcement of the reality of her bodily loss—a fleshly linguistic act that produces consciousness. Linguistically, we also recognize the power of the gap here: what is missing—breast and language—can influence us strongly, and we may fill in the gaps of Lorde's suffering narrative with our own memories of ordeals that we have endured or our imaginings of adversity that we fear having to undergo, thereby increasing the personal impact of her narrative on us.

Linguistic acts such as her analogizing of the pain in her chest to "someone . . . stepping on my [lost] breast . . . with hobnailed boots" convey the raw cruelty of this pain (45). The image of her breast being squeezed in a vise will evoke a wincing pain for female readers who have undergone a mammogram.

Still other linguistic acts enable Lorde to comprehend her bodily transformation, her difference after the mastectomy. One act is the telling of case histories or anecdotes about two other mastectomees who denied their difference, Lorde argues, by accepting the prostheses of a heterosexual, patriarchal culture that cannot bear the reality of the breastless female. Her argument is militantly feminist, discounting the idea that some women, homosexual and heterosexual, would not wish to display their physical differentness after a mastectomy. Lorde, however, is an unblinking realist. She uses *heteroglossia* to explore her sense of otherness and fragmentation and to define the new breastless reality that she must accept. She counterpoints the Reach for Recovery woman's patriarchal, cheery spiel of denial—pointing out its hegemonic cultural assumptions—to her own interior voice of the lesbian self. The interior lesbian voice poses a litany of questions: how will her lover react to her body, how will they fit together, will she still be found physically "delicious," how will she endure the loss of pleasure formerly felt during lovemaking in her right breast (43)? These questions would certainly occur to heterosexual women, too. She also juxtaposes her firm and serene "voice-over," her sage retrospective voice, the one that knows she has endured and triumphed, once again to the shaky voice of her journal entry for the fourth day after surgery, which records pain, grief, and silences, as she struggles with "words like cancer, pain, and dying" that float around constantly in her head. Through it all, she expresses her commitment to make the act of writing this journal useful to other sufferers, to help them accept their bodily transformations (46). Writing the journal affirms the reality of Lorde's ordeal and its potentially positive consequences.

Lorde also recounts a scene of herself before the mirror that tests reality. She eyes her altered self and in words captures her recognition of that alteration. The woman's gaze into the mirror, a moment present in many novels and autobiographies of aging, marks the opportunity either to deny or to acknowledge the ravages of illness and aging. Kathleen Woodward's mirror stage of old age is relevant here. In addition to the social aspect of the mirror stage of old age discussed in chapter 2 of this book, there is the (Lacanian) psychoanalytic aspect, which Woodward contrasts to that of the mirror stage of infancy. When the infant gazes in the mirror, he or she reacts lovingly toward the reflection, whereas the elder gazes with repulsion at her or his reflection: "In the mirror stage of old age, one is libidinally alienated from one's mirror image. If the psychic plot of the mirror stage of infancy is the anticipated trajectory from insufficiency to bodily wholeness, the bodily plot of the mirror stage of old age is the feared trajectory from wholeness to physical disintegration, . . . [and the sense that] this aging body is not my self" (67). Lorde struggles against this feeling of repulsion or alienation from her altered self; she attempts not to follow the trajectory from wholeness to physical disintegration but to create another trajectory toward wholeness and integration of body with mind.

She is at first taken aback by her disfigured anatomy; the mastectomy estranges her body from her self: "I looked strange and uneven and peculiar to myself" (44). Yet instead of rejecting her one-breasted body when she gazes at herself both with and without the lamb's wool prosthesis, Lorde determines to reject the lamb's wool and embrace her surgically altered self without the prosthesis as "ever so much more myself"; the lamb's wool sits incompatibly on her chest, "awkwardly inert and lifeless, and having nothing to do with any me I could possibly conceive of" (44). It is, furthermore, the wrong color, reminding her of her marginalization as an African American, just as the Reach for Recovery woman's language marks Lorde's marginalization as a lesbian. Lorde in this dramatic moment gazes at the mirror, antici- pates in its vision her body's trajectory toward disintegration, and yet decides that she will lovingly guide her body in its path: "either I would love my body one-breasted now, or remain forever alien to myself" (44). She chooses to embrace her altered body, and this act of courage distinguishes her deci- sion from the ordinary impulse of the mastectomee and, as Woodward sees it, of the old person too: "Strangeness, the uncanny, old age, decrepitude, death, fear, danger—all are linked together in this momentary drama of the mirror stage of old age . . . [where] the narcissistic impulse directs itself *against* the mirror image" (Woodward, 68). Lorde fully accepts the reality of her one-breasted body and those of other mastectomees. Like an elder facing extreme old age and death, she will take no "psychic reprieve" (Woodward, 69) from the reality of her lost breast, the aging of her body, and the hovering of death; she takes these things for her companions.

As her gaze turns, shortly after this mirror passage, from oblique reflection directly to the changed landscape of her body, the distance between herself and her body narrows, and she begins to familiarize herself with the new terrain, "the strange flat plain down across which I could now for the first time in my memory view the unaccustomed bulge of my rib-cage" (45). Again, she compares her transformed landscape to the bodies of the young Dahomey Amazons and seeks strength from this linkage to her ancestors, who were able to adapt to bodily changes demanded by their cultural beliefs. She acknowledges that she will have to learn a new physical posture with her one-breasted self (47). These notions join with her recording of her act of masturbation after the surgery (40), another willed act of self-love, to suggest Lorde's increasing self-affirmation, physical and psychic.

Also counteracting the severe physical pain and initial dislocation from her altered body is the healing love of the women in Lorde's life, "the woman energy" that she responds to with a corresponding energy that wills her survival (39–40). Lorde's language captures the erotic sensations of this love flowing into her, its warm maternal quality. It is an amniotic fluid surrounding her, as if she were "floating upon a sea within a ring of women like warm bubbles keeping me afloat upon the surface of that sea"; there is "a texture of inviting water just beneath their eyes" (39). The women's energy soothes her body so that her body is no longer her enemy. Interdependence, community, warm and wet motherly love, all float her toward a womanist recovery. These communal energies counteract her feeling of isolation and the wrenching separation from her breast, which she had likened to the child's agonized individuation from the mother.

Lorde's return home from the hospital heralds a more concentrated effort to tackle the philosophical questions and choices in her altered existence, those kept in abeyance by her physical pain in the hospital. As she has to face a new physical posture with regard to herself after the mastectomy, so must she formulate a new metaphysical posture, born out of a direct dialogue with death. Lorde considers being on speaking terms with death a necessary "developmental and healing task" (47). Facing death immediately forces her to interrogate her lifelong conceptualization of time and to reconsider what she wants to accomplish in her work and relationships with people. How to finish current writing projects and whether to begin new ones must be considered, as must whether or not she has the time to begin new relationships with people (46–47).

She learns from her meditation that isolation from people kills, and she describes such killing in the language of the subaltern: women who have lost a breast may feel they have "gone into purdah," they may experience exile, "the status of the untouchable"—which "you can die of" (49). Here her language crystallizes the interlocking oppressions of race, ethnicity, age, and illness, representing their power to isolate the victim. To resist being exiled, Lorde adapts one guiding truth for her life: the central importance of her relationships with family and old friends. If she has dialogued with death, *they* are the counterdialogue of life. As Lorde learns, these women are "fundamentally supportive of a life force within me" (47). To live easily, but not too easily, with death, Lorde knows she must remain immersed in these life-giving relationships. She discovers, "The only answer to death is the heat and confusion of living; the only dependable warmth is the warmth of the blood" (47).

The other life-giving activity that Lorde ponders metaphysically is her work. With postmodern self-reflexiveness, she talks about how her act of writing is now different after her brush with death. Love and work become partners in a new metaphysical "life dance" for Lorde, similar to the one L'Engle describes at the end of *The Summer of the Great-Grandmother*. The imagery of dialogue or *heteroglossia* used earlier to describe Lorde's jostling, competing subject-positions makes way for this new imagery in her metaphysics-building: counterpointing rhythms in the "life dance" that Lorde begins to perform at home. The rhythms of her "family women" dance beside the poet's internal rhythms, the waning dreams move along beyond those dreams realistically worth pursuing, all accompanied by the rhythms of the "ghost of [her] right breast" (47). She creates philosophical underpinnings for her new life dance by sharing her thoughts with other lesbians who have had mastectomies, sharing their "stories across age and color and place and difference" (49). Sharing enriches her writing.

As she writes, her changed perception of time influences her. She attains awareness of her (and everyone's) temporary earthly status. Moved by this awareness, she writes in order to make each millisecond count (52). She extracts the sweetness and awe from each minute (53). She lives in the center of the moment. In this commitment to seizing the moment, she strikingly resembles May Sarton (see chapter 2). Lorde's narrative underscores what she had said about time during her convalescence: time no longer could simply wash over her unheralded as she drifted in abstract reverie. Her desire would be to make even a dull hour permanent, an impossibility unless you freeze it through language, as Keats did in "Ode on a Grecian Urn." Browning similarly longed to freeze the good minute in "The Last Ride Together" and "Two in the Campagna." I take pleasure in the irony of placing canonical white male poets Keats and Browning beside this black feminist lesbian poet. Yet she belongs with them because they share the language of time and try to manipulate time, ever mindful of mortality. I celebrate Lorde's ability, sharpened through the experience of her illness, to extend the moment in a gendered way; each moment is contextualized by her black lesbian poetic sensibility. The linguistic magic of *The Cancer Journals* records the marvels and fears of each minute, for herself and for other women who might need them. Working with words in this way employs Lorde's fears productively and at the same time siphons them off: a doubly efficacious use of time.

Lorde ends this central chapter of the *Journals* with another dialogue between herself and herself. Dated 20/28 February 1979, this dialogue sums up the chapter's search for new directions in Lorde's life. It is an enabling pair of lines, following a passage where she envisions her work as a way to address her fear. In these two lines she convinces herself that she can handle her fears of the future through her commitment to living in this scary moment and staying involved in her work with language:

> Isn't there any other way, I said.
> In another time, she said. (54)

This, now, is the time to live. Working and loving are the best way to do this living right now.

The third and final section of *The Cancer Journals* further politicizes the body politics of breast cancer, challenging those who characterize it as a "cosmetic problem" solvable through prostheses. Lorde vehemently opposes this solution for two reasons. First, it symbolically sidesteps the truth that a mastectomy means a brush with death that necessitates some changes in a woman's behavior and outlook. Second, she feels that prostheses encourage

women to finesse the reality that they have changed, physically, psychologically, and philosophically, after mastectomy; wearing a prosthesis, women
live in the past instead of contemplating a changed future (57). Prostheses and
implants silence the reality of mastectomy, while Lorde's words and single-
breastedness voice that reality. Finally, she claims that prostheses isolate
women from each other, especially other cancer patients (61), and we know
by now that Lorde equates isolation with death. All that Lorde has struggled
to achieve, to speak, in chapter 2, would be undermined by the symbolism
and the use of breast prostheses; prostheses impede the fulfillment of "the
need for every woman to live a considered life" (57). The unconsidered life is
not worth living.

For Lorde, prostheses ensure a shallow, unexamined life for women and
a childish dependency. They also encourage an apolitical outlook that does
not question the American Cancer Society's failure to educate American
women adequately about links between breast cancer, animal fat, and hormones (58), an outlook that accepts our victimization by the environment's
pollution, radiation, and food additives (60). (Lorde's last point would probably not be addressed in the 1990s, as the public is becoming more informed
about research linking cancer to diet and environment; perhaps the activism
of feminist writers like Lorde encouraged this research and public access to
the results of medical studies). To illustrate her view of the infantilization of
women through prostheses after breast surgery, she analogizes the prosthesis
to the candy given a child after an injection (64); both offer an illusory, destructive sense of comfort. Lorde wants to apply her experience to writing
that resists infantilization of women, that reveals the desirability of living a
considered life.

The politicization increases in this chapter through Lorde's use of anecdotes based on her own experience as a mastectomee within the patriarchy.
First she recounts her dialogue with a nurse in her breast surgeon's office
who scolds her for not wearing the prosthesis because it is bad for morale
at the doctor's office; clearly these medical professionals are ostriches, and
they assume the patients are, too. She compares her visible single-
breastedness as a woman warrior battling cancer to the patch that Moshe
Dayan wore over his empty eye socket, overt symbol of his war wound: if
the world considers that an acceptable lesson in the horrors and sacrifices of
war, Lorde asks, why shouldn't her "body symbolism" be visible in the fight

against cancer? It is not acceptable, she concludes, because our culture is "woman-phobic" and sees women as decorative sex objects (60); anything that detracts from women's decorativeness is to be dismissed or disguised. Her feminist voice is firm and angry here.

Lorde opposes the sexist-ageist view that paints women as fading and sexless in middle age by narratively valuing her own increased beauty, strength, emotional complexity, and creativity. Erik Erikson and colleagues have written about the growth that comes with aging: "As we see it, and as many of our subjects demonstrate, the early years of the long span of aging are open for creative living: experimentation with new life-styles or exploration of new activities . . . [or] a delightful expansion of one's range of interest and appreciative experience" (324). Aging, intensified by cancer, brings Lorde self-actualization, as a result of which she can reject the female role of sex object and move beyond our youth-loving cultural icons. Loss through a mastectomy can, ironically, contribute to a woman's self-development. The prosthesis interrupts the middle-aged woman's blooming. This is why she argues against prostheses: to encourage middle-aged women who are finding their voices and experiencing true ripening at last to continue to do so, but realistically. Besides finding a voice, establishing a more tolerant and affectionate relationship with one's body is possible more than ever in middle age—if women perceive their bodies not through the male gaze but through female eyes. She even advocates designing clothing—comparable to maternity wear—that accommodates the aging body and a woman's gaze upon herself (65).

Up to this point in the chapter, I reacted with tolerance, prompted by my feminist sympathies, but was not in complete agreement with what I thought was Lorde's somewhat extreme argument that prostheses are a destructive political and psychological lie and a sop to a patriarchal society. I thought that were I in this situation, I would adjust to the change in my body with great difficulty and would seek to avoid exposing myself to added social tensions by not "flaunting" my mastectomy publicly; a prosthesis would protect me from others' fear and prejudice. However, Lorde shocked me into taking her side of the argument by citing evidence that women who have had mastectomies lose jobs and promotions, even if they wear prostheses (66). Not surprisingly, she likens this workplace discrimation to racial oppression, comparing the marginalization of the female cancer patient to that of the African

American in our society: "Suggesting prosthesis as a solution to employment discrimination is like saying that the way to fight racial prejudice is for Black people to pretend to be white" (66). The conflict, then, is between self-denial and acceptance of one's difference; no good can come of the former, and the latter is requisite for psychological adjustment to one's altered life. This analogy struck me as very revealing of the body politics and economics of the American breast cancer industry.

The American Cancer Society is also indicted by Lorde for its adherence to the profit motive in its research on treatment of cancer, not prevention, and in its neglect of unconventional (often eastern) modes of treating breast cancers, which reflect its "western medical bias" (73). Lorde marshals evidence and a militant argument for a wider and more creative research effort on breast cancer. She urges women to take charge of their bodies and their health, to arm themselves with new medical knowledge beyond the traditional western patriarchal sources. She tells women readers, "Every woman has a militant responsibility to involve herself actively with her own health" (73). Lorde herself has done that, and by writing *The Cancer Journals,* she has galvanized many more women to do the same, including elderly women who are often neglected by the medical establishment.

Lorde's text does not end on a purely political note, however. It turns to interrogate the psychosocial phenomenon of blaming the victim: pointing the finger at the cancer victim as having courted her illness by not being happy enough. Women are not to blame for their cancers or for aging; Lorde claims that our polluted, oppressive environment is to blame. She asks how anyone can be truly happy in our violent, racist, polluted, hungry society. She asserts that all women of color must in self-defense know and prepare daily for this violent hatred. She concludes, "We are equally destroyed by false happiness and false breasts" (75). Truth telling, in carefully crafted language acts, will help to protect our collective mental health.

Lorde ends with a selection from one last journal entry dated 30 March 1979, in which the sources of her true happiness come into sharp focus as she considers all that she would refuse to give up in exchange for her lost breast: her lover Frances, her children and other women she loves, her poetry, her arms, her eyes (76). She sees one self in the journal entry successfully fighting another self, "the devil of despair"—the trophy being a third entity, her soul. In claiming this spiritual trophy, this dialogical victory, Lorde has won her sanity, gained peace of mind, located her "well of feeling" and her sexuality within herself, an older woman of color. In a real sense she has come home to Audre Lorde (77). Concluding thusly, she encourages readers to believe in their ability to undertake their own difficult journey and reach a happy destination in their later years.

Maya Angelou: Homilies on Aging and Life's Journey

Writer Maya Angelou's *Wouldn't Take Nothing for My Journey Now*—not strictly an autobiography or memoir but a collection of personal essays, meditations, sketches, and homilies resonant with autobiographical passages—gives us some contemporary insights into the workings of race, gender, and age in the author's life and American culture. Her insights grow out of her own life's journey. As with the other works in this chapter, Angelou's book focuses more on the subject-positions of race and gender than on age. Nevertheless, the title, in particular the word *now*, suggests that the author is an elder since her life's journey has been going on for some time, it has taught her some valuable lessons that she wants to pass along to others, she has much invested in it, and its richness is beyond price, not tradeable for another's life journey or for material goods.

Angelou is conscious of her age when she discusses her own continuing journey in search of answers about God and religion in one of the essays, titled "Power of the Word." Here Angelou observes with amusement those people who have already concluded that they are Christians: "Many things continue to amaze me, even well into the sixth decade of my life. I'm startled or taken aback when people walk up to me and tell me they are Christians. My first response is the question 'Already?' It seems to me a lifelong endeavor to try to live the life of a Christian" (73). Her notion of the search itself as the process of achieving moral goodness, as well as her contention that she is still caught up in the search even though she is in her sixties, reveals Angelou's energy and optimism about her later years. She rejects our culture's stereotype of aging as spiritual stagnation and philosophical cynicism. Erikson would consider her another example of an elder vitally involved in life, one who can "share in the responsibility of the generations for each other" while she keeps seeking the meaning of life (337). Angelou lives in the wonder of the search and can celebrate both her rejoining of "spiritual growth [with] physical aging" and the persistence of her quest for existential meaning (47). Her wisdom and spirituality are evident in the sermonic mood of her brief essays. As Anne Whitehouse has observed, these sermonettes "are simple but not simplistic. They are generous evidence of a life fully lived" (18).

Gender is also preeminent among the subject-positions that shape Angelou's identity, as seen in the piece Angelou chooses to begin the collection, "In All Ways a Woman." In this essay, the difficulties of living as a woman in a patriarchal culture and the need for toughness of character to protect one's interests are asserted. The toughness must be tempered by tenderness so that women do not simply become facsimiles of "those men who value power above life, and control over love" (7). She does, however, factor in the element of age in this piece. To live to be an old woman presents its own challenges, part of the challenge being to learn to live as a tough *and* tender woman. An old woman must have the luck to avoid being hit by a truck and a favorable genetic makeup, things beyond her control. Most important, however, is the active sense of humor that will enable the woman to live a long life; this she must cultivate.

Through several sketches of her elderly female relatives, Angelou gives us recipes for wit and longevity. She also shows us how the older generation of women can coach the younger into extended survival and a growing relish for life in the later years. Historical gerontologist Lois W. Banner observes that this bond between the younger and older generation of African-American women may be inspired by West African societies, where "special deference was accorded to the elderly because of older people's perceived closeness to revered ancestors . . . [and where] grandparents characteristically preserved and passed on family and tribal history, the lore and the wisdom of the folk" (341). That elder's role of passing along family history and ethnic tradition is also undertaken by Herman Roth with his sons in *Patrimony* (see chapter 1). Angelou's essay "Living Well. Living Good" shows us her reverence for her female elders and respect for their wisdom in her warm portrait of seventy-nine-year-old Aunt Tee.

Angelou describes Aunt Tee's skin as the color of "old gold" and notes her tough, thin build (61). These are positive images of aging that challenge stereotypes of decay and atrophy. Aunt Tee, servant in her later years to a wealthy aging white couple, is contrasted to the couple in their approaches to living and aging. The couple become less and less sociable, succumbing to "dry silence" (63), growing less hungry for life, as reflected in their increasingly insipid, invalid-like meals. Aunt Tee watches them age but does not enter the "mirror stage of old age" or see her own senescence in them; perhaps the race factor subverts the common operations of the psychic mirror here.

More significant in forestalling a disengaged old age for Aunt Tee is her own increasing humor and sociability. She dates a chauffeur who lives nearby, entertaining him and another couple every Saturday night in her quarters, cooking them an African-American soul-food feast of fried chicken, greens, pigs' feet, potato salad, and banana pudding—in pointed contrast to the white couple's bland fare. Instead of the dry silence of the white couple, music, dancing, joking, and card games liven up these evening entertainments: laughter and fun fill their lives. No longer really living themselves, the white couple ask Aunt Tee to leave her door open when she entertains so they can see her and her friends having a good time, see life being lived fully.

Aunt Tee and her white employers suggest a good and a bad model for aging. In the good model, the person continues to participate actively in life and creates her own pleasures; in the bad model, the person withdraws from life or becomes merely a voyeur of life's pleasures. As Angelou concludes after this sketch of Aunt Tee, "living well is an art which can be developed" (65). This art can be developed and practiced in later life, too. She counsels readers to cultivate the art of living well by developing a forgiving attitude toward others, the capacity to enjoy "small offerings" from life, an awareness that the world owes us none of these offerings, and the ability "to invent new scenarios" in our lives (66). The Aunt Tees of the world, elders who engage with life intensely, are loved by life and receptive to its gifts.

If there is a racial component to this message, it is perhaps that whites, even those gifted with wealth and power, do not always know how to age wisely, to have fun living, and they can learn from "people who may differ . . . in political stance, sexual persuasion, and racial inheritance . . . [how to] be founts of fun" (65). In fact, an African-American racial, or tribal, inheritance may be the liberating conviviality that stretches into old age, preserving a person's length of days and joie de vivre. As the Delany sisters observe in what their long-lived mother taught them about aging, those who take care of themselves and surround themselves with love will extend their years (181).

Aunt Tee takes her place beside Angelou's mother and grandmother as life's adventurers, flexible and imaginative in creating new paths for their life journeys when the old paths no longer satisfy them. Her mother, Vivian Baxter, never learned how to spell failure and "practiced stepping off the road and cutting herself a brand-new path any time the desire arose" (80). Her grandmother railed against complainers, asserting that whining does not cure dissatisfaction: "What you're supposed to do when you don't like a thing is change it. If you can't change it, change the way you think about it. Don't complain" (87). Activism and a realistic understanding of the boundaries circumscribing a person's actions characterize this feisty elderly relative's philosophy of life. Both female relatives are vigorous pathfinders whose enthusiasm in old age has clearly been contagious for Angelou. Readers are likely to "catch" the energy and optimism from Angelou's lively prose portraits of these women.

Such women of the older generation have given her a positive anticipation of her own old age. Angelou juxtaposes these female elders to negative elderly women who widen the generation gap, resenting youth and urging them, wrongly, "not only to grow up, but to grow old, and that immediately" (97). She insightfully notes that such adults' attitudes reflect "regret for a misspent youth"; in contrast, the elderly women who encouraged her in her youthfulness had really enjoyed their youth, had taken pleasure in their lithe bodies, and therefore did not "envy me my youth" (96). Angelou's perspective suggests a comfortable mingling of the generations and the mutual regard of young and old, as well as the assumption that active, pleasurable living is possible for the individual across the age continuum.

I am struck, in general, by the lack of attention to ageism in the work of Angelou, Lorde, and Clifton and by their dismissal of the ageism of our culture. As Banner argues, old black women in our culture—like Native Americans and Hispanics—earn respect and veneration because they come from "a matrilineal past and a tradition of goddesses [as symbols of female strength]" (335). Many aging black women also experience strong support of community and kin, unlike many aging white women. Research shows that aging black women display "a more positive attitude toward life than any other group within American society" (Banner, 336). They are resilient, adaptable, optimistic. Angelou, Lorde, and Clifton think of themselves as evolving, capable of changing as they age.

The Delanys also desire change in old age but realistically assert that changing the world and changing oneself are hard, though possible (115). They themselves change. For example, as centenarians they take up yoga, and at age seventy they started over by moving to Mount Vernon—at the same time racially integrating the neighborhood. In the latter act, race is again foregrounded over their advanced age. In chapter 2, we also see Doris Grumbach address the issue of embracing change, of moving to Maine, at age seventy, but race is an invisible factor in her narrative since she is of the dominant white race. After overcoming a lifetime of sexism and racism, the Delanys do not feel especially circumscribed by their age. Despite somewhat slower reflexes, they note that in their dreams they are always young, and in their waking moments they usually forget that they are old (201). Bessie also confesses to the capacity for surprise even at age 101, couching her confession in terms of race, gender, and age: "I never thought I'd see the day when people would be interested in hearing what two old Negro women have to say. Life still surprises me" (209). Bessie clearly enjoys this change in our culture's attitudes toward the ideas of African Americans, relishes readers' receptiveness to the wit and wisdom of old women, and is gratified by the publishing industry's willingness to print their book.

The Delanys' book has, indeed, become a popular bestseller, and as I have noted elsewhere, books on and by aging women are in general sought after. Books by and about aging African-American women have a particularly bright future. Readers are increasingly interested in considering how age and race as well as gender and age work together to shape the experience of old age and accord it a new dignity denied by white patriarchy in the past. In fact, one proclamation of Bessie's about her aging blackness could well speak for the other women studied in this chapter: "The Lord won't hold it against me that I'm colored because He made me that way. He thinks I am beautiful! And so do I, even with all my wrinkles! I am beautiful!" (130). Not only is blackness beautiful, but so is old age for these stalwart women, the Delanys, Angelou, Lorde, and Clifton. And I, a middle-aged white woman, feel a surge of energy and optimism about the future from reading their words.

Velma Wallis: Autobiography and Tribal Legend

I would like to end this chapter with an examination of an autobiography of aging by a Native American that is as optimistic about old age as the works already discussed here. Velma Wallis, a member of the Athabascan tribe of Alaska, does not, in *Two Old Women* (1994), write a strictly autobiographical narrative. Instead, she appropriates an ancient legend of her people that is quite revealing about her culture's attitude toward elders, a tale that she had heard many times from her own mother. Wallis recasts the tale through her own imagination, lyrical style, and moral perspective. In these respects her work resembles the fictive story of Fa Mu Lan, the Woman Warrior, as re-told—or, rather, created anew—by Maxine Hong Kingston in her autobio-graphical work, *The Woman Warrior*. However, Wallis gives the tale an overtly autobiographical context by framing it with an introduction about herself, her mother, the tale's origins, and her family's values.

Wallis sets the introduction at the Porcupine River, close to where it emp-ties into the Yukon. She and her middle-aged mother have pitched a tent here and are chopping wood for winter. Mae Wallis, in her early fifties, is still agile and strong at her work, proud that her body challenges old age's limitations. She is another Aunt Tee. Velma marvels at her mother's abilities and pro-claims her as the role model she will emulate when she becomes an elder. Like Angelou and Clifton, Mae and Velma recall Velma's grandmother and other family elders, people who did not succumb to a passive old age but who "kept themselves busy until they could no longer move or until they died" (xii). Both praise these elders' generativity.

Mae's recollection and narration of the Legend of the Two Old Women come directly out of their conversation and their mood: "Mom remembered this particular story because it was appropriate to all that we thought and felt at that moment" (xii). All that they are thinking and feeling is epitomized in the legend's moral: "This story told me that there is no limit to one's abil-ity—certainly not age—to accomplish in life what one must" (xiii). This moral actively resists our hegemonic culture's ageism. The story also depicts how even elders can face hardships and change their complaining, passive attitudes toward life; I recall here Angelou's grandmother and her view of complaining versus change. Elders can summon their resourcefulness and creativity and become strong survivors on their own. The two old women of the legend are role models that challenge negative stereotypes of elderly women.

Wallis's story, furthermore, explores distrust and distance between the generations as well as rapprochement. The tale shows the younger genera-tion's growing respect for the knowledge and wisdom of the elders and the elders' capacity to teach and humanize the lives of the young. Thomas Cole and other gerontologists have warned us that with our nation's economic problems, especially problems with the federal budget deficit, there is an increasing "possibility of intergenerational warfare between young and old"; Cole calls for "generational equity" (234). Texts like Wallis's join Angelou's and Clifton's in offering us measures to defuse this intergenerational warfare. The two old women in the tale come to be regarded as wise experts on living, sought after by their younger kinfolk. The legend of their feats acts as a gift "given by an elder to a younger person" (xii). Mae's narration of the tale is her gift to the next generation as represented by her daughter. That Mae's gift is gratefully accepted by Velma is evident in the reverent tone of her narrative. Wallis's depiction of her tribe's increasingly positive attitudes toward aging agrees with Banner's research on the concept of "vigorous [and] productive aging," as pursued in Chinese and Native American ethnic groups (317, 320). Banner observes, "In China, as among Native Americans, people regularly inflate their age upward because of the veneration accorded aging wisdom in these societies" (321).

Reinforcing Wallis's introductory statement of personal commitment to the elderly of the tribe and to the cultural study of aging is the author's dedication of the book to a long list of tribal elders whom she acknowledges for their influence on her: "This book is dedicated to all of the elders whom I have known and who have made an impression in my mind with their wisdom, knowledge and uniqueness" (vii). Wallis equates the elder with the sage in her tribe. (See chapter 4 for a discussion of other texts' increasing association of aging with becoming a sage.) The dedication also reflects autobiographical impulses of her writing: to thank her elders and to preserve their wisdom in writing. In addition, the acknowledgments in Wallis's book reveal her literary and moral debt to her mother, Mae: "Without you, this story would not be, and I never would have developed a desire to be a storyteller. All those many nights that you spent telling us stories are greatly appreciated" (ix). Velma's storytelling becomes a way for her to extend her dialogue with her mother.

All of these elements suggest that *Two Old Women* may be examined as autobiography, so I turn to it briefly as a revealing and fascinating autobiographical text on aging in the context of a Native American ethnic group.

Wallis's written version of the oral tale tells us what happens when two old women, Ch'idzigyaak (age eighty) and Sa' (age seventy-five), are cast out from the midst of "The People" during a very severe winter when the tribe is half-starving. The two have been known for their complaining about the aches and pains of old age and have walked with a cane to emblematize their aged bodies. However, they had been provided with food, shelter, and firewood, and their goods were transported by others as the nomadic tribe moved from camp to camp. In exchange, they had tanned their kinsmen's animal hides. With his tribe in dire straits, the chief decides that if the group is to survive, the two weak and dependent (not truly dependent because of their contribution of tanned skins) old women must be left behind. Surreptitiously, Ch'idzigyaak's daughter leaves behind a bundle of *babiche* (a multipurpose moose rawhide). Her grandson leaves his hatchet. The chief allows the women to keep their own shelters. With these tools and the renewal of the skills of their youth, the women begin their struggle to survive, determined to prove their people wrong and to outsmart death (28).

Wallis's narrative emphasizes the women's increasing strength and flexibility as they adjust to the new demands placed on them. Readers witness the women's growing resourcefulness as they learn again how to hunt, how to build shelters and fires, how to create rabbit-skin clothing and caches for the fish they capture, how to seek out the right campsites, how to marshal their energies: in short, how to push their aching old bodies to do more and more. Wallis writes their bodies vividly and shows how their minds control and expand their bodily capacities (49).

Wallis also depicts through flashbacks the recollections of the two heroines that in their youth they too had faced this issue of care for the elders. These recollections help them to see that their past experiences enable them to endure in their present exile and give them the skills as well as the vision to change their tribe's cultural practice with elders. Ch'idzigyaak recalls the tribe's abandonment of her blind and deaf grandmother during a particularly severe winter of her youth when she herself felt constant hunger; she reports that some kin returned to kill her grandmother to end her suffering. Sa', more fiery and stronger than her companion, recalls how as a teen she courageously—and outrageously—argued with the chief not to abandon another old woman. The chief decided that Sa' would remain behind with the woman. The outcast Sa' survived, but the woman perished in the severe winter. These recollections reassure the women that they have endured hardships in the past, that they have survival skills, and that they can challenge a bad tribal practice.

The outcome of this saga is that they survive not only the winter but the whole year and into the next winter. They stop complaining, throw away their walking sticks, and work very hard. Like Audre Lorde, they triumph over adversity and are strengthened as they face the future. In fact, they flourish, building plentiful stores of food for the winter, making more clothing than they can use, securing their shelter and supply of firewood. Their despair, hopelessness, anger, and humiliation also heal as they become stronger, more independent, more determined to live. Both women are no longer hungry and are much healthier. Sa', now "lithe and energetic," is hard to identify as an older woman from afar (85).

When they again encounter their kin, nearly starving in the dead of the next winter, their subject-positions are reversed. The women, overcoming their earlier resentment and suspicion of The People, offer the means of relieving their suffering, of saving them, with their hard-won stores.

The two women also become a symbol of hope for the whole tribe's future if both generations work together. They have proved to the younger generation that they are still "of use to this world" (28). Daagoo, the man who acts as guide and liaison between the two women and the tribe, notes admiringly how both women have changed, have become like strong warriors: "the two women were ready to fight whatever they had to face. These were not the same women he had known before" (112). Daagoo, an elder himself, is inspired and transformed by the women's reconceptualization of old age: "he knew that he never would believe himself to be old and weak again" (116). *Old* and *weak* are words that do not need to be linked. The young, moreover, now accord the women due respect for the wisdom and experience of the older generation that the two women deserve. Never again will The People ever abandon an elderly person. The two women acquire power and status, illustrating a cross-cultural phenomenon that David Gutmann describes as "the unofficial matriarchy of later life . . . a shift toward greater female dominance" (156). Furthermore, in returning to the tribe, the two female elders again experience "worry-free sleep" at night (121); they have learned how important it is to be a part of a large group (65). Community helps stave off both the dangers of nature and human loneliness. It strengthens the women's desire to live.

As in other ethnic narratives of aging and illness examined in this chapter, and even in Roth's *Patrimony* (see chapter 1), *Two Old Women* emphasizes what the older generation can offer the younger generation in its stories and its wisdom grounded in experience. It also stresses how the generations are bound to one another, urging mutual respect and mutual responsibility of young for old and old for young. Wallis's own respect for her mother and grandmother, expressed in the introduction, resonates in her characterizations of Sa' and Ch'idzigyaak.

Finally, Wallis's reinvented tale redefines old age as potentially useful, reconceptualizes elders as heroic, salvational, and inspirational to youth. It rejects American stereotypes of old age as deterioration, passivity, hopelessness, and dependency. As readers travel through Wallis's narrative of Sa' and Ch'idzigyaak, they may, further, be reminded of what recent medical science has said about the salutary effects of vigorous exercise on the elderly. This strenuous activity combines with both women's attunement to the rhythms of nature and the seasons, their consumption of untainted food (although their diet is high in meat content, they eat small quantities), their breathing of fresh air, and their use of leisure time for meditation on family, tribe, and the sources of contentment, to make their lives healthful and blessed. Many readers will leave the book convinced that they have discovered the fountain of healing and happiness in Alaska.

Less concerned with racial or ethnic oppression than either Clifton or Lorde, but as concerned with the values of her ethnic group, Wallis focuses on age as a catalyst to test the humanity of her tribe. Readers may be shocked at the callousness of the chief in casting the women out into the cold, shocked enough to reconsider the ways in which our culture may metaphorically, if not literally, cast our elderly out into the wilderness. Wallis's tale raises my consciousness about mainstream America's cruelties to old folks and about the ways in which we fail to use the rich gifts that elders would willingly give back to society. The fact that the Athabascans change and come to appreciate the two old women gives me hope for an evolution of attitudes in our own culture.

4

Aging Autobiographers: Philosophical Musings and Deepening Wisdom

WESTERN CULTURAL CONVENTIONS have usually placed the elderly at two ends of the mental spectrum: either as self-indulgent, doddering old fools, or as wise and spiritually profound elders whose acquired knowledge and experience give them the sibylline powers of the sage and whose generous nature prompts them to share their wisdom. In this chapter we turn to autobiographical works that emphasize the latter: Howell Raines's *Fly Fishing through the Midlife Crisis* (1993), Donald Hall's *Life Work* (1993), and Florida Scott-Maxwell's *The Measure of My Days* (1968).

Raines comes to his book with an extensive background in journalism, major editorial positions at the *New York Times,* and a Pulitzer Prize for a *Times* article, "Grady's Gift." He also has published a book on the Civil Rights movement, *My Soul Is Rested,* and a novel, *Whiskey Man.* Hall is one of America's preeminent poets, the author most recently of *Their Ancient Glittering Eyes* and *The Museum of Clear Ideas* and winner of the National Book Critics Circle Award for his volume of poems *The One Day.* He is, additionally, a prolific writer of nonfiction, literary criticism, and children's literature (including the prize-winning *Oxcart Incident*). Scott-Maxwell had a variety of careers as actor, writer of short stories and dramas (her major plays are *The Flash-Point* and *They Knew How to Die*), and psychoanalyst trained under Carl Jung. She also was an activist for women's suffrage and for a time a traditional mother and homemaker. Her books include *Towards Relationships* and *Women and Sometimes Men*. She died in 1979.

All three are clearly professional writers who bring a wealth of observation and diverse experiences to the contemplation of old age and life's meanings. In this chapter I sound the intellectual and spiritual depths achieved and expressed by these aging authors, examine the constellation of philosophical concepts, especially involving time and mortality, with which they grapple, and consider the literary methods that convey the "X-ray vision" of aging writers.

I myself turned to the authors in this chapter for their ability to burn away excrescences and get to the heart of existence so that one can, in May Sarton's words, live close to the marrow. They enabled me to see the pristine, luminous core of life. I sought them, in my own midlife passage, because of their capacity to value time by extending and intensifying the moment and because of their ability to make me value time more. I do not include Sarton's work in this chapter because one of her journals is the subject of chapter 3, on the passage to seventy, and I want in this book to convey a sense of the wide variety of writers who have taken up the autobiography of aging. Nevertheless, Sarton embodies the philosophical older writer in expressing her desire toward time, through a sentence from *After the Stroke* that I quoted in the introduction but that I repeat here because it is central to this chapter: "I want to live in the instant, the very center of the moment" (48).

Raines, Hall, and Scott-Maxwell, through different activities, meditations, and evocative uses of language, find and sometimes inhabit the center of the moment, describe it, explore its benefits, and in the process challenge some outworn notions of time and aging. They enable readers to dwell intermittently in the center of the moment. These autobiographers also raise as many existential questions as they try to answer. Their questions, and the ones they prompt in readers, provide strong incentives for continuing the journey toward wisdom and greater spiritual depths. They also suggest ways of making time count, of numbering our days to create a meaningful existence in old age.

The Cultural Climate Inviting
Philosophical Autobiographies of Aging

A growing number of popular writers on aging cultivate readerships for these more complex literary autobiographies that philosophize on aging. For example, Betty Friedan, in *The Fountain of Age*, complements and reinforces the autobiographies by offering good reasons and multidisciplinary research (sociology, psychology, history, popular culture) to interrogate the stereotypes of old age. Friedan insists that age brings increasing intellectual capacities and wisdom. She associates this greater wisdom with Erik Erikson's notion of the older person's main developmental or conceptualizing tasks: to acquire wisdom about life through reconciliation with death and to take a realistic appraisal of one's skills and limitations, as well as one's loves and friendships over a lifetime. Completing such a multidimensional, integrative task results in a new knowledge and more creative thinking. Friedan defines this new sageness as "the ability to see the picture whole, and its meaning deep, and to tell it true: wisdom" (216). She contends that many seasoned elders have the wisdom to understand the vagaries of human existence, the essences of the human condition (602).

Another recent writer on aging, Rabbi Zalman Schachter-Shalomi, also develops these notions of the elder as sage and of old age as a new phase of human development in his book *From Age-ing to Sage-ing: A Profound New Vision of Growing Older,* coauthored with Ronald S. Miller. Schacter-Shalomi's idea of "sage-ing" as we age, of "spiritual eldering," embraces, even more than Friedan's notions of the elderly, an intense spirituality that deepens one's wisdom. Schachter-Shalomi also insists on late-life generativity, recognizing the older person's capacity to contribute to his or her community, to pass on to the younger generation a legacy, the riches of a lifetime of experiences and contemplation (2). "Sage-ing" thus has these elements or aims: "to become spiritually radiant, physically vital, and socially responsible 'elders of the tribe'" (5). As mentioned earlier, David Gutmann also observes transcultural examples of the elder statesman or "culture tender" role. Instead of withdrawing from society, elders may "become the interpreters and administrators of the moral sector of society. . . . [O]lder people . . . relish and sponsor the . . . vital dimensions of social stability and continuity" (228, 226). The elder's increased self-knowledge and serenity, as well as evenly balanced powers of judgment, may be given back as "consecrated service to the community" (Schachter-Shalomi and Miller, 5). The driving idea of Schachter-Shalomi, an evangelically optimistic elder himself, is that through "conscious aging," most individuals can achieve spiritual radiance and wisdom and enrich their society.

In this spiritualized conception of the elder's function, Schachter-Shalomi seems to heed the call of gerontologists like Thomas Cole to join "the growing search for ideals of transformation, self-transformation, and wisdom" in late life (Cole, 242–43). Cole, Gutmann, Schachter-Shalomi, and Friedan all argue that old men or old women should not become pariahs or sit in rocking chairs by the fire. They have the potential to remain actively involved in the life of the community, not as worker/drones, but as spiritual and intellectual guides, even visionaries, for the next generation.

In an unusual collection of self-reflective autobiographical essays edited by George Pollock, *How Psychiatrists Look at Aging*, several aging psychiatrists examine the assumption that elders are wiser than the young by considering whether they have personally achieved wisdom and what sort of wisdom they may have acquired. They also meditate upon how changes in their personalities over the years have altered their attitudes toward work and relationships. Many of the contributing authors stress the opportunities for new intellectual and artistic growth as well as older peoples' ability to integrate the pieces of their lives, to unify mind and body (see, for example, Kirkpatrick, 147). Samuel Atkin, in an essay coauthored with his son Adam, eschews false modesty and acknowledges his work with patients is effective, bolder, and better in these later years (21). The increasing capacity to teach well is noted by Edward D. Joseph (120). Samuel Atkin also observes that since patients look upon him, at eighty-eight years old, as "a sage, a Confucius," he is "in a good position to educate them" (20). Atkin's language here echoes that of Schachter-Shalomi and Friedan.

Atkin also describes a greater vigor and an almost erotic intensity in his work, despite physical fatigue: "I am bolder, more forthright in my interpretations. I sally forth like Don Quixote from my exhausted state through an act of willing. I rise to virility and produce" (18). This passage reflects a newly energized idealism and perceptivity in his professional performance, a confidence and wisdom born of experience. I note some of the same elements in passages from Hall's *Life Work* when he reflects upon his writing. Like Hall,

Atkin takes real joy in his work: it is central to his life's purpose. For Atkin, the experience of eighty-eight years does not produce stagnation and cynicism.

The wisdom of the aged, in psychiatrist Chester M. Pierce's view, becomes more complex because it contains a postmodern wariness about certitude or "The Truth"; this wariness about oversimplifying truth makes teaching more difficult for Pierce as an older man: "It is now more difficult to teach, since I am less certain and more tentative about what I profess to be true or worthy of retention or in need of disposal" (187). Unlike Atkin, Pierce suggests that the older he gets, the more likely he is to question the importance of concepts and principles, the more likely he is to frame questions than to possess the certitude of answers. Friedan similarly notes that older people are good at posing "questions of central meaning and basic value" (244).

This interrogative tendency presents opportunities for emotional and spiritual growth. Questions about prioritizing work, family, and friendships also lead Pierce to declare the centrality of friendship and a loving family in the meaning of his own existence (188). Like the other essayists in the Pollock collection, he is immersed in generativity and is also performing the Eriksonian integrative function of connecting the parts of his life in a larger picture.

Books such as *How Psychiatrists Look at Aging, The Fountain of Age,* and *From Age-ing to Sage-ing* suggest a growing tendency among the general public to interrogate cultural stereotypes of old age as past the capacity for intellectual growth and the ability to contribute spiritually to society. Literary autobiographies join these books in exploring elders' capacity for visionary wisdom, spiritual depth, and complex integrative skills.

Acknowledgment of the development of a new form of wisdom in elders is often coupled with the urge to share this wisdom—especially about work, love, and mortality—with the next generation. In literary autobiographies of aging, the desire to share and teach often prompts the writer to tell his or her life story. Yet the authors examined in this chapter do not pontificate about all they have learned in a professorial or parental tone. In fact, much of what autobiographers of aging have to say out of the wisdom acquired over a lifetime is couched in tentative language, language appreciative of the complexities of potential "answers" to existential questions.

More often what they say is speculative about life's meaning, work, their futures, their relationships with others. Autobiographers of aging have sur-

vived major changes, painful losses, serious illnesses, or other traumatic experiences that lead them to ask a wide variety of ethical, ontological, and
epistemological questions. Perhaps simply framing such questions, no easy
task, entitles them to the title of sage. Answers, sparingly offered, take readers to a new plane of insight.

In this chapter, I consider how Howell Raines, Donald Hall, and Florida
Scott-Maxwell explore the larger questions of human existence and the ways
of creating meaning in one's life. Their topics are time, work, leisure activities, love, and friendship, all pursued from the perspectives of the creative
artist, the spouse, the parent, the friend, the elder. As Raines, Hall, and Scott-
Maxwell write, they show us how they make contact with the center of the
moment each day of their lives.

Howell Raines: Moments of Leisure, Nature, and Acceptance of Mortality at Midlife

For Howell Raines, author of *Fly Fishing through the Midlife Crisis,* the center
of the moment is most often found in the mountains beside the Rapidan
River. There he can "hear the sigh of the Eternal" (17) while he pursues his
passionate avocation of fly fishing. Fly fishing is a form of devotion and prayer
for Raines, as work is for Donald Hall. Although Raines eschews the more
formal religion of the Southern preachers from his boyhood, through fly
fishing and his book about it he searches "for wholeness, if not holiness" (32).

Holy moments exist in this book's language about fish, sometimes blending spirituality with wit: "as I reflect more deeply on the fish's history as a
mythic symbol and religious icon, I begin to wonder if having fish shapes
around me is a way to stay in touch with the ideas of Jesus without having
to go near the people who do business in his name" (108). Sometimes the
prayerful quality of fly fishing is solemnly stated: "The point of fly fishing is
to become reverent in the presence of art and nature" (33). Raines's book
celebrates the magic of brushing up against the otherworldly quality of trout
and bass: "[Fishing] brings these creatures from the realm of mystery into
the world of reality" (107). Contact with these beings in waters ringed by
mountains in itself spiritualizes one's perspective on life.

Hence, fly fishing becomes more than catching fish for Raines; it becomes *midlife turn to nearer* (handwritten margin note)

time and space for meditation, for asking important questions about his own life at its midpoint. Writing about fly fishing is a vehicle for writing contemplatively as well as poetically on these questions. As reviewer Nick Lyons observes, Raines uses fly fishing as "metaphor for change and growth and some steady stay against the stupidity and ambiguity of much of life" (Lyons, 7). Fly fishing is the eye at the center of life's whirling senselessness and elusive mystery.

Writers who join fishing with philosophical meditation and lovely prose and who analogize fly fishing to life journeys have a long history, and Raines names some of his literary models, such as Norman Maclean and Ernest Hemingway (30). The philosophical link is apparent to him: "If we can discipline ourselves to cast a line with perfection, perhaps we can impose order on—or perceive some inherent order within—the chaos of daily existence"; fly fishing is a useful and common literary device to contact "the heart of life's abiding mysteries" (30). Yet even more than Maclean's and Hemingway's work, Raines's prose and his aim in writing *Fly Fishing through the Midlife Crisis* remind me of Henry David Thoreau's *Walden,* in which he explores ways to cut through the trivial details that fritter away our lives and reach the essential bone of meaningful existence, "to suck out all the marrow of life," to become truly awake (Thoreau, 62).

It is surely no coincidence that Thoreau published *Walden* in 1854 at age thirty-seven (although he had begun his Walden Pond experience nine years earlier, his reflections upon the experience occurred in his later thirties), and Raines began to feel the twinges of unhappiness and restless anxiety that signaled the start of his midlife crisis at age thirty-eight (56–57). Like Thoreau, he turned to nature, in the form of fly fishing, to ask existential questions and (re)configure his life's priorities. I was thirty-eight when I was drawn to literature about aging and took up research in literary gerontology; writing about the literature of aging from an autobiographical perspective intensified as I traveled through my forties in quest of a more meaningful later life. The late thirties and early forties, early middle age, prompt many of us to reflect upon where we have been, the kind of existence we have hitherto constructed for ourselves, the degree of its meaningfulness, and the variety of directions our lives can still take into later life. As Erik Erikson suggests, this stage of adulthood generativity "must 'take care' of what is being procreated, produced, and created. . . . [There is] the widening concern for what has been generated by love, necessity, or accident" (37). That is, productivity continues, but with the consciousness that products (for example, the products of love: relationships) must be cared for and reflected upon. Raines and Thoreau display this deepening concern for what they themselves and their often trivializing cultures have produced.

Rereading *Walden*'s famous passage about time and fishing helped me to understand Raines's intentions and the transcendentalist mood of his book. Thoreau says, "Time is but the stream I go a-fishing in. I drink at it; but while I drink I see the sandy bottom and detect how shallow it is. Its thin current slides away and eternity remains. I would drink deeper, fish in the sky, whose bottom is pebbly with stars" (68). Thoreau recognizes the thinness, the insubstantiality of quotidian existence: it does not satisfy his philosophical thirst for substance or essence. He must probe deeper, move beyond time, leap into the sky, the essence of eternity. Like Thoreau, Raines fishes linguistically in "the sky"; he fishes for deeper, sweeter, more spiritual notions of living. He fishes and writes about fishing so that he and his readers can make contact with the center of the moment, use time more meaningfully, since in midlife time is in shorter supply, and push the boundaries of time into the blue of eternity.

Raines's reverent exploration of fly fishing takes readers beyond study of the sport to meditations upon nature, human interactions, and the passage of time. Especially featured in the text is Raines's relationship with his fly fishing mentor, Richard C. Blalock. The book offers a biographical portrait of Blalock and describes his great influence on the author. Dick Blalock is Howell's elderly sage, who teaches Raines about fly fishing. Yet he also offers philosophical lessons about "living easefully in the world of nature" (20), about friendship and father-son relationships, about the sweetness of life and the naturalness of death as the end of life's journey. Blalock is responsive to the questions and the neediness of a man in midlife crisis and helps Raines to perform major psychic tasks of the middle-aged man. He helps Raines in the way any true mentor would: "Rather than abort the mentee's quest by providing answers the mentor deepens the person's ability to keep the questions alive while journeying through the nourishing dark" (Schachter-Shalomi and Miller, 193). Many of the questions plaguing Raines are about aging and death.

Raines-as-narrator explores some common elements of the midlife passage and his own difficulties in getting through it. He characterizes himself as one American male who has successfully navigated a midlife crisis of about five years' duration, which his research suggests is average for an intense midlife passage. His purpose is to act as mentor: to offer advice, raise further questions, and share the wisdom born of his own maturing journey with other men in the throes of the voyage. Raines epitomizes the depression and anxiety haunting victims of the midlife crisis as "the black dog." Sympathetically he addresses the many who are lost and struggling against this black dog. He warns them that the midlife passage is a "severe journey—a soul-rending passage that will either heal you or wreck you" (80); he has been through it. Although each man must make his own version of the journey in his own way, Raines implies that sharing his experience with others might help them not to feel so lost or isolated.

Out of the thirty-eight chapters in Raines's book (thirty-eight being apt since the author's own midlife crisis began at about that age), only five (chapters 2, 6, 9, 13, and 24) address the concept of the black-dog midlife passage directly. However, the entire book tracks the author's journey through it to survival, renewal, and wisdom. In the earlier of the five explicit chapters, Raines defines the midlife passage and gives his own symptoms. The crisis begins for Raines with mild sensations of "dread, disappointment and restlessness" (57) but worsens. He defines the midlife crisis with stoic restraint: "[It is] five years of steadily intensifying anxiety or depression or some satanic combination of emotional torment" (79). In addition to the image of the black dog hounding him is the image of the "taste of ashes on the tongue" (29). Life has become for Raines dry, insipid, routine, unnourishing, deadening.

Subsequent sections on the midlife crisis bring these general symptoms into clearer focus for readers. His self-denigrating estimates of his own "middling" skill as fisherman and of his unexceptional work as journalist provide windows on Raines's general malaise, angst, and disappointment: "I had spent countless hours at fishing of all kinds, but I was truly expert at no kind" (77); and "They call it journalism, but some days it felt like stenography" (77). On the subject of his work, Raines differs most from Donald Hall. While Hall lives for his work, Raines feels that he is wasting his time and that he has produced no writing of lasting value. Like a hamster on a wheel (163), he is trapped in his routine job, and financial obligations keep him at the wheel.

The feelings of hopelessness and oppression surround him, "palpable as a blanket" (163), and nearly suffocate him. In midlife, a man in our culture longs for expertise and recognition of that expertise through satisfying work or leisure activities (preferably both). Hence, his failure to achieve the status of expert or sage unleashes disappointment and depression. (I would add that although Raines's book focuses almost exclusively on men, women at midlife long to be recognized for their expertise, too; this is increasingly so for professional women—no settling for the "mommy track" in the professions.)

This longing for the title of "expert" is directly connected by many a middle-aged person to a sensation of the acceleration of time and a fear of death. If people think they have not already acquired expertise or enough fruits to show for their efforts, the time remaining for this achievement seems to shrink alarmingly. There is no longer world enough and time to achieve all the promise of youth. Raines grapples with these feelings in his narrative. For example, he recounts a scene from the recent past in which he compares the increasing expertise in fishing of his sons Ben and Jeff to his own level of skill in midlife. While his elder son Ben fishes upstream a little, Raines chats with a stranger, an older man who praises Ben's casting. The praise prompts a confession from Raines that Ben is a better fisherman than he is. The stranger's reply is the harbinger of Raines's old age, decline, and death: "Of course he's a better fisherman. . . . He's younger than you are, so he's got better eyes. . . . He's got quicker reflexes, so he's going to miss fewer strikes. And he's taller than you are, so he can cast farther than you can" (164).

The stranger's words trigger more than a little friendly father-son rivalry in Raines, elicit more than the lust for expertise. The words remind him that while his son is developing into a skilled young man with potential for further growth, he, Howell Raines, is moving inexorably toward death. His mentor, Dick Blalock, reinforces this lesson of mortality conveyed by the stranger. Raines paraphrases Blalock: "Inextricably braided into the joy of having sons is the fact that their growth is a reminder of our mortality" (164). That our sons—and daughters—may grow up to surpass us in expertise adds a bittersweet tinge to the pain of facing, through them, our own mortality.

What does acquiring expertise give a person? Does expertise bring us happiness, and if so, why? Raines suggests that achieving mastery of fly fishing and adopting its discipline may fill for some older men "the holes in their souls," holes caused by unfulfilled yearnings and undeveloped potential (112).

Having expertise, "the feeling of artistry" (154), in one area gives the individual a sense of control over life, assures a person that he or she has acquired the knowledge adequate for effective living, is a badge of one's self-reliance and maturity. From a psychosocial perspective, Erik Erikson sees the importance of continually renewing "a sense of competence based on resources from within, on demands from outside, and on opportunities that arise"; he contends that especially as we age and our physical powers are diminishing, "a lifelong sense of effectiveness is a critical resource" (147). Raines would agree with Erikson's contention.

He illustrates how Erikson's idea works for himself when he describes a scene in which he entertains an unfamiliar and problematic fishing situation: no surface feeding. He deals successfully with it: the fish are eating nymphs, he deduces, and so he ties on a nymph tie; the fish bite. At this moment near the book's end, he recognizes that he has attained such knowledge not only of fly fishing but of himself, knowledge that he can apply to meet many of life's challenges: "It was one of those rare moments in fishing—or in life, for that matter—when you can feel the weight of acquired knowledge and take pleasure in the fact that it is adequate for the problem that confronts you" (253).

Raines comments elsewhere about the qualities of expertise in any field: "It involves close observation and a momentous act of self-trust" (261). The expert acquires enough skills and knowledge to trust himself or herself in new situations and observes the terrain of each new situation carefully in order to meet its demands. Successfully negotiating his midlife passage, Raines by the end of the book is a man who trusts himself, and he reports both a sense of satisfaction with the level of expertise he has achieved and acceptance of his limitations. He knows that he is no genius but that he can display flashes of genius in his sport: "as a man approaching fifty, I knew that I would [and did] hit a ceiling [in the progress toward expertise in fly fishing], and I thought: So be it" (207). Donald Hall feels the same satisfaction in his own expertise and awareness of limits to his capacities as he wrestles with the wording of a poem and finds some, but not all, of the language to meet his aims.

Be it at work or at a leisure activity one treasures, both Raines and Hall would concur that acquiring expertise and using it are ways to live in the center of the moment. Both have learned the elder-sage's approach to time:

"time is *stretchable,* not linear, so we can reframe and reshape it using contemplative techniques" (Schachter-Shalomi and Miller, 93). These two writers become expert in ways to stretch and re-create time in contemplative moments, either fishing amid nature or within the mind creating poetry.

The term *expertise* expands for Raines over the five-year period of his midlife crisis beyond work and fly fishing to include expertise at friendship and parenting. He increasingly values, records, and celebrates these relationships in his text. He learns much about relationships from Dick Blalock, whom he eulogizes at Blalock's funeral as "an expert in the art of friendship," a person who showed younger men that "a man in the course of his life can be father and brother to those with whom he has no familial kinship" (329). Blalock himself illustrates how older men can mentor younger men, pursuing what Schachter-Shalomi and Miller celebrate as "the art of intergenerational bestowal by which elders pass on to younger people the living flame of their wisdom" (189). Blalock assumes the mantle of elder who acts as "repository of high-status knowledge, practices, and qualities" (Kaminsky, 47). He instructs Raines while they fish. Fishing is for Blalock, and increasingly for Raines, an opportunity to socialize with friends, to meditate, to philosophize. More often, fishing gives Raines the time and space to listen to Blalock's monologues and to learn about relationships, especially father-son relationships, from an elder statesman of fishing waters and of life.

One of the important lessons the author passes on to readers derives from their discussion of the competition between the father and the son over their expertise in fly fishing; but readers can substitute tennis, or hunting, or any activity jointly pursued by fathers and sons. Blalock teaches Raines from his own experience as the son of a domineering, competitive father. He notes that the dynamics of the father-son relationship are such that a son is vulnerable to damaged self-esteem if the father is not careful to control a "consummate capacity to belittle" his son's developing powers (165). Blalock's father was not careful.

From Blalock's story of his father's verbal abuse, Raines gleans this nugget of wisdom: "Dick's story illustrated something no father should forget. In the arsenal of familial emotions, fatherly condemnation is a nuclear weapon" (169). The potency both of a father's condemnation and of this epigram can raise the consciousness of many fathers reading Raines's book, as Blalock's story did for the author. Blalock's words gave Raines "a chance to clean up his act" before dying or before turning his son into a candidate for the psychotherapist's couch (170); he hopes to do the same for readers through his epigram. Raines confesses that Blalock's story, together with some remarks his wife reports about their son Ben's sensitivity to his barbs, compels him to stop nagging his fishermen sons "for good" (170). So struck was I by this passage from Raines's book that I showed it to my spouse, a very loving, but at times critical, father to our son. Sometimes we do not realize the power we wield over the children in our households. Prose like Raines's can endow us with insight.

Dick Blalock thus helps to sharpen Raines's expertise as a father and opens him up to the center of many moments of affectionate companionship with his two sons, snapshots of whom grace the inside covers of the book and literary snapshots of whom appear in several passages of the text. One especially moving episode Raines presents is the last fishing trip of his younger son Jeff's boyhood, just before Jeff's departure for college. Raines tells Jeff of his pride in him, his confidence in Jeff's ability to succeed in college, and his pleasure in Jeff's company: "I told him I wanted him to know how much fun it had been to be his father and what a deep joy it had brought me to watch him grow up. . . . I told him that notwithstanding the fact that he was my son, he was a man whose company I would choose on any day, on any stream" (197). What an eloquent tribute to the father-son relationship Raines gives his readers here! It is comparable in intensity of love and mutual respect to the relationship between Philip Roth and his dying father, Herman, described in *Patrimony*. As Raines's narrative moves toward closure, we have come to understand that his early words about his sons, "They are my favorite beings in all of creation" (53), are not inflated rhetoric but intensely meant language written from the heart's core.

Blalock also wisely encourages his friend Howell Raines to confront and settle from another angle (that of himself as son to an elderly father) the "unfinished business between fathers and sons," to acknowledge the baggage of the years, clear up the hurts and misunderstandings that create barriers to communicating love. Midlife is the time when you must "balance your books with the people you love" (340). The specter of time's rapid passing and intimations of one's own mortality or of a loved one's approaching death prompt such reconciliations. Raines himself dissolves the feud of several years with his father and brother (on a fishing trip, of course) and rejoices in their friendship and the memories and stories they share on the last two pages of the book. I will not forget, in my own family life, the rapprochement after almost a decade's estrangement between my mother and her brother at the graveside of their mother. Dick Blalock's death and Raines's mourning for him open Raines's heart and lips to express his love to his own brother and father. Life is too short to waste on petty grievances.

There is one noticeable gap in Raines's narrative of expertise in relationships here: the one concerning the relationship between him and his wife. Although he briefly mentions how Susan came into his life, indicates her presence on the family fishing trip before Jeff's departure for college, and makes several allusions to the deepening rifts of his marriage, I experienced disappointment at the absence of discussion of this relationship from his narrative. Reassessment of a marital relationship is a major psychic task of many midlife crises, and he avoids discussing his own reassessment.

Raines offers no apology for this omission but defends it as necessary because the story of their marriage is Susan's as well as his: "The winding down of any long marriage is a complicated story and a sad one, too, if the marriage has been a very good one for a very long time. I am not going to tell the entire history of that marriage, because the story does not belong to me alone" (198). Issues of privacy always face the autobiographer, but I suspect that in this case Raines is using his former wife's privacy as an excuse to avoid grappling with a topic that troubles him and reveals too many of his own flaws or mistakes. Perhaps if his reassessment of their marriage had ended in reconciliation and reaffirmation, as did the author's reunion with his father and brother, their story would have been a part of this narrative. But resolution of their problems through divorce is cursorily dismissed by Raines; it is not as successful a negotiation as he would like the other resolutions of his midlife crises to appear.

And so I trust a little less Raines's presentation of his midlife passage because this passage is even harder and messier than he allows us to see. This narrative decision is also unfortunate for readers since glimpses into the process of "reading and talking and hiring of experts that serious, caring people do" during the time preceding divorce would have provided valuable help to readers enduring their own marital conflicts at midlife (198).

Raines's narrative is especially successful, in contrast, on the matter of mortality. Underlying the middle-aged man's sense of time's rapid passage and his need for expertise or intensity in relationships, fly fishing, and work is the realization of his mortality. His narrative focuses on it especially in chapter 24. Acceptance of death is, for Raines, essential to understanding and facing the black dog of the midlife crisis. The black dog is not so different from an hourglass image that haunts Donald Hall when he faces cancer. To absorb the reality of his own mortality and comprehend death as the natural completion of a person's biological destiny (201), Raines again seeks the wisdom and guidance of Dick Blalock. Midway through the book Blalock faces a serious bout with heart disease and eventually dies. In the months before his death, Blalock recognizes life's sweetness and the shortness of his remaining time (256). He teaches Raines that each day of life is a gift, not to be dissipated, that a lifetime is finite. Blalock has lived intimately with death since his teen years during the Korean War and within his own family, which viewed death with equanimity. Therefore he can teach Raines, in whose long-lived but death-denying family there had not been a death for fifty years, that death is intertwined with life.

Chapter 24 is, in part, a confession by Raines of his fear of death (204). It is also a revelation of his family's characterization of death as an interloper in life (200), a view that until midlife he accepted. Finally, chapter 24 is a renunciation of his family's view and an embrace both of Blalock's perspective and of the outlook of some Native Americans, represented in a mythic figure, Skeleton Woman. Raines enthusiastically presents Skeleton Woman as a figure who undergoes both death and rebirth and epitomizes "the way in which death is braided inextricably into the process of living" (200). Observing Blalock as he defies doctors' orders and ventures upon the arduous trails and canoe routes where fly fishing beckons, Raines can understand this blending of living with dying. Adopting the Cheyenne warrior's shibboleth that "It is a good day to die" and writing it daily on a piece of paper, he confronts his fear of dying and exchanges it for a sense of death's natural place in daily life. With this exchange, he experiences a new freedom in living.

Raines feels the naturalness of death most when he dwells in nature. There the Cheyennes' slogan enters his soul. He sets the scene at the end of chapter 24, fittingly at the magical hour of sunset, as the shadows deepen on a day of fishing in the beautiful canyon of the Gros Ventre Mountains, where he had once talked with his college-bound son Jeff. Then he describes the visceral knowledge he has acquired: "Beside those waters, the death song of the Cheyenne entered me, filled me up, and I knew that it *was* a good day to die" (205). One hundred seventy-six years earlier, on a tender night, a Romantic poet filled with the ecstatic, soulful song of a nightingale understood the same thing: "Now more than ever seems it rich to die" (Keats, "Ode to a Nightingale," ll. 55–58). When is a good day to die? Any day, if you subscribe to the Cheyennes' perspective and apply it to yourself personally, especially any day spent in the center of the moment, in the heart of nature, open to its pleasures, in synchrony with its rhythms.

Although Raines claims here to have assimilated the Cheyenne concept of death as daily present in his own life, I think he tempers this calm Cheyenne perspective near the end of his book with the wish for a long life in the way he phrases what I will call his "personal mortality statement." He makes this statement as he accepts and "transcendentalizes" Dick Blalock's death: "I believe he is in all the waters we knew together, and on some good day, I will enter them, too. [But] I am not ready yet" (335). This desire to meet death later in life is expressed in the last sentence of this passage and in the "plea bargaining" that follows it. He confesses, all too humanly, that he is not ready to die because he would like to live to meet his grandchildren, take them fishing, and teach them Blalock's notions about fishing and nature. Such a desire only makes clearer the difficulty of attaining the Cheyennes' philosophical conviction of death's presence and naturalness.

Despite confessing this desire to defer his death, Raines, nevertheless, manages to convince himself and his readers in many other passages of the book that an especially good day to die is one lived in the center of each moment, any day that extends time by extracting every drop of pleasure or ecstacy from it. As he increasingly accepts the inevitability of his death, Raines also develops the sense that he must grasp and enrich the time he is living, use his time to seek pleasure; here he does sound like a bit of a hedonist: "We are not on this earth for long. Part of what a midlife crisis is about is figuring out what gives you pleasure and doing more of that in the time you have left" (298–99). Raines tempers the carefree tone of his hedonism, however, by asserting sensibly that pleasure comes from what he considers a balanced life: to combine fishing, working, and time for friendships and family, and to pursue as many as possible of these activities outdoors (299). Pleasurable, intensely lived moments, for this latter-day Thoreau, abide most often in the natural world.

Moreover, pleasure in nature for Raines moves beyond animal-like hedonism into a spiritual dimension. Erikson has observed this "abiding faith in nature" among his older research subjects from a variety of religious backgrounds (225). They express a reverential sense of kinship with the natural world and a soothing conviction of its continuity, "a deep sense that they and their lives are but one part of a world that has comprised everything we recognize as life and that will continue to do so as long as life continues to exist" (226). Raines describes similar feelings. He experiences a reverence for mountains, rivers, and wildlife and suggests that for him fly fishing is a form of praying (108, 304). Elsewhere he describes the magical, supernatural act of fishing: "The appeal is the same as that which resides in pulling a rabbit out of a hat. We have reached into a realm over which we have no explainable mastery and by supernatural craft or mere trickery created a moment that is . . . phenomenal" (107). Such a phenomenal moment gathers one briefly into the noumenal spaces of the universe. In a natural setting, Raines exchanges the temporal for the eternal, which moves him to confront death and to intensify time on earth. He is the sage who lives in "*durative* time, which orients his life against a background of transcendent meaning and purpose" (Schachter-Shalomi and Miller, 138).

We can leave Raines's book understanding more how the spirituality obtained from fly fishing and natural landscapes takes us into the center of the moment and extends or transforms time. In fact, we are treated to a vivid description of an epiphanic experience of fishing at Minn Lake, where Raines's hook engages the snout of a fish while the borders blur between dream and reality, between time and eternity: "For just a bit, the circle of water, sky and light in which I found myself seemed to have slipped the bonds of sidereal time, and this fish, my fly and I converged according to the elongated beats of dreamtime" (122). Such moments at Minn Lake enable Raines's narrator to apprehend a new kind of knowledge and to feel a new openness to learning—about fishing and about life. It is a slow, not overly avid or self-conscious, receptivity, "an act of relaxation, a surrender, a submission to the knowledge one wishes to possess" (123–24). The language here suggests a relinquishing of the fearful struggle against acquisition of new ideas, an end to aggressive, exclusively rational approaches to fishing and living, in exchange for a gentler, more personal, and more intuitive or spiritual interaction between man and fish, between man and new knowledge. This receptivity may explain fly fishing's attraction for *middle-aged* men of lowered testosterone levels (296), and it may be the impulse behind such men's desire to write lyrical, self-revealing, and contemplative works like *Fly Fishing through the Midlife Crisis.*

Time is the stream in which our narrator goes fishing, but occasionally he fishes more deeply into the sky of eternity. Reflections upon such moments enlarge his vision and "age his heart" into a new wisdom, answering the question in the epigraph from Gian Carlo Menotti in Raines's book ("How can one age the heart? / What wound, what memory will ever teach it wisdom?") and echoing the title of the last chapter, "Aging the Heart." The wounds of his life and the memories of these concentrated, epiphanic moments bestow wisdom upon Raines. Casting his line over the water at such centered moments, he touches "the weightless tongue of time itself," time lightened by its contact with eternity (335).

Contact with Howell Raines's lyrical language and transcendent vision also briefly lightens the burden of temporality and mortality for readers like me, those of us engaged in the midlife passage, opening for us a window into pleasure, tranquillity, and order.

Donald Hall: Life as Work, Work as Life

Author Donald Hall at age sixty-three considers the centrality of his work as a writer to the meaning of his life in his slim meditative volume, *Life Work.* The life and the work under scrutiny are primarily his own, so, as reviewer Robert Kelly points out, this book is "in a lovely, delicate sense, . . . in fact, an autobiography" (11). As the title suggests, life and work are interchangeable for Hall; Kelly says, "we can almost feel the ampersand between the words" (11). Work and pleasure are also closely associated in this autobiographical text. Hall frees the term *work* from any onerous connotations, claiming not to have "worked" a day in his life: "because I loved my work it was as if I did not work at all" (4). Work is a treat or reward after *chores.* (This distinction reminds me of the first time I taught a literature class. I thought in amazement, "They are *paying* me to talk about literature; I should pay *them,* it's so much fun.") Hall also explores what he has come to recognize as a sacred component of working: its devotional power and prayerful nature when the worker is wholeheartedly committed to the work (9). As he examines his feelings about work, Hall's reflections invite readers to reconsider their own life's work, their attitudes toward working.

The passion of this meditation on and paean to the work of the writer is intensified midway through the text when Hall must pause from work to fight the recurrence of cancer in his body and cancer's disruption of his life. Work and mortality then become intertwined in Hall's ponderings on what constitutes a meaningful existence. This book becomes a powerful example of what Kelly names "our strange new genre, autothanatography, . . . logging the spiral down the road to death" (Kelly, 11). As with Audre Lorde, when time seems about to be foreshortened for Hall, he must look at his work plans in a new way; he must reprioritize his projects. Yet despite what his illness has in store for him, Hall, like Lorde, knows he must keep on writing.

From the beginning of his book, Hall characterizes work as a major determinant of contentment in his life. To him, absorption in work, with its accompanying loss of self-consciousness, is comparable to the absorption and self-abandonment of lovemaking. Work brings contentment because of its unself-conscious devotional element; he even defines his wife Jane's gardening as work because this avocation is for her, as for May Sarton, "a devotion undertaken with passion and conviction; because it absorbs her; because it is a task or unrelenting quest which cannot be satisfied" (33–34). Central to his notion of meaningful life's work is that it does not end, it arches over the life span into the future—like the rainbow arch of experience that Tennyson's Ulysses relentlessly follows, believing that "old age hath yet his honor and his toil" (l. 50). Like this Victorian Ulysses, Hall is a believer in work as continuous quest.

Underlying his conceptualization of work is the conviction, passed on to him by his Victorian grandfather Henry Hall at age ninety, that work harbors the "secret of life," giving one's life length and substance. Work promises longevity because it energizes; it is an essential ingredient in the elixir of life. Henry Hall associates work with health in the concise syntax of his motto: "keep your health—and woik-woik-woik" (14).

Grandson Hall argues that work only energizes and prolongs our lives if our noteworthy work is willingly and freely pursued; slavish workaholism is not vitalizing (37). Moreover, we must work strenuously, the demands of our work stretching us beyond our proven capacities. Hall would approve Robert

Browning's famous line in "Andrea del Sarto": "A man's grasp should exceed his reach / Else what's a heaven for?" Hall underscores the ideas of work as pushing us into greater capabilities and work as the source of contentment by quoting sculptor Henry Moore: "The secret of life is to have a task, something you devote your entire life to. . . . And the most important thing is—it must be something you cannot possibly do!" (54).

Hall does not, however, glorify the working state for the older writer. He acknowledges that at age sixty-three he is unlikely to be doing his best work any longer, but he still maintains the hope that he might be capable of producing fine work now (20). That raises an important question about what we mean by the prime of our life, our fertile period of creativity and productivity. Often people assume that the middle is the prime, that we have learned enough and experienced enough to have the powers of synthesis and generativity in full swing in our forties and fifties. Hall believes he is past his prime at sixty-three; perhaps his body subliminally warns him of the incursions of his illness, or he is aware of the fatigue of age that limits his hours of productivity.

Yet, as Anne Wyatt-Brown has written about aging in relation to creativity in later life, many artists plagued by physical illness, depression, or fear of death develop a new sensibility that results in innovative and more complex art (12–13). Although Hall may have to reduce his daily hours of productivity, what he writes may be "enriched by . . . [his] battle against despair" (Wyatt-Brown, 12). Moreover, he shares with us how he has learned to manage his fatigue and husband his energies to produce his art in ways that he might not have known about in his younger days, when creative energies were carelessly dissipated.

Such careful husbanding of creative energies can allow one to have what Hall identifies as "best days," days that flow smoothly with complete concentration—when one loses track of time and of self so that *"absorbedness* occupies [one] from footsole to skulltop. Hours or minutes or days—who cares?—lapse without signifying" (41). On best days, he makes progress on multiple projects and intersperses work with chores, naps, lovemaking, cooking and dining, and the leisured viewing of a ball game to cap off the evening. Hall chronicles a hypothetical "best day" for us (41–48). In doing so, he invites us to revisit some of our own best days of working.

I remembered some hours (clearly not all the hours) spent before my word processor, writing of what moved me, writing to move others: distilling in language the essence of the transformative experience offered to me in Toni Morrison's *Beloved,* with its revelations about slavery and motherhood; or visiting the Holocaust Museum in Washington, D.C., and writing with awe about how it teaches us; or discussing Paul Monette's *Becoming a Man* with students in a senior seminar and then writing with a colleague about ways to teach Monette to homophobic students. These hours removed me from time and self-absorption, made me feel that I lived fully and meaningfully. But they also made me question how I spent many other hours of each waking day, made me wonder why I wasted such hours and how I could avoid such waste in future. Living fitfully in the center of the moment on a "best day" raises these questions about colorless moments and empty hours. Yet Hall, finally, shows me that having *some* best days as a writer or teacher leaves open the possibility of producing more of my own "best work." Hall's best work makes his life and his readers' lives meaningful because it extends and deepens consciousness, his own and his readers'(37).

This extension of consciousness revitalizes Hall's writing. When writers become more conscious of the layers, nuances, and complexities of existence, they create more choices for daily life, more options for the future, more reasons to keep going, more curiosity about the unknown, more longing to extend the perimeters of consciousness further. Writing compels us to envision multiple angles on issues of importance to us, so that we no longer feel forced to behave and believe in just one way. The older a writer is, the richer the complexity of the perspectives he or she may develop. Writing is potentially an act of liberation for aging elders; it counteracts the constraints of physical deterioration or the set of lifetime habits by widening the elder's perspectives.

Zalman Schachter-Shalomi, writing with Ronald Miller, describes the potential expansiveness of "elder consciousness." He notes that one of the methods that initiates a person into the elder's heightened consciousness is creative activity, such as painting or writing poetry; through these activities, we "evoke the Inner Elder . . . [and] connect . . . with the deeper, more meditative aspects of consciousness" (152). Developing the "elder archetype" within himself (Schachter-Shalomi and Miller, 152), Hall can deepen his writerly consciousness and experience many best days.

Hall juxtaposes a best day to its counterpart, a "worst day," in which consciousness shuts down, work cannot proceed, and blank pages haunt the writer, increasing apathy and depression (61–62). He gives sculptor Henry Moore's description of a worst day as "lethargy, discouragement, conviction of failure" (113). If we are fortunate to have the kind of personality that allows it, Hall suggests, we can get through a worst day by keeping at our work, although on a worst day nothing may be produced. It is enough of a triumph just to get through the day (113).

Even Hall's worst days, however, still focus on the desire to work. This unquenchable desire suggests that working may be our primary means of survival. Contemplating the worst days enables Hall (and readers) to understand that we work "in defiance of death" (62). In *The Cancer Journals,* Audre Lorde also proclaims the resistive energy of her writing, fighting against the force of her breast cancer: writing is *eros* in struggle against *thanatos.* Hall recollects a hiatus in his work two and a half years earlier as he fought colon cancer; he recalls having wept not only for his mother, wife, children, and grandchildren, who stood to lose him, but also "to think that [he] would have to stop working" (62). Work is humankind's way of resisting death's efforts to make us passive, silent, and unconscious.

This phrase "in defiance of death" ends part 1 of Hall's two-part text. It forebodes the dreaded event in his life that is the focus of part 2: the recurrence of the carcinoma to which he had sacrificed half his colon and, temporarily, his work.

When the news that his cancer has recurred reaches the author, he sardonically reflects in part 2 on whether the title of this text should be changed to "Work and Death." He rejects this change, partly, I think, to avoid wallowing in self-pity. He will maintain a stoicism about his mortality. Moreover, the original title must stand in order for Hall to reassert that work is still the central focus of text and *life;* he must work "not only in defiance of death but in plain sight of it" (68). I do not detect in Hall's spare and restrained prose many traces of excessive self-pity, nor am I overwhelmed with pity for him because his fear of death is infused with a brave awareness of its eventuality. But we readers may feel pity for ourselves and our own mortality, through Hall's "mortality tale"; as Kelly wryly says, "If we're smart readers, we think, Poor us, that we must die" (11).

And yet, death fuels our work. Gerontologist Robert Kastenbaum notes that many older artists, preoccupied with death and the shortness of time, write in an adventurous and innovative style: "Late style may be an out-come—or casualty—of the aging individual's confrontation with the pros-pect of cessation and the hope of renewal" (301–2). Hall, like Lorde, emphasizes the death watch's powerful incentive to his writing, the push to work while there is yet time. The barbell shape in the ultrasound of the lesion on his liver metamorphoses into an hourglass, with the sands of his allotted time running out (66). Writing provides the only respite from his relentless speculations about how much time he has left to live.

Writing temporarily stops his obsessive replaying on the projection screen of his mind the film clip with the hourglass shape on his liver. Having read the medical literature on his disease, he reports that his prognosis of having more than three years left is poor (113), and he wonders about the condition of his mind and body for work in the third year. Still, he parries and bargains mentally for more time. I am reminded of a mental game I play with the concept of my own health and speculation about the time allotted for my life when I schedule a mammogram in my birth month, turning the frightening reminder that such a medical test gives me of my own mortality into both a celebration of my birth and silent petition for my continuation. As we age, we need such mental games, but even more, we need tasks to absorb us each day, to divert fruitfully this preoccupation with death and time's foreshorten-ing. Death's presence can be a tonic to the serious, committed worker, but the worker must not stare unblinkingly at it.

Writing helps keep Hall's thoughts anchored in the present: no reveries permitted of dancing at his newborn granddaughter Abigail's wedding (71). Writing gives him a modicum of control over his illness, as if language about the ordeal can somehow diminish the ordeal: "Writing about cancer allows me to transcend my cancer by the syntax or rhetoric of dread and suffering" (68). He ponders writer Henry James's words about the death of an author-protagonist in midlife in "The Middle Years," published when James turned fifty: Hall agrees with James that the idea of a second chance at life is illusory for all, not just for those who die at fifty. Writers must keep going with the life they have been given, the one life they have been developing themselves. James becomes for Hall another emblem of the artist still creating on the bed of his illness, writing through the exhaustion, confusion, and weakness, writing in defiance of death (116). As people who deal in the word understand, writing is a way of knowing, an art demanding full concentration in the here and now, and for these reasons alone, it is therapeutic, cathartic, a transformative experience.

Hall writes the interpersonal situation of the cancer survivor exceedingly well. He weeps over the possibility of Jane as a widow. (There is bitter irony here for readers who know that Jane Kenyon died in the summer of 1996, tragically, of leukemia at age forty-seven.) He comments wryly on other acquaintances' discomfort about his health, during the preoperative period: "Oh, it's a burden for us *morituri*, the way we frighten everybody" (79). You can hear the irony in his tone, the amusement about "us *morituri*" since all of us fit into this category: we are all about to die, in a sense, and yet most people—ostriches—rarely care to acknowledge this fact. To jolt the ostriches, Hall writes the body of the cancer survivor in detail. He tersely describes the hospital procedure and his time there in one paragraph, choosing to focus instead on his physical and mental recuperative time at home and on the gradual resumption of consciousness, routine, interest in his work, and energy for it. Three days after his return home he starts examining his poems; seven days after his return he is back at *Life Work*. Writing also enables him to contemplate chemotherapy and to face unflinchingly the idea of another lesion in his liver (113). He anticipates the poison of the chemo in his veins killing cancer cells, imagines the loss of appetite and the diarrhea, the lassitude afterwards (124). In the conclusion to *Life Work*, Hall, by setting down the words, can will himself to know that the chemotherapy may not be effective, that he may no longer have the energy to work.

Life Work is also Hall's vehicle, as he "turn[s] old," for exploring memories of his boyhood relationship with his grandfather. Now he can identify with his grandfather's pleasure in talking to the boy about the experiences of a lifetime (80). In these passages portraying his grandfather, Hall shifts from autobiography to biography, or to the blend of the two genres that has been a continuing topic of discussion in this book (see, especially, chapter 1). Interweaving his present recuperation with reminiscences about his physically active youth, he recalls the hard labors of his grandfather on the farm during the summers of boyhood, when Hall helped his grandfather run the place, doing scythe mowing and trimming fields for hay. He explains the old work ethic, sprung directly from the Victorian doctrine of work, in turn descendent from the Puritan ethic, an ethic by which Hall was raised: "Things were done because it was the way to do them, an aesthetic of work, old habits bespeaking clarity and right angles, resolution and conclusiveness" (87).

Hall shares with readers memories of several grandparents and great-grandparents, focusing on what Wesley, Kate, and his other relatives taught Hall about work and its saving capacity. Living now in his grandparents' home gives a physical reminder that Hall has patterned his own later life after theirs: "work, love, and double-solitude" (75). He is particularly impressed by the unrelenting nature of Grandmother Kate's work in the home and by her energy in meeting the demands of homemaking; in an efficient, terse sentence, Hall marvels at her work capacity: "Kate never kept lists, she just kept moving" (98). He enjoys cataloging her labors of cooking and canning, sewing and darning, cleaning and caring for the sick, just as he takes delight in describing Wesley's farm chores of milking, mowing, and caring for cattle. What he notes most often is their pleasure in tasks well completed and the length of their workdays, the length of the workweeks for both grandfather and grandmother.

While Hall's values may in some respects be traditional, he is clearly committed to sexual equality in his valuing of the work contributions of women and men. For him, work humanizes all of us, challenges us to cultivate the best we have to give. Therefore, the enforced idleness of an earlier generation of middle- and upper-class Victorian women was, in his view, the worst kind of punishment that men inflicted on women, a virtual assault on their psyches, their souls (106–7). He knows this from his observation of his mother's history, which increasingly challenged idleness. He encapsulates her history in a miniature portrait for readers: widowed at fifty-two, Lucy gradually increased her workload, working first as a volunteer in a hospital and then returning to teaching for a wage for another decade. Hall notes her growing energy and mental liveliness as she aged and worked; she blossomed "in a high pride of work and accomplishment" (113). His mother is another of Hall's industrious role models who ascribe to work not only an energizing power but also a curative one.

These memories of his own youthful labors and those of his family contrast with Hall's present physical situation, and the painfulness of the contrast is underscored by the way the book is structured, alternating memories of the farm life with recent medical experiences. In the present Hall briefly notes his physical pain and the sleepiness induced by painkillers, which he dreads for its interference with his work. He weeps once a day, discouraged by tiredness and insomnia, anxious about new unidentifiable pains that tether him to that hourglass, aware of the vulnerability of his "thin slack body" (89). He cites Freud's ideas about work as "a major palliative" to civilization's discontents, but he somewhat bitterly observes that the palliative effect is diminished by bodily suffering (92–93).

Hall's narrative tracks the positive signs of the recuperative process too, using his growing capacity to work as a gauge of recovery. The patient-author notes that gradually he is acquiring more mental energy, enough to move beyond the easy reads of mystery tales to the demands of philosophy and poetry. From writing one page at a sitting he has progressed to four. He is again hitting his stride. Because, like Freud, Hall loves achievement, he begins again to live by the clock, by what his body allows him to produce within the boundaries of time. Cancer is not the real "wasting disease" for Hall: like his farmer ancestors, Hall believes that "if work [is] life, working badly [is] a wasting disease"(96).

Even as he works, however, the looming presence of death influences his work. When he begins a new longer poem, "The Daughters of Edward D. Boit," his latest brush with death is reflected in the poem, which "gives off a posthumous odor" (106). Bowing to his mortality, to the uncertainties of time, he declares at the end of Life Work that he will undertake no new large-scale projects, only little poems, short stories, essays, as well as revisions of current works. The only long-term task he will take on is dying. Now he wishes to retrace and reassess his past, a stage described by Erik Erikson as the "reexperiencing of earlier stages in a new form . . . a growth toward death" (327).

Throughout these ruminations about the past, work, and death run the cross-currents of Hall's relationships with people. He frames lingering questions about how well he has balanced work, love, and friendship in his life. Except for Jane, his mother, his children and grandchildren, at this juncture in his life, Hall would cheerfully exclude the rest of his friends from his daily life (keeping in touch by letter only). He acknowledges himself among the "aging workers desperate to work" (117), choosing work over people. Resurrecting memories of his own children's childhoods, especially Andrew's, he confesses to his own imperfections as a constantly working father: "Because

I was impatient to write and read, I did not play catch with [Andrew] as much as I might have done" (74). Readers will hear regret in the tone of this simple observation and Hall's tentative questioning of his priorities. Readers like me may recall with a pang the times they chose to grade papers and prepare for class, write that legal brief, finish that speech, instead of reading to their son or sitting down to a game of chess with their daughter.

However, Hall's questioning about his priorities here does not seem to reveal intense inner conflict over family versus work: he was raised by his father to do what he wants to do, and Hall, with pleasure, continues to do just that. There is little guilt because work indisputably took precedence during Donald Hall's prime. These are, I would argue, the choices of a traditional male; female authors with children might feel and express with more angst the lacerating choices between work and home that professional women make daily. Only now in his sixties and facing death can Hall shift his priorities occasionally, tear himself away to be with his grandchildren and his children. David Gutmann, citing studies of the rising estrogen levels in men as they age (and the rising testosterone in women), observes that having more estrogen is one way to explain older men's increasing interest in nurturing relationships (182–84). Whether such interest is hormonally induced, in Hall this change is muted. Making more time for children and grandchildren may be a sign of the deepening "androgynous" wisdom of older men (Gutmann, 184), but work is still Hall's top priority: his life is his work; his life is not his children or his grandchildren.

Almost as an afterthought, the final pages of *Life Work* focus directly on Hall's religious faith as a Christian. Not surprisingly, he ties his faith to his work by conceptualizing work as a form of prayer. Work is to Hall what fly fishing is to Raines: a source of pleasure as well as a conduit to the spiritual dimension of existence. Unlike Madeleine L'Engle and Doris Grumbach, Hall has an almost apologetic, embarrassed tone in his confession of faith in and love for Jesus on these pages. He questions aspects of this faith, not concerning Jesus, but concerning God, for "the cloud of unknowing remains thick over my head" (122). What I notice most in these final pages, however, is not his commitment to his faith (he is a deacon) but the absence of the spiritual in his discussion of his writing. He justifies this lacuna by arguing that his work is a form of religious activity: "my work is my devotion. Thus, to write *Life Work* as I walk (temporarily) from the tomb is my devotion" (122).

Sharing his devotion to Jesus and to his writing is the spiritually nurturing figure of Hall's wife, Jane, who is a strong presence in *Life Work* (though a silent one: Hall uses no dialogue to give us Jane's voice). Jane daily rubs her husband's body and, like Jesus, lays healing hands on his abdomen, as if "she is praying or meditating the cancer out" (123). Their increased physical and spiritual intimacy is the gift born of Hall's illness: "I feel as if I had crawled into her body through her pores" (123). Their love and mutual devotion are as impassioned as is their devotion to work. We learn that Jane, also a poet, encourages Hall's work. He is never happier than when he and his wife are working in absorbed silence near one another.

Work and love, love and work: pare down life to its essence, contemplate losing it, and these are what we would regret to leave behind—if, like Donald Hall, we are fortunate enough to have had them in the first place.

Florida Scott-Maxwell: From Work and Leisure to Essence, Consciousness, and Clarity

I have shown how Hall focuses on work and Raines on leisure activities that lead them into the essence of their existence. In contrast, writer Florida Scott-Maxwell is past work and leisure: past leisure because it can be understood only in juxtaposition to work, and she has moved far beyond work. Instead, she explores in her journal, *The Measure of My Days*, internal states of temporal being and pathways to the essence of life. Katherine A. Allison argues in her dissertation that Scott-Maxwell, having acquired economic security, a supportive circle of female friends, and gender equality in old age, finds her true voice as person and writer (1235-A). The strength and philosophical depth of her voice are apparent in *The Measure of My Days*, which has become a canonical text of the literature on aging.

Scott-Maxwell records how, through intense existence—living in the center of the moment—she contacts life's essence, where she experiences a heightening or deepening of her consciousness. Heightened consciousness intermittently brings her to clarity: clarity about her identity, about external reality, about the human condition, about truth, about death and beyond. Harry J. Berman points out that Scott-Maxwell's situation, as a woman in her eighties, encourages her clarified perspective: "this woman's increasing frailty and a concomitant reduction of activities create the conditions for an intense involvement with the essence of life, with the nonphysical aspects of humanness" (1994, 150).

This clarity does not inhibit the author's impulse to raise questions and to sketch different sides of an issue. In fact, the clarity she describes encourages both multiple perspectives on truth and the individual quest for personally conceived truths: "I wonder if old people want truth more than anything else. . . . Perhaps truth is diversity so each seeks his own" (87). Because of her long life, Scott-Maxwell feels closer to the truth (142), but specifically to her own truths—and she argues that other people should apprehend their own truths. Relativism and subjectivity are assumed as she encourages readers to construct their own truths about the larger philosophical issues that her journal raises.

More than Raines and Hall, Scott-Maxwell examines human relationships and the tools for self-knowledge and self-development. Naming the tasks or sacred duties required of one in old age, Scott-Maxwell sees as paramount the completion of the self and truthfulness to that self (21). Each person is obligated to "realize [his or her] uniqueness" (Berman 1994, 151). In this respect, Scott-Maxwell's Jungian training is evident; for her, Jungian analysis is a "rich and searing process of gathering a centre where you know what you are and are not" (56). She depicts with extraordinary vividness and candor her center, the inner architecture of identity in old age. Without ignoring the difficulties of existence for the old, she shows how age is an exciting time of discovery about oneself: "If at the end of your life you have only yourself, it is much. Look, you will find" (142). The completed self becomes a unique and rewarding companion in late life.

Although *The Measure of My Days* explores diverse moral, social, and political issues, I would like to focus mainly on Scott-Maxwell's insights into a woman's identity and existence as shaped by senescence, aloneness, ill health, and the imminence of death. Through these situational factors, which may seem negative, inhibitory, or depressing to the uninitiated, the author ascends into the state of intense being leading to clarity and wisdom. As Erik Erikson argues, wisdom is the ultimate condition achieved in late life, "the final strength": "Wisdom is detached concern with life itself, in the face of death itself. It maintains and learns to convey the integrity of experience, in spite of the decline of bodily and mental functions" (37–38).

As an old woman, Scott-Maxwell can integrate the experiences of her life-time in order to formulate wise truths. Indeed, Scott-Maxwell observes that many old people possess "apocalyptic" wisdom (12): they are able to see visions of the future based on their vast knowledge of the past; they can divine truths in the present that lie hidden to the eyes of the young. Like Plato and other ancient Greeks and Romans, she attributes spiritual wisdom and imaginativeness to aged women especially (Banner, 59, 109, 116). Schachter-Shalomi, writing with Miller, similarly describes an archetype of the Wise Old Woman, "a personification of the psyche that has panoramic knowledge that is unavailable to normal consciousness" (145). With her wide purview, Scott-Maxwell assumes the mantle of guru or crone, participates in the cultural tradition described by Lois Banner, in which aged women, like the sibyls, are portrayed "as wise, as progenitors of knowledge and insight" (118).

Scott-Maxwell fashions herself as a sibyl in the way she deliberates on topics: her tone is assured, but not out of hubris, and softened by the tentativeness and complexity of her statements of truth. Creative imagery and autobiographical anecdotes bespeaking the diverse experiences of Scott-Maxwell's past hint at the depths of the sibyl's perspective (discussed later in this chapter). Even the form of the text promotes the sibylline quality of her pronouncements. The text's ideas are presented as dazzling apothegms in fragmentary entries, some as short as a sentence or two, and ideas are frequently not continued from entry to entry. In fact, many individual sentences could stand alone as philosophical epigrams applicable to many other contexts. In addition, many of these epigrams are mystical and allusive in their enigmatic phrasing, drawing readers into the mysteries of their meanings. So this meditative journal by an aged female is itself apocalyptic or epiphanic. It contains the writings of a sage who reveals for younger readers some roads into psychological and spiritual clarity and in what that clarity consists.

From the beginning of her journal, Scott-Maxwell yokes clarity to self-knowledge, a desirable state even when acquisition involves struggle and pain. She observes that people who can struggle through the clashing elements of their nature and can hold themselves accountable for many facets of their own personality achieve "clarity, a deepened awareness" (10–11). Elsewhere she acknowledges the painfulness of coming to consciousness, of confronting all the qualities of one's character (56); but the reward of this process is that one "experiences eternal truths that give dignity to man" (57). Greater consciousness is a sentience that complicates yet crystallizes, placing her in the center of the moment.

One way that this clarified consciousness is conceptualized in the journal is through the image of a crystal prism. This prism splits one's univocal, dull consciousness into facets or multicolored perceptual filters of reality. Scott-Maxwell posits that we may occasionally become prisms when we experience intensity of being and self-knowledge: "It is the possibility that all intense experience is an increase of energy. It is the intensity of being and knowing ourselves that turns us into prisms, we split consciousness into qualities and we have to endure the passion of doing this" (128). The painful passionateness of achieving this multiple consciousness, of embracing all colors of the perceptual spectrum (not unlike the personal epiphany described by Madeleine L'Engle that undergirds her spiritual faith), is Scott-Maxwell's ontological and psychological goal. She seeks it because multiple consciousness enables her to see the order of the universe.

Scott-Maxwell solemnly commits herself, moment by moment, to this task of attaining and maintaining clear consciousness, of "keep[ing] the crystal clear that the colours may assume their order. . . . I must live so that clarity produces the order of diversity" (129). She measures her days against the standard of this variegated clarity, and the beauty of her language about this prismatic percipience invites readers to seek it. The challenge is to keep oneself sentient and open to experiences that will change one's perceptions—the opposite of the stereotypical elder as impassive and rigid in outlook. This open sentience is like the relaxed receptivity to learning that Raines describes. One of Scott-Maxwell's apothegms is relevant here: "It takes great courage to open our minds and hearts, yet it is required of us to our last breath" (70–71). With open mind and heart, a person can embrace change.

Change is the key word in Scott-Maxwell's thinking; no less than "the creation of a change of consciousness" is what this radical woman seeks in her eighties and would have other elders seek as well (129). She seeks change of consciousness because it will burn away excrescences and bring us face to face with our essence. Scott-Maxwell does not advocate changing the essential self or the unconscious (one cannot, by the very definition of the unconscious, modulate changes in it). Instead we must alter our active consciousness in order to tap into the unconscious, where our essence dwells. Contacting essence is the sacred duty that gives any life meaning: "the purpose of life may be to clarify our essence, and everything else . . . allows the central transmutation. It is unstatable, *divine* and enough" (129; emphasis added). Contact with the unconscious is a gift, Scott-Maxwell declares, because it lets one experience the immortal forces that govern us, and such an experience is transformative (76).

The "deep unconscious," for Scott-Maxwell, has a numinous or visionary dimension, in that entering it even briefly bestows on her "convincing proof of order and meaning in the universe" (108). Contacting the unconscious is almost like believing in God or in the ingenious structure and purpose of the universe God created. In an essay on the unconscious, Françoise Meltzer observes similarly, "the [psychological] concept of an unconscious can be made to dovetail nicely with certain theological beliefs" (147).

This notion of the sacred essence of the self is evoked in Victorian poet Matthew Arnold's "The Buried Life," which helped me to understand Scott-Maxwell's thoughts. For Arnold, the buried life is the core within the self that remains buried—in the unconscious, as Freud and Jung would say—in order to protect it from the potentially harmful fluctuations of one's external life. Such fluctuations might alter the sacredness or sacrifice the integrity of the essential self. In Arnold's poem, contact with the buried life does not automatically bestow panoramic knowledge of the order of the universe; the scope is deep and internal, rather than wide and external. Nevertheless, Arnold posits that a lover can place one in touch, fleetingly, with the buried self. This contact enables one to understand his or her origins, future goals, and central core, to distinguish what one is from what one is not. Does Scott-Maxwell agree that love can initiate this central transmutation or changed consciousness where we meet our essence? Aside from love, does she suggest other means by which to experience this divine, indescribable clarification of one's essence?

Love *is* a means to make contact with the unconscious, with our essence, and it is a way to initiate changed consciousness, according to Scott-Maxwell, but only if we understand it in its relation to pain, since pain assures intensity of being. Throughout the journal, she includes important epigrams on love. For example, she describes the necessity and difficulty of "walking on the egg-shells of affection" to avoid hurting those she loves: "All this is very tiring, but love at any age takes everything you've got" (15). Even more than its demanding nature, she stresses love's power to hurt, especially through loss:

"Love opens double gates on suffering. . . . Parting is impoverishment. . . . The going away of someone loved is laceration. . . . love and suffering are the same" (42–43). Loss is a theme winding through *The Measure of My Days.* Loss is something octogenarians experience on a regular basis, through people's departures for other homes and through their deaths. These pained notions of love are concretized for readers through Scott-Maxwell's focus on her family, the love and hope she feels for each of her children, and the separation from them that she must endure. Love-pain in the old is also portrayed through an architectural image: the self that loves and suffers can change, can transmute the way sorrow and loss are felt, can reach a "citadel where there is a wounded quiet, knowing strength" (43). This inner citadel is the central place that merges pain and pleasure, where we meet our essential but elusive self, "the core of our being" (43).

A mother's love for her children is pleasurably intense, but the author also characterizes it as a painful burden, "the weight of hope for those she bore" (16–17). There is, furthermore, the continuing maternal fear that she has not loved her offspring enough, that she has somehow failed them, and this fear is felt as the deepest sort of stab (66). Although love can heal and soothe, it is precisely because the failure of maternal love or the loss due to separation devastates her that love becomes for the author a way into *clarity* and a "glimpse of transcendence" (66–67). Scott-Maxwell describes the loss of love vividly in passages marking the departure of the boat that takes her son and his family away from England. To readers she expresses sorrow and anger at this separation, but she must repress these emotions and appear happy before her family, for good opportunities are offered her son by this move. Yet she is amazed at how the pain energizes her, makes her feel more alive, brings her to prismatic consciousness (126–28).

She demonstrates this prismatic multiangled perspective in this way: as the family is sailing through the English Channel, she imagines their progress and vicariously experiences their excitement and pleasure ("I have all this clear in my head" 127); but she also experiences the perspective of the loving mother left behind, "bereft" because she is "losing contact with their dearness," their essence. She does not describe herself as experiencing the liberatory energy of the older mother observed by gerontologists such as David Gutmann: "the ending of parental restraints liberates unused, blunted potentials, and . . . these become available for new satisfactions and uses" (213).

Instead of being energized by a reduction in the constraining responsibilities of motherhood (and a growing distance from her adult children), Scott-Maxwell is caught within a painful knot of maternal love intensified by separation. Love, pain, and intensity of being lead to her clarity of perception.

Scott-Maxwell tends to conceptualize in terms of bipolar opposites, or as Robert Yahnke puts it, she sees the Taoists' yin-yang tension in all things; so it is not surprising that she sees the possibilities for achieving clarity not only in love relationships but also in aloneness. In this respect she resembles May Sarton, who from middle age on saw the imaginative possibilities of solitude. As Scott-Maxwell frequently reminds us, the common lot of the very old is solitude. Yet solitude actually has rewards. Because aloneness for the very old is often accompanied by inactivity, there is focused opportunity for a "swelling clarity as though all was resolved. . . . a degree of consciousness which lies outside activity" (33). Solitude may become a seedbed for truth by sharpening perceptivity and fostering intensity of being. It thus helps to crystallize and modulate Scott-Maxwell's views on identity, time, and death, eliciting from her the wisdom of the sage.

It is in solitude, suggests Scott-Maxwell, that one best explores the interior architecture of the self, the citadel already mentioned. Solitude also makes room for more inner space in which to dwell. As their exterior world narrows and as they lose frequent direct contact with it, the old usually exist in a world they have constructed for themselves (137). Kathleen Woodward observes in the elderly Jean-Paul Sartre the sensation of dwelling in an empty body that accompanies his (externalized) inactivity; but the empty body leaves room for reverie building: "For Sartre the empty body in old age was at times associated with the *pleasures* of inactivity. . . . But we could say instead that he was musing, resting, or daydreaming . . . content to merely exist" (179). Like Sartre, Scott-Maxwell does much pleasurable musing, especially about herself, in solitude. Solitude gives her the courage to be herself, to know the reality of that self, and to exist fully: "I feel most real when alone, even most alive when alone" (14). Solitude nurtures companionship with oneself. Alone, finally, one has an intense relationship with oneself, the loss of which would be the most difficult for an elder to bear, in Scott-Maxwell's view (46). When alone, she knows she is a person of fine quality.

There is also a spiritual turn to the aloneness and emptiness of elders' days, "days when emptiness is spacious and non-existence [for which read:

uncluttered, noneventful external life] elevating" (119). This invigorating inner and outer spaciousness frees the narrator to intuit the human soul's creativity and to discern the spirit abroad or within (141). Solitude thus ushers her into spiritual contemplation, into clarity, into the center of the moment. Howell Raines, standing alone in an icy stream surrounded by mountains, would undoubtedly agree with Scott-Maxwell's notion that solitude opens us up to wonder and mystery: "It is undeniable that one needs the absence of others to enjoy the magic of many things" (Scott-Maxwell, 24). Among these magical things she enjoys are self-knowledge and knowledge of nature. When alone, she is convinced of her immortal essence and confident of her strength to "stand by what [she] is . . . the sacred identity within [her]" (24, 121–23). Conviction about the sacredness of personal essence is what makes Scott-Maxwell the sage, shedding prophetic light on the meaning of life. In solitude, her psychoanalytical views join with her theological beliefs: she argues for the value of personal essence and the immortal quality of the soul.

Solitude also teaches Scott-Maxwell to value time differently. Unlike the stereotype of elders as stuck in their pasts, Scott-Maxwell is firmly rooted in the present: "What matters is what I have now, what in fact I live and feel" (7). Solitude energizes her so that she is receptive to the uncomplicated and immediate pleasures surrounding her (14). In fact, she sounds rather sybaritic as she describes the desire of the old for comfort, the sensuous pleasures of baths, food, and drink. She asserts unabashedly that cultivating the capacity for sensuous delight allows one to thrive in old age (88).

Sensuous pleasure is only one of many reasons for the old to take each day as a precious gift. This becomes clear to Scott-Maxwell after she undergoes gall bladder surgery. Readers watch the process of her increasing clarity in the aftermath of the operation as her physical pain eases. She records her movement toward clarity as she convalesces in the same way that Hall, after his surgery, travels toward the ability to work. Surviving this operation, Scott-Maxwell sees with added vision that each extra day is an opportunity to "gain some new understanding, see a beauty, feel love, or know the richness of watching my youngest grandson express [himself]" (90–91). To do these things is to make the most of each day, to live in the center of that day's moments. "Heightened awareness"—seeing beauty and feeling love—is an important element of Scott-Maxwell's increasingly vital involvement in life.

Experiencing euphoria as she recuperates, Scott-Maxwell wishes to embrace even more of life: not only the present but also a future for herself. I am reminded of Herman Roth's ecstatic joy and energy after his cataract surgery. Scott-Maxwell sounds like a bold pioneer as she records the memory of this feeling, "I was still eighty-two . . . and I wanted to scale the sky" (95). Like Raines and Thoreau, Scott-Maxwell would use her future time to reach for the sky, beyond the terrestrial and the temporal, to journey into the transcendent spaces of existence that yield up timeless spiritual knowledge.

Finally, our author writes an entry in which she proposes two oppositional ways of categorizing time from the perspective of the old, leaving us with questions and without closure on the issue and uses of time. Readers are left to choose for themselves whether the old should dwell in a present in which they must remain sentient since the future is uncertain and the past stale, or whether they ought to excavate memories of the past and fantasize about the future since the present is empty (137). This passage reveals Scott-Maxwell at her most sage-like and instructive in that the passage compels readers to become their own sibyls, to construct their own versions of the truth on how to spend one's time meaningfully in old age.

Using time and solitude to acknowledge and comprehend all she has done and been, Scott-Maxwell suggests an elder can finally create a centered, integrated self, fully grasp reality, and prepare to leave it. Like Erikson, she sees as the major late-life task the establishment of personal integrity, balancing "the tension between a sense of integrity, or enduring comprehensiveness, and an opposing sense of despair, of dread and hopelessness" (Erikson, 37, 54). Some cannot balance the tension, and as Jaber Gubrium has observed in the narratives of nursing home patients, they sink into a slough of despair, consumed by thoughts of mortality and "worried to death" about signs of their own mortality (19). Scott-Maxwell does not worry about dying. She sees her condition of completed selfhood and apprehended reality as the best preparation for death: "When at last age has assembled you together, will it not be easy to let it all go, lived, balanced, over?" (42). Although she does frame this serene view of death as a question, there seems to be no trace of despair, dread, or hopelessness in her vision of the relinquishment of life.

Scott-Maxwell's meditative journey through old age is comparable to Thoreau's trek into the woods; both are epistemological and ontological quests to apprehend reality and to live fully before dying. As Thoreau says, "I went to the woods because I wished to live deliberately, to front only the essential facts of life, and see if I could not learn what it had to teach, and not, when I came to die, discover that I had not lived. I did not wish to live what was not life, living is so dear" (62). Scott-Maxwell is convinced that she *has* lived to grasp the dearness of life by experiencing both the intensity that fosters spiritual clarity and the completion of self, both the deep unconscious and love for others. Knowing life's dearness, Scott-Maxwell is ready for the next stage of consciousness, the transmutation into death.

As with Hall's and Raines's works, death itself is a major focus of Scott-Maxwell's journal, a topic that synthesizes all she says about identity, time, solitude, and spiritual clarity. Having discovered and developed her self, having reinforced her belief that she is worthy of immortality, and having sought and obtained greater spiritual awareness and clarity, not surprisingly Scott-Maxwell also seeks awareness that human life is finite, that she is dying. In this respect she belongs to a trend in contemporary culture that Thomas Cole describes: "A growing element in our contemporary culture seeks not to avoid but to transform its fate into a journey to self-knowledge and reconciliation with finitude" (244). Scott-Maxwell welcomes death as a deeper spiritual experience of clarity. The gall bladder surgery, again, assists our journal keeper in exploring her desire for consciousness of death, and it also concretizes her desire.

In an entry that is very confessional and that almost made me feel like a voyeur prying into the anxious interior monologue of the preoperative patient, Scott-Maxwell tells readers that she hopes she will not slip into death unconsciously on the operating table: that would cheat her of clarity and the capacity to die well, that is, fully aware of and absorbing the new experience (90). Although she does not wish to court death, she is not reluctant to die because she is convinced she has fully lived. She also expresses curiosity about "the great mystery," which she would like to satisfy (90). Schachter-Shalomi and Miller argue that "dying people [can] use their transitions as occasions for inner awakening" (178). Scott-Maxwell describes this inner awakening of the dying in the womanist imagery of pregnancy. Like Madeleine L'Engle, she compares life to a pregnancy for the gestating self and death to a birth, or an ascension of the self from consciousness, imagination, and self-awareness into a new dimension of spiritual clarity (76, 150). Affirming this optimistic concept of ascension, she concludes the journal.

Readers should not leave *The Measure of My Days*, however, thinking that the author writes only about intensity of being, about her flaming, wild, and radical heart that leads her to completion of self, full living, and celebratory embrace of death (12, 131). These states she names in direct defiance of the stereotypical image of passive, worn-out old age. She is well aware of ageism, and undermining the stereotype is one of her purposes in her journal. Early in the journal, she declares: "my eighties are passionate. I grow more intense as I age" (13). No tired blood for her in late life! Yet because Scott-Maxwell conceptualizes through bipolar opposites, her final juxtaposition of intensity with a state of tranquillity is to be expected. By the end of the journal, tranquillity comes to be valued as much as intensity. This tranquillity is an actively won state of mind (143). It is associated by the author with a feeling of the naturalness of being old, and it may be obtained through facing how age changes us. As Cole advocates, Scott-Maxwell finds "ways to integrate the ancient virtue of submission to natural limits with the modern value of individual development for all" (Cole, 251).

Is this active tranquillity also a vehicle to clarified perception? Two autobiographical anecdotes appearing near the end of the journal suggest her answer, and I end with an examination of them. These anecdotes illustrate an approach to living that does not assume life is a struggle to be fought through, but, rather, that takes life lightly and effortlessly. She posits "a genius for ease," in which the person is unaffected by the modulations of reality (144) and assumes both that life is to be enjoyed and that one ought to have what one wants.

The first anecdote takes readers back in the author's memory to a zoo visit in which she watched a young, pregnant female monkey. She remembers and records the monkey's graceful movements: the monkey swings from the top bar down to the floor, and then "with languid elegance" creates for herself a "rug" of straw, casting at the author-observer a withering "look of unconcern" as she takes her ease and consults her own pleasure (145–46). Scott-Maxwell's message here seems to be that the "skill of being effortless" comes down to humankind from our primate ancestors and that it is an essential biological element residing in the human brain. This skill reminds me of the nonchalant motions of fly fishing described with awe by Raines. Like Raines, Scott-Maxwell admires effortless mastery and is "spellbound by ease" (146).

Scott-Maxwell pairs this monkey anecdote with another depicting a human version of skilled ease: she remembers a performance by a man in a music hall fifty years earlier. The man strolled onstage, bearing a walking stick. He sang a song once and then again silently, faintly mocking his first performance, "living the rhythm with exquisite accuracy, and masterly indifference"; she and the rest of the audience responded tumultuously to "the man who dared to be so unconcerned" (147). His creation of the tension between song and silence with easeful indifference changes her, leaves her pleased and relaxed, deepening her consciousness about the range of modes available for happy living. Ease, accompanied by intensity, leads to completion, to full grasp of reality and of the seriousness of death. Ease may even lead us to conviction of "the possibility of some form of continuity" after death (138).

With these concluding anecdotes, Scott-Maxwell balances her sometimes impersonal, sibylline insights, offsets the fragmentary nature of her journal entries, takes an accurate summative measure of her days, and displays her clarified vision. She leaves me slightly off balance, unsettled by the tension between her journal's paired oppositions, but prompted to address the questions and issues central to old age. By offering readers both tranquillity and intensity, she leads us into the center of the moment, where the meanings are. If we choose to linger there, she has given us some philosophical and psychological tools with which to do so.

Afterword: Philosophical Autobiography and Beyond

I chose Scott-Maxwell's work to end this final chapter of my book for three main reasons. First, I sought a work that unequivocally emphasized very old age and the philosophical issues of this time of life, to compare with the works of early middle age and young old age by Raines and Hall. Clearly *The Measure of My Days,* by a consciously philosophical octogenarian, does both of these things well.

Second, since the first two works in the chapter are written by men, I wanted a literary work that could represent one woman's views on aging and that would help me to consider how gender contributes to the development of a heart and mind of wisdom in senescence. In her intense scrutiny of maternal feelings and responses to familial separation, Scott-Maxwell distinguishes herself as a female and provides instructive contrasts to Raines and

Hall; both were fathers and involved with their children, yet neither were viscerally wrenched by separation from family in the way that Scott-Maxwell confesses to be. She affirms that into old age, a woman remains a mother, with all the intensity and range of feeling that relational term implies.

Still, I was a bit surprised not to find more presences of gender in *The Measure of My Days*, particularly since Scott-Maxwell considered herself a feminist and fought for women's suffrage. I marked a passage in which she critiques gender stereotypes' negative effect on men when they are forced to compete in the workplace (24), and another passage in which she wryly observes men's limited understanding of the social status of inferiority and the condition of invisibility experienced by many women and third-world people (61–64). She considers the insensitive white male a poor role model for third-world people to emulate as they develop themselves.

Finally, I noted a more complex passage in which Scott-Maxwell reminds readers how men's cruel and insistent assumption of women's social inferiority wounded Scott-Maxwell and, undoubtedly, other women too throughout their lives (100–102). She asserts that this assumption of inferiority in women is culturally supported by men's comparisons of ordinary women to the ideal of the Virgin Mary (100–105). She calls for women to construct their own identities by merging the highs and the lows with which men have characterized them. Scott-Maxwell would refuse the honor bestowed upon the super-human woman on the pedestal and spurn the representation of women as inferior. Instead, she would want women to be honored as people. Here, as elsewhere in her journal, she stresses the quality or essence of people, of women: "At my age I care to my roots about the quality of women, and I care because I know how important her quality is" (104–5).

These three passages, especially the last one, appealed to my feminist sensibilities and kept me politically and emotionally attuned to Scott-Maxwell as she philosophized on other topics throughout her text. Yet the small presence of gendered ideas in relation to the rest of the text made me wonder whether gender fades in significance and in one's consciousness as one attains very old age. Raines, tongue-in-cheek, alludes to the diminishment of testosterone and increase of estrogen in middle-aged men as an explanation for their attraction to the delicate, noncompetitive style of fly fishing that he praises. We have already noted Gutmann's studies of late-life hormonal shifts in men and women that result in blurring of gender roles (182). Perhaps

Raines and Scott-Maxwell envision a new domain of androgyny or gender neutrality developing as we age, one that could subvert our culture's sexism and ageism. If so, then the paucity of passages on gender in Scott-Maxwell's text could be read as positive indicators that cultural biases against women loose their hold as women age. With a future population dominated by elders (the baby boomers turned gray), the fight against both sexism and ageism could stand a good chance of ending in victory—in the twenty-first century.

There is a third reason I chose to close with Scott-Maxwell's text: because the book's philosophical wisdom has helped me to deal with the terminal illness of a contemporary, a cousin of mine by marriage, who valiantly fought a malignant brain tumor for three years but who in 1995 succumbed to the cancer. His struggle has raised many questions for me over the past few years. How does a person take the measure of his days on his deathbed and decide he is ready to die, without regret? Does the measuring differ if you are ninety-six (as was Scott-Maxwell, living eleven years after the publication of her journal) or half of that, forty-eight (as was my cousin)? Does time expand or contract and concentrate as one struggles for one more day of life (or struggles against it) when the body increasingly resists life? How is love sustained and even nourished despite the endurance of illness by the patient and the backbreaking, heart-wrenching work of tending the dying, as it was for my two cousins, husband and wife?

The Measure of My Days grapples with some of these questions. Like the texts by Raines and Hall, it shows me how to infuse time or being with new, nonsynchronous meaning. I might not have been receptive to such writings a decade earlier; I practiced avoidance of such "foreign" subjects as aging and death in my thirties, and I was not attuned to their relevance for me. But in middle age such texts take on added significance and power. Reading them teaches me that a man dying at forty-eight is not robbed of time if he has made use of time more intensely than most of us do on any average day. There are no average days when a person practices intense being.

All three works discussed in this chapter have eased my own anxieties about aging into death, especially death in the prime of midlife, by nudging me to move beyond mere chronological measurement of my days on earth. Sarton's journal *At Seventy* and Lorde's *Cancer Journals* similarly take each day in new ways and show me how to avoid trivializing the units of time in my life. Many of the works examined in this book deepen time through spiritual experiences, especially those by L'Engle, Raines, Grumbach, Wallis, and Scott-Maxwell. The hours in the lives of Clifton, Roth, and L'Engle are enriched by intimate interactions with their elderly parents, by participation in family history, and by the transmission of "generational memories" that preserve cultural continuity (Myerhoff, 231–32). Grumbach, Lorde, and Sarton describe the expansion of time through networking with women friends and through their openness to the myriad experiences that keep transforming them. All resist a biological essentialism regarding the trajectory of elders' lives that intones: "Slow down, deteriorate, reach stasis, die."

The works examined in this volume join a resonating choir of autobiographical voices on aging that support the work of such gerontological researchers as Erikson, Myerhoff, Cole, Gubrium, and Gutmann. These autobiographers insist that we can remain vitally engaged with life in old age, that our later years are a time of rich intensity and opportunities for psychological and spiritual growth. Literary autobiographers are creating a cultural dialogue that is changing people's minds about old age. Autobiography in its very form is fictional, yet these works are having a true-to-life, positive impact on readers like me, who are obtaining from them spiritual and psychological guidance on the pathways into old age.

Works Cited

Primary Works

Angelou, Maya. *Wouldn't Take Nothing for My Journey Now*. New York: Random House, 1993.

Clifton, Lucille. *Generations: A Memoir*. In *Good Woman: Poems and a Memoir, 1969–1980*. Brockport NY: BOA Editions, 1987.

Delany, Sarah, and A. Elizabeth Delaney, with Amy Hill Hearth. *Having Our Say: The Delany Sisters' First 100 Years*. New York: Kodansha International, 1993.

Du Bois, W. E. B. *The Autobiography of W. E. B. DuBois: A Soliloquy on Viewing My Life from the Last Decade of Its First Century*. Millwood NY: Kraus International, 1968.

———. *In Battle for Peace: The Story of My 83rd Birthday*. With comment by Shirley Graham. New York: Masses & Mainstream, 1952.

Grumbach, Doris. *Coming into the End Zone: A Memoir*. New York: W. W. Norton, 1991.

Hall, Donald. *Life Work*. Boston: Beacon Press, 1993.

Kingston, Maxine Hong. *The Woman Warrior: Memoirs of a Girlhood among Ghosts*. New York: Alfred Knopf, 1976.

L'Engle, Madeleine. *The Summer of the Great-Grandmother*. New York: Farrar, Straus & Giroux, 1974.

Lorde, Audre. *The Cancer Journals*. San Francisco: Aunt Lute Books, 1980.

———. "Age, Race, Class, and Sex: Women Redefining Difference." In *Sister Outsider: Essays and Speeches*, 114–23. Trumansburg NY: Crossing Press, 1984.

Raines, Howell. *Fly Fishing through the Midlife Crisis*. New York: William Morrow, 1993.

Roth, Philip. *Patrimony*. New York: Simon & Schuster, 1991.

Sarton, May. *After the Stroke: A Journal*. New York: W. W. Norton, 1988.

――――. *At Seventy: A Journal.* New York: W. W. Norton, 1984.

Scott-Maxwell, Florida. *The Measure of My Days.* New York: Viking Penguin, 1968.

Thoreau, Henry. *Walden* and *Civil Disobedience.* Ed. Sherman Paul. New York: Houghton Mifflin, 1960.

Wallis, Velma. *Two Old Women.* New York: HarperCollins, 1994.

Secondary Works

Allison, Katherine A. "Florida Scott-Maxwell: Biography of a Woman/Writer." Ph.D. diss., Univ. of Washington, 1990. Abstract in *Dissertation Abstracts International* 51, no. 4 (October 1990): 1235-A.

Angel, Rabbi Marc D. *The Orphaned Adult: Confronting the Death of a Parent.* New York: Human Sciences Press, 1987.

Appiah, Kwame Anthony. "Race." In *Critical Terms for Literary Study,* ed. Frank Lentricchia and Thomas McLaughlin. Chicago: Univ. of Chicago Press, 1990.

Atkin, Samuel, and Adam Atkin. "On Being Old (A Psychoanalyst's View)." In *How Psychiatrists Look at Aging,* ed. George H. Pollock, 1–24. Madison CT: International Universities Press, 1992.

Bakhtin, M. M. "Discourse in the Novel." In *The Dialogic Imagination,* ed. Michael Holquist, trans. Caryl Emerson and Michael Holquist, 259–422. Austin: Univ. of Texas Press, 1981.

Banner, Lois. *In Full Flower: Aging Women, Power, and Sexuality.* New York: Random House, 1993.

Baughman, Ronald. "Lucille Clifton." In *Dictionary of Literary Biography; American Poets since World War II,* ed. Donald J. Greiner. Vol. 5, pt. 1: 132–36. Detroit: Bruccoli Clark and Gale Research, 1980.

Beauvoir, Simone de. *The Coming of Age.* Trans. Patrick O'Brian. New York: Warner Books, 1972.

Bell, Susan Groag, and Marilyn Yalom. *Revealing Lives: Autobiography, Biography, and Gender.* Albany: State Univ. of New York Press, 1990.

Benstock, Shari. "Authorizing the Autobiographical." In *The Private Self: Theory and Practice of Women's Autobiographical Writings,* ed. Shari Benstock, 10–33. Chapel Hill: Univ. of North Carolina Press, 1988.

Berman, Harry J. *Interpreting the Aging Self: Personal Journals of Later Life.* New York: Springer, 1994.

――――. "May Sarton's Journals: Attachment and Separateness in Later Life." In *Research on Adulthood and Aging: The Human Science Approach,* ed. L. E. Thomas, 11–26. Albany: State Univ. of New York Press, 1989.

———. "Sarton's Journals: Interpreting the Aging Self." Paper presented at the annual meeting of the Gerontological Society of America, Washington DC, 20 Nov. 1992.

Bleich, David. *The Double Perspective: Language, Literacy, and Social Relations.* New York: Oxford Univ. Press, 1988.

———. *Subjective Criticism.* Baltimore: Johns Hopkins Univ. Press, 1978.

Cixous, Hélène. "The Laugh of the Medusa." Trans. Keith Cohen and Paula Cohen. In *The Signs Reader: Women, Gender, & Scholarship,* ed. Elizabeth Abel and Emily K. Abel, 279–97. Chicago: Univ. of Chicago Press, 1983.

Cole, Thomas R. *The Journey of Life: A Cultural History of Aging in America.* New York: Cambridge Univ. Press, 1992.

Dasenbrock, Reed Way. "Fish, Stanley." In *The Johns Hopkins Guide to Literary Theory and Criticism,* ed. Michael Groden and Martin Kreiswirth. Baltimore: Johns Hopkins Univ. Press, 1994.

Davidson, Cathy N. "Critical Fictions." Guest column, "Four Views on the Place of the Personal in Scholarship." *PMLA* 111, no. 5 (October 1996): 1069–72.

Denzin, Norman K. *Interpretive Biography.* Newbury Park CA: Sage, 1989.

Eakin, Paul John. Foreword to *On Autobiography,* by Philippe Lejeune, trans. Katherine Leary. Minneapolis: Univ. of Minnesota Press, 1989.

Erikson, Erik H., Joan M. Erikson, and Helen Q. Kivnick. *Vital Involvement in Old Age.* New York: W. W. Norton, 1986.

Freire, Paulo. *Pedagogy of the Oppressed.* Trans. Myra Bergman Ramos. New York: Continuum, 1993.

Friedan, Betty. *The Fountain of Age.* New York: Simon & Schuster, 1993.

Gates, Henry Louis, Jr. "'Tell Me, Sir, . . . What *Is* 'Black' Literature?" (introduction of special issue). *PMLA* 105 (January 1990): 11–22.

Gilligan, Carol. *In a Different Voice: Psychological Theory and Women's Development.* Cambridge: Harvard Univ. Press, 1982.

Gubrium, Jaber F. *Speaking of Life: Horizons of Meaning for Nursing Home Residents.* New York: Aldine de Gruyter, 1993.

Gutmann, David. *Reclaimed Powers: Toward a New Psychology of Men and Women in Later Life.* New York: Basic Books, 1987.

The Holy Scriptures: According to the Masoretic Text. Vol. 2. Philadelphia: Jewish Publication Society of America, 1966.

Isenberg, Sheldon. "Aging in Judaism: 'Crown of Glory' and 'Days of Sorrow.'" In *Handbook of the Humanities and Aging,* ed. Thomas R. Cole, David D. Van Tassel, and Robert Kastenbaum, 147–74. New York: Springer, 1992.

Joseph, Edward D. "Have I Achieved Wisdom?" In *How Psychiatrists Look at Aging,* ed. George H. Pollock, 109–22. Madison CT: International Universities Press, 1992.

Kaminsky, Marc. Introduction to *Remembered Lives: The Work of Ritual, Storytelling, and Growing Older,* by Barbara Myerhoff, with Deena Metzger, Jay Ruby, and Virginia Tufte; ed. Marc Kaminsky. Ann Arbor: Univ. of Michigan Press, 1992.

Kastenbaum, Robert. "The Creative Process: A Life-span Approach." In *Handbook of the Humanities and Aging,* ed. Thomas R. Cole, David D. Van Tassel, and Robert Kastenbaum, 285–306. New York: Springer, 1992.

Kelly, Robert. "Mortality Tale." Review of *Life Work,* by Donald Hall. *New York Times Book Review,* 3 October 1993, 11.

Kirkpatrick, Martha. "Aging, Like a Woman." In *How Psychiatrists Look at Aging,* ed. George H. Pollock, 141–47. Madison CT: International Universities Press, 1992.

Lejeune, Philippe. *On Autobiography.* Trans. Katherine Leary. Minneapolis: Univ. of Minnesota Press, 1989.

Lentricchia, Frank, and Thomas McLaughlin, eds. *Criticism and Social Change.* Chicago: Univ. of Chicago Press, 1983.

Lyons, Nick. "It's Not about Catching Fish." Review of *Fly Fishing through the Midlife Crisis,* by Howell Raines. *New York Times Book Review,* 19 September 1993, 7.

Marcus, Jane. "Invincible Mediocrity: The Private Selves of Public Women." In *The Private Self: Theory and Practice of Women's Autobiographical Writings,* ed. Shari Benstock, 114–46. Chapel Hill: Univ. of North Carolina Press, 1988.

Meese, Elizabeth A. *Crossing the Double-Cross: The Practice of Feminist Criticism.* Chapel Hill: Univ. of North Carolina Press, 1986.

Meltzer, Françoise. "Unconscious." In *Critical Terms for Literary Study,* ed. Frank Lentricchia and Thomas McLaughlin, 147–62. Chicago: Univ. of Chicago Press, 1990.

Muske, Carol. "Notes on Current Books: *Generations: A Memoir.*" In *Contemporary Literary Criticism,* ed. Sharon R. Gunton. Vol. 19: 108–11. Detroit: Gale Research, 1981.

Myerhoff, Barbara, with Deena Metzger, Jay Ruby, and Virginia Tufte; ed. Marc Kaminsky. *Remembered Lives: The Work of Ritual, Storytelling, and Growing Older.* Ann Arbor: Univ. of Michigan Press, 1992.

The New Encyclopaedia Britannica. 15th ed. Chicago: 1988. *Micropaedia 2,* 102–3, under "Benin"; *Micropaedia 3,* 848, under "Dahomey."

Parry, Betty. "A Conversation with Lucille Clifton." *Passager: A Journal of Remembrance and Discovery* 1 (spring 1990): 21–25.

Peppers, Wallace R. "Lucille Clifton." In *Afro-American Poets since 1955,* ed. Trudier Harris and Thadious M. Davis. Dictionary of Literary Biography series, vol. 41: 55–60. Detroit: Bruccoli Clark and Gale Research, 1985.

Pierce, Chester M. "Concerning an Aging Psychiatrist." In *How Psychiatrists Look at Aging,* ed. George H. Pollock, 179–89. Madison CT: International Universities Press, 1992.

Pollock, George H., ed. *How Psychiatrists Look at Aging.* Madison CT: International Universities Press, 1992.

Price, Reynolds. Review of *Generations: A Memoir,* in *Good Woman: Poems and a Memoir, 1969–1980,* by Lucille Clifton. In *Contemporary Literary Criticism,* ed. Sharon R. Gunton. Vol. 19: 110. Detroit: Gale Research, 1981.

Rosenblatt, Louise M. *Literature as Exploration,* 4th ed. New York: Modern Language Association of America, 1983.

Schachter-Shalomi, Zalman, and Ronald S. Miller. *From Age-Ing to Sage-Ing: A Profound New Vision of Growing Older.* New York: Warner Books, 1995.

Selden, Raman. *A Reader's Guide to Contemporary Literary Theory,* 2d ed. Lexington: Univ. Press of Kentucky, 1989.

Viorst, Judith. Review of *The Place He Made,* by Edie Clark. *New York Times Book Review,* 16 July 1995, 15.

Walker, Alice. *In Search of Our Mothers' Gardens.* San Diego: Harcourt Brace Jovanovich, 1983.

Waxman, Barbara Frey. *From the Hearth to the Open Road: A Feminist Study of Aging in Contemporary Literature.* Westport CT: Greenwood Press, 1990.

Whitehouse, Anne. "Meditations." Review of *Wouldn't Take Nothing for My Journey Now,* by Maya Angelou. *New York Times,* 19 December 1993, p. 18.

Woodward, Kathleen. *Aging and Its Discontents: Freud and Other Fictions.* Bloomington: Indiana Univ. Press, 1991.

Wyatt-Brown, Anne M. "Aging, Gender and Creativity." Introduction to *Aging and Gender in Literature,* ed. Anne M. Wyatt-Brown and Janice Rossen, 3–13. Charlottesville: Univ. Press of Virginia, 1993.

———. "Literary Gerontology Comes of Age." In *Handbook of the Humanities and Aging,* ed. Thomas R. Cole, David D. Van Tassel, and Robert Kastenbaum, 331–51. New York: Springer, 1992.

Yahnke, Robert. Presentation on Florida Scott-Maxwell's Taoist Philosophy in *The Measure of My Days* at the convention of the Association for Gerontology in Higher Education, Baltimore, March 1992.

Index

AGE STUDIES

Anne M. Wyatt-Brown and Janice Rossen, eds.
Aging and Gender in Literature: Studies in Creativity

Margaret Morganroth Gullette
Declining to Decline: Cultural Combat and the Politics of the Midlife

Jaber F. Gubrium
Living and Dying at Murray Manor

Barbara Frey Waxman
To Live in the Center of the Moment: Literary Autobiographies of Aging

Idea for a series of essays (a book)
How to Make Love to a Feminist

Midlife spiritual autobiogs.
Flyfishing Through The Midlife Crisis,
Howell Raines